T

CH

BLUE NT

Other books by Padma Aon Prakasha

The Nine Eyes of Light: Ascension Keys from Egypt

The Power of Shakti: 18 Pathways to Ignite the Energy of the Divine Woman

THE
CHRIST
BLUEPRINT

13 KEYS TO CHRIST CONSCIOUSNESS

Padma Aon Prakasha
with the Christ Council

FINDHORN PRESS

ISBN 978-1-84409-173-7

Cover art and interior symbols by David Andor,
    www.wavesource.com.au
Interior design by North Atlantic Books.

British Library Cataloguing-in-Publication Data.
A catalogue record for this book is available from the British Library.

Printed in the European Union.

1 2 3 4 5 6 7 8 9 10 11 12 13 14 15 16 17 16 15 14 13 12 11 10

Published by
Findhorn Press
117-121 High Street
Forres IV36 1AB
Scotland, UK

t +44(0)1309 690582
f +44(0)131 777 2711
e info@findhornpress.com
www.findhornpress.com

CONTENTS

I pray . . . that they may be One in us.

—Yeshua, in John 17:19

PREFACE

The Christ Blueprint was revealed through a miraculous process of Communion with each of the thirteen Apostles and Masters of Christ. Communion is the bridge from the dream world into the present moment, the bridge between you and the soul living in all beings. It is in this Presence, revelation, and inspiration that the greatest things are revealed to us about life.

The way to access this directly is by raising your state of consciousness, to allow yourself to ride into and be swept away by inspiration, love, and the universal mind. This is Gnosis, energy and wisdom that transforms you. Gnosis does not try to explain or prove the soul—it serves to change it, to melt the dross into gold, to burn away all impurities in order for you to embody love.

Gnosis is direct knowing, the "download" directly from the Source of Being. It is a fluid Intelligence; clear, direct, instant. Just as love cannot be proved, such is Gnosis. It is there whether we acknowledge it or not. It is a state of being, accessed through lived experience, becoming the Gnosis itself.

The Gnosis of the Christ Blueprint contained within these pages all started to be revealed when I arrived in the beautiful seaside town of Saintes-Maries-de-la-Mer, in the heart of the mystical Camargue region of southern France. My partner and I were on a road trip through the sacred sites of France for two weeks, or so we thought.

Saintes-Maries-de-la-Mer is the place where Mary Magdalene, Marie Salome, Joseph, and other disciples of Christ arrived upon fleeing Palestine after the Crucifixion and Resurrection of Christ Yeshua.

Within two hours of arriving, we sat down to dinner opposite the small church built to honor these brave men and women, the disciples of Christ. As we sat down, a form appeared right in front of us, followed by two others. It was a woman, radiant, beautiful, soft, and very present. Behind her was a shadowy figure of a man. She turned and looked toward me, and my heart stopped. It was Mary Magdalene.

Her rich sensual presence brought me to joy instantly. I started to laugh, feeling the warmth, the sensual aliveness deep in my heart, bubbling up. It overtook me and I gladly surrendered, for it felt like life's desire itself, which is only the joy of love.

She started to speak openly and humorously both to me and to another glowing, powerful, yet equally feminine figure, whom I later found out to be Marie Salome. They were both so wise and beautiful, playful and womanly, sisterly to us and to each other, laughing freely and with abandon. So human yet so divine, so natural in poise and grace, which they both innately emanated. It felt like we were with family, and I felt at home.

Magdalene told us that we would find an apartment to live in there within three days, and we should rent it for three months. We let her know what we wanted, and she smiled, saying yes to our every request. The next day we found a tiny apartment that went beyond all our stated requirements. Quiet, beautiful, and thirty feet from the Mediterranean Sea, it was nestled into a water spa complex with sauna, steam room, and numerous water-massage pools. Needless to say, we moved in exactly three days later. The first miracle!

Later that day, walking along the seafront, Magdalene again appeared, and in a pressing, urgent, and direct manner that left no room for doubt or hesitation, she started to talk about the womb and womb-man. My partner started to transcribe what was being said through me about the mystery, empowerment, and crucial role of woman and sacred marriage, and then the whole process of revealing this book started in earnest.

All of this began with the astonishing revelations about the secret lineages of the ancient mothers that Mary Magdalene and Salome held for Yeshua, and how they assisted him in his work with the Feminine Wisdom born from harnessing the power of the womb, one of the greatest secrets of ancient Egypt. Synchronously enough, my partner's womb then started to open with these revelations about the true power of woman. She started to experience deep, rich fertile joy in the womb, as well as feeling all of humanity in her womb, all within a few days!

Each day Magdalene, and Salome too, revealed further truths about the Christ Blueprint. As each quality of the Blueprint landed in our bodies, minds, and souls, we went through deep, felt experiences and shifts in ourselves as we aligned to each of the thirteen aspects of Christ. Different lessons and healings happened on a daily basis, resulting in huge accelerations in both of our consciousnesses.

We could notice in each other the transformation after each Apostle was revealed; so quick were the shifts that there was a "before" Peter and "after" Peter only two days later! At one point our brains were hurting so much in an intense twelve-day process that our bodies gave out on us; we literally passed out, so powerful were the transformations that were occurring on the deepest levels.

It became clear that Mary Magdalene stood behind Yeshua with Salome and Mother Mary as his main supports. It also became clear that in the twenty-first century the roles are reversed: Mary Magdalene stands first, and Yeshua stands behind her as her support. Magdalene is now the main portal for those who wish to enter Christ Consciousness, and it is through the Feminine Christ that all thirteen of Christ's original teachings and pathways will be fully revealed and lived.[1]

---

1. The Feminine Christs are the quartet of Christed Women: Mary Magdalene, Marie Salome, Martha, and Mother Mary, who were given Keys to the powers of love, power, birth, and life to share and spread what they call "the Womb of the World."

Some of these Keys were shared with me on the windswept beaches of the remote peninsula of Saintes-Maries-de-la-Mer, the first town in the world to have a Christian church and the sacred site where the Feminine Christ first landed on earth. Each Key and revelation was mirrored in my own life and relationships. Each seed planted in the fertile soil of my body, mind, and soul by Magdalene flowered and bloomed over time to present to you this overview of Christ Consciousness. In this blooming, each quality of Christ Consciousness, each Master and each Apostle, arose within me as it was required to. Some were more of a challenge to learn with, and from, than others.

The process of embodiment never ends, for even the greatest masters are always growing, learning, creating, and playing in myriads of ways, more and more and more . . . for there are indeed worlds without end to explore and delight in.

—Padma Aon Prakasha
November 2009

Introduction

INTRODUCTION

Christ Consciousness in this age was reactivated by Christ Yeshua and the twelve Apostles surrounding him two thousand years ago in the form of the Christ Blueprint. It is a map of equal interconnected relationship where each part of the Blueprint, each part of each person in relationship, is honored, recognized, and loved in order for all parts to function to their highest potential.

Life is relationship. We come into existence only through relationship. We are like a circle, a web of relationships that create who we are and how we feel, think, and act. When any one relationship is not balanced, then "you" are not balanced. The same applies to our own bodies, minds, souls, and DNA. They too are a web that when woven together in harmony can produce a Perfect Human, or Christ.

All thirteen qualities working together create Christ Consciousness.[1] In order to bring our lives into the lived expression of all thirteen, all aspects must together become a fluid and easily accessible part of our expression. Each of these thirteen is a pathway, and each pathway is but one aspect of the whole. If we go too far down one pathway, we can lose sight of the others, for no single pathway in the Christ Blueprint will bring us into Christ Consciousness; only all thirteen working together will.

---

1. These Apostles include many but not all of the traditional biblical Apostles, for the Christ Blueprint is formed by those Apostles who anchored Christ Consciousness onto earth consciously, many of whom were women who were conveniently left out of the original twelve by male Bible commentators. There have been many variants of the original twelve, the last variant being that there were thirteen, a feminine number in tune with nature's innate organic rhythms, with the thirteen-moon calendar of natural time cycles and with life's flow itself.

It is your job, those who are accessing Christ consciousness, to embody all thirteen in action as Christ, the embodiment of God in form, a fully unified being woven together in unconditional love. Yeshua Sananda, the last full representative of Christ Consciousness on earth, embodied this through sacred relationship with all the aspects of himself that he gathered around him, the thirteen Apostles. Each Apostle represents a part of the Christ, an aspect of Christed Consciousness, with all of them unifying and collectively contributing to reawaken Christ Consciousness on earth.

Yeshua needed his Apostles around him, as they all formed the body of Christ, one unified consciousness. Without him they were nothing; without them he was nothing. Each link in the chain was totally interdependent, each needing the other in order to become whole and anchor Christ Consciousness on earth. The body of Christ is a holographic consciousness, with all identities and names being fluid and interchangeable, like seeing through multiple perspectives and eyes simultaneously; in one moment you are seeing through John the Baptist's eyes of ruthless compassion, fire, and power; in the next moment through Magdalene's eyes, the eyes of Holy Love; and in the next moment through Yeshua's eyes. Equally, you could in one moment be seeing through the eyes of pride or Lucifer's shadow, and in the next moment be seeing through the eyes of unworthiness, the shadow of Martha.

All thirteen Master qualities and their human vehicles, the Apostles, create twenty-six aspects of Christ Consciousness. The shadow aspects then create twelve more, so there are thirty-eight aspects to work with, almost like a Tarot of Christ Consciousness. To embody and integrate all of them in action on earth, here and now, is to enter sacred relationship with all the aspects of yourself.

In learning about these many and varied qualities of Christ Consciousness, both the light and the dark, one comes to a deep understanding that this life is not just about integrating one or two of these qualities; it is about fully embodying all of them as a Christ-conscious person. It is not about being stuck or fixed on only incorporating Mary Magdalene or Isis; it is about bringing them all into union and harmony within *you,* embracing *all* aspects of Christ Consciousness. Only this can truly fulfill you, and it is an open invitation for you to live in it every day.

THE THIRTEEN QUALITIES

One eventually becomes able to shape-shift into any of the thirteen qualities according to what is appropriate for the highest potential to manifest in that moment. In real and accessible terms, the Christ Blueprint gives us the inspiration and the map to embody Christ Consciousness here and now. It is both eye-opening and heart-opening, providing a deeper connection with the Christ within you. All of the thirteen qualities create Christ Consciousness. Christ Yeshua integrated all twelve qualities of the Apostles and masters to create the thirteenth—himself.

Christ Consciousness embodies forgiveness and humility as a return to wholeness. We let go of the past and whatever we think people have done to us, or what we think we have done to them. In these actions we free ourselves to embrace the present without the need to continually refer to and reenact our past, the source of much fear, guilt, and anger.

Forgiveness sees that no harm has ever been done, and you and the "other" are innocent. The two people who embodied true forgiveness and humility as a quality of love are the Apostles John Zebedee and Master Paramahansa Yogananda. In forgiveness and humility, one overcomes the shadow side of false humility, projection, blame, guilt, and shame in order to step into the present moment.

Christ Consciousness embodies true service, giving and serving all beings with the totality of your body, mind, and soul. The female Apostle Martha embodied service, for to serve another becomes the obvious natural expression of the free flowing life force, of joy itself, when one sees that the other is but an aspect and a reflection of yourself. Christ Consciousness overcomes unworthiness, lack of self-love, selfishness, lack of passion, confusion, and doubt in order to serve one's deepest, most passionate heart's desire, which is true service.

Christ Consciousness embodies compassion, beauty, and gratitude. Gratitude becomes a way in which we recognize the perfection of all things, seeing nothing as a mistake, and that we have never failed or taken a wrong turn. Everything is in perfection, and everything given to you in each and every moment is for the unfolding of the soul's journey and purpose. We can thank and transmute everything that repels or hurts us, as gratitude becomes an alchemical process through which our hurts become opportunities to heal and deepen into love's embrace. Gratitude leads into the full embrace of what is; it leads us to becoming fully present in the now. Gratitude becomes a journey into a world of soft, considered openness that leads into limitless possibilities. Gratitude leads into a deep, felt trust that everything that is occurring in your life right now is perfect.

Christ Consciousness integrates the qualities of ruthless compassion and Divine willpower as embodied by the prophets Elijah and John the Baptist. Divine Will and ruthless compassion are the abilities to confront and cut through the ego in order to serve the best interests of the soul, even if it is painful or judged to be "wrong." Willpower is what sustains and drives us, what brings us into dynamic action, penetration, and persistence in achieving goals of any kind. When aligned to the Divine Will or the Divine Plan, willpower becomes the foundation for love's actions.

Christ Consciousness embodies the qualities of embracing an unconditional love, traveling into the deepest darkness and bringing love there out of compassion. These qualities were embodied by Mother Mary and her higher Self Isis in their embrace and compassion for all life. Christ overcomes the shadow of contraction, selfishness, and the fear that keeps the heart closed in order to do so.

Christ Consciousness embodies the lived direct experience of faith and trust in life and loyalty. Loyalty is choosing to be loyal to love in every moment. In this choice, we enter peace, the peace that arises as a result of the mind shifting its identity and values to love, by placing trust and loyalty only in that which loves. Apostle Joseph of Arimathea embodied these qualities, and one has to overcome cynicism, fear, and temptation in order to live this.

Christ Consciousness embodies surrender, the easiest act for the soul, and the hardest act for the ego; to simply let go. Surrender breaks you down and reorganizes every part of you when you sincerely ask for love to enter your life, and for you to live this life, beckoned by the call of the soul that desires to recognize itself. Surrender makes us gentle, soft, and transparent. In surrender, all the things you have to fight for, or against, are conquered, and a new way of living arises. Apostle John the Beloved and Master Kuthumi embodied these qualities of loving wisdom. Christ Consciousness overcomes deep struggle, seeking, sloth, and inertia in order to do so.

Christ Consciousness embodies holy desire and holy love in the desire for transformation and union within your own heart and with your partner. By sharing the fruits of these unions with all, in the overflowing healing and sharing actions of holy love, Christ Consciousness fully includes your own personal side in this embrace, leaving nothing out. How else are we to fully experience our humanity and serve its flowering? The Master Lady Nada, higher Self of Mary Magdalene, helps us to overcome codependency and attachment on every level in order to do so.

Christ Consciousness embodies the feminine power of fertility and manifestation, the power of cocreation with the Ancient Lineages of Mothers, the sacred feminine lineages that have been on earth since the beginning of creation. In this power of cocreation the seeds were planted for the Christ Blueprint to anchor and flourish Now, to birth from the womb of creation. Cocreation is the basis of an enlightened civilization, where there are many Christs working together, not just one. The Apostle Mary Salome and her higher Self Ishtar helped Yeshua in this connection, assisting him to overcome, as we all must, lust, competitiveness, and male-female inequality in order to do so.

Just as Yeshua needed to connect with the lineage of ancient mothers throughout history, so he had to connect to its masculine equivalent through the vehicle of Apostle Peter, a Priest of Lord Melchizedek. Many millennia before Yeshua this Master created the Melchizedek Priesthood, a priesthood dedicated to the creation of love and wisdom in our societies on earth through dedicated service. Apostle Peter was the first to recognize Yeshua as Christ. In recognizing the best in ourselves and others, one draws out their soul in unexpected ways, bringing them into new expression and full manifestation. The soul becomes free when it is seen. Christ Consciousness grounds, anchors, and makes real its Presence through lived, powerful, and authoritative action in the world, the Key of Peter.

Christ Consciousness embodies the witnessing quality of pure consciousness, seeing all that is happening around you for what it truly is without interpretation, projection, and preference coloring or distorting anything. Apostle Thomas was the vehicle who saw the big picture, enabling every part of the body of Christ to fulfill its role, allowing us to access the power of regeneration or Resurrection, as embodied by the Master Babaji. We all have to overcome the shadow side of witness consciousness, which is isolation and separation from our feelings, from relationship, and from the feminine, in order to do so.

Christ Consciousness embodies Holy Law, the law of evolution, the evolutionary drive that pushes humanity forward into its next unfolding. The Apostle Simon Zealot embodied this fierce, deep passion for evolution, which is why he was guided by Prophet Moses. To live in

Holy Law, Yeshua lived totally in the moment while following the previous impulses of Creation and the Divine Plan as laid down by Moses in order to do so.

Christ Consciousness embodies the diamond mind of creative intelligence, clarity, discernment and lightning power of penetration. This diamond mind manifests in navigating, and seeing through, the law of the mirror. The mirror of Judas is where the projection of our minds, and wounds, gets displayed onto the world and people around us as a reflection of ourselves and our own creations. Lucifer, the higher Self of Judas, is the principle of polarity. Polarity is vital in order to manifest matter, the earth, and creation. Without it there would be no matter, no yin and yang. Lucifer has played this role, of creating through polarity throughout history in obedience to Divine Will, for which he has been vilified and judged because of peoples' own projections about the nature and purpose of light and dark. To learn and integrate this crucial dynamic allows us to live fully embodied on earth, in sovereign freedom, with full acceptance of matter, of earth, of the feminine. To do this we have to overcome persecution, judgment, pride, and vanity.

Christ Consciousness embodies the Divine or Golden Child of innocence and openness that has the ability to touch all people regardless of race, religion, or culture. Yeshua set the foundation to allow the Indigo and Golden Children to be able to arrive on earth today. In order to fully integrate Christ Consciousness we have to overcome the Antichrist force: all the shadow sides of the twelve Apostles, the twelve shadow qualities of Christ Consciousness we need to integrate in order to live a loving, healed, and blessed life.

Using the Christ Blueprint to navigate through life allows us to see and fulfill within all the aspects that create Christ Consciousness. In this seeing of all aspects, our highest potential is to allow ourselves to become fluid and embody each of the different qualities of Christ Consciousness, as and when it is required.

We can identify which aspects of Christ Consciousness we need to integrate, and then work with them with the goal of embodying all aspects. Of course, you will all feel drawn to a few aspects in particular, which are your strong points, the aspects you already know and love about yourself, the aspects you feel comfortable with. This then becomes the foundation for you to explore the remaining qualities that you have not yet integrated, and the shadows that you are still living with. In this, we become centered in the Self, allowing the limitless to take hold in our lives, fulfilling the promise stated so clearly by Yeshua: you are Christ.

The Christ Council

THE CHRIST COUNCIL

The Christ Council is a Council of Enlightened Masters who create, oversee, and implement the Blueprint of Christ Consciousness. They are the teachers and supporters of the Christ throughout all times, the Ones behind Christ. They have always remained behind the scenes in order to serve their purpose. They have created and held the seeds for the evolution of humanity since the beginning of the Divine Plan, to culminate in the birthing of Christ Consciousness in this age: the age of shadowless joy and constant celebration.

The Christ Council oversees, organizes, and executes the Blueprint of Christ as established by the thirteen Apostles of the Body of Christ two thousand years ago. They are responsible for birthing Christ Consciousness in this age now through the revealing of the secret teachings of Christ and his inner circle of close Apostles. The Masters are thirteen in number, and were responsible for overlighting, or supervising, the bodies of the twelve Apostles of Christ Yeshua when they were alive.

The Christ Council are the Lineage of Christed Masters throughout history, from the beginning of time, the beginning of Creation. They are drawn from four main sacred traditions: the Indian, the Tibetan, the Hebrew, and the Egyptian. There are also four female Masters sitting in the Council who are just now starting to reveal their Keys en masse.

Christ Yeshua embodied the Keys from all of these traditions, including the Feminine Mysteries of Birth and Cocreation. Yeshua is the last in a long line of Christs, and he embodied to make these Keys available to humanity now in the twenty-first century: the flowering of the seeds of the Christ Blueprint on a mass scale.

DIVINE DESCENT

The Christ Council are responsible for activating quantum shifts in Christ Consciousness among the Christ family by sharing practical tools and transmissions that rapidly accelerate consciousness, leading to the eventual descent into the physical body of Christ Consciousness.

Divine descent is seen as part of the flowering of the Christ Blueprint and will lead to global transformation on a mass scale. Imagine the qualities of the Christ Council fully embodied: by their mere presence alone, millions of people in suffering will be instantly counterbalanced by their light. This is the next step for those committed enough to become empty vessels of the Christ Light.

The crown is where this Divine descent occurs. This Divine descent is what made Yeshua the Christ, by Christ descending into Yeshua so he became Christ Yeshua; it is the process by which Maitreya entered Shakyamuni to make him the Buddha. Shiva also entered Ramana on his enlightenment to make him a maharishi, and on his death was seen to leave his body in a blinding flash of light witnessed by hundreds. The Apostles after his Resurrection were also overlighted by the Divine Mother, who gave them all the power to heal and share the Christ energy with many others.

Some traditions refer to this process as being "overshadowed" or "overlighted" by the Masters. Some speak of it as the "baptism of the Holy Spirit." This Divine descent is similar to the process of enlightenment. Before enlightenment, most of us identify ourselves as a "self," as an entity fixed in time and space with a history, personality, and individual memories distinct from any other. Upon enlightenment, we discover that this sense of a fixed or permanent self is an illusion, that we are simply a witness to a series of personalities that come and go.

The Divine descent takes this one step further. We begin to dissolve many of these human personalities that govern our existence. We become more and more identified with the Divine personalities that take over our lives and destinies. This Divine descent is one of the aims of the Christ Blueprint: to enable bodies on earth to embody these qualities of enlightened consciousness. These states of consciousness come to those who are fully ready to serve as vehicles for the transformation of humanity and are fiercely dedicated and willing to go the whole way in the full embodiment of the Christ Light.

This is an unprecedented move. The Christ Council are uncloaking themselves in a way never done before, stating to us all, "Here we are; we are here to provide the Quickening. This is what you have to do to descend the Christ Light."

They are offering help, support, guidance, and practical transformation on an unprecedented scale right now to you. They are opening the doors to the Council of Christ, amplifying the descent of Christ Light onto earth now, because it is time. The Antichrist has almost fully descended onto earth, and now it is time for the Christ Light to shine clearly in its full power, majesty, joy, and love. To gain access to direct teaching, one must be available by clearing away all obstacles along the rainbow bridge or antakarana that connects your crown chakra to Source. These clearings allow for direct initiation and guidance from the Apostles or Masters within the Christ Council that you are most connected to.

CHRIST CONSCIOUSNESS

Christ, through love, embodies all of humanity within itself. It holds the world in the crucible of our own consciousness and helps to transform it. In Christ Consciousness one sees the perfection in all beings and simultaneously sees the correcting that is required that obstructs others from realizing Christ.

One can experience a lot of human beings at once and what is occurring within their consciousness. This means that many people very soon can be vessels that shift and impact mass consciousness directly, working on large numbers of people and on towns and cities themselves. Conversely, one is also more able to help others by holding them in prayer in a powerful, felt way that deeply transforms them.

Christ is God acting out God's wishes for Itself. As you are God acting out your own wishes, you realize that there is truly nothing to do; and yet the actions flow through your empty vessel, actualizing the wishes that have already happened.

The purpose of the Christ Blueprint is to create leaders, teachers, and bringers of the new paradigm, to guide those who are ready and who know deep within themselves that they are here to establish the foundation for an enlightened civilization on earth. These revelations are the final parts of the secret teachings of Christ. The rest are being revealed, or have been revealed, by others. The purpose of these teachings is to bring wisdom, ripeness, and joy so that what Christ is, and who the women are, can be known, felt, and reenacted once more on earth by those who dare to step up—by those who dare to take life by the horns and live it fully.

This is what we did two thousand years ago.

Are you ready to complete the final steps?

The Blueprint was anchored then; this is the flowering time for those seeds to activate.

There was only one Yeshua; but there will be many Christs.

As Yeshua said, "There are many who will come after me who will do greater things than I." This could be you, and in fact it is your birthright, what Yeshua died for. For many are called, but few choose themselves.

Holy Desire

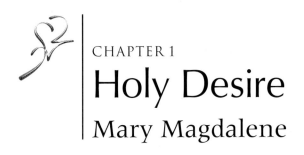

CHAPTER 1
Holy Desire
Mary Magdalene

I, Mary Magdalene, open the doors to holy desire and holy love. As soul mate and twin flame to Yeshua, our holy and alchemical union played a crucial role in igniting and grounding the body of Christ Light into earth.

My burning desire to give all, both to my flame and to God, through the marriage of both of our human and Divine forged me into a transparent, open, receptive vessel, both to Yeshua as a man and Yeshua as the Christ. Through this complete vulnerability I found myself, in Self-knowledge and unconditional love.

It was holy desire that ignited my love to complete my mission, and it was love that then mastered me.

Holy desire always wants to embrace all aspects of the heart, from the most universal and impersonal to the most deeply intimate and personal heart, allowing all the possibilities for love in its infinite expressions. In this, the truth that Yeshua gave to me was made real: to love one being fully, completely, and unconditionally is to love the whole of humanity.

We give in order to give, not give in order to receive. Through the giving we receive.

HOLY DESIRE

As a guardian of sacred relationship, I ask all those interested in the purpose of tantra and sacred sexuality, which is to reach Self-realization, to raise their vibration to that of unconditional love and to practice this first and foremost. This is the essence of the practice, and then the worship in the bedroom can continue everywhere else also.

Sacred sensuality leads into orgasmic levels of passionate presence, free-flowing life fueled by holy desire. Holy desire is a wanting, an inner burning that propels you, fuels you to keep deepening into the Divine. Holy desire is not motivation; it is the deep inner yearning of the soul that can never be stopped, that does not change or waver. Holy desire is passion: passion for the soul, passion for the Divine, passion to fulfill the soul's deepest urges and yearnings. To desire oneness is to live in this passion, always open to following this thread wherever it may appear and wherever it may take you.

Nothing can be achieved without the energy of desire. Desire lies behind every thought, action, and word we utter. It sparks the will to do, to move, to live; it is life in action, linking us to Divine Will as desire fuels will. Holy desire makes us give our all. It makes us place our very soul at the altar of the Divine, to allow Divine Will to flow through us unimpeded, for the soul's keenest desire is to be reunited with God in the bridal chamber of the heart in sacred relationship.

If you do not desire, you are not moving toward anything. Desire is the energy that makes all things grow, flower, and bloom. It enables the soul to expand and reach for the infinite, and to surrender to the infinite when it comes, despite the fears that may arise. Holy desire never ends, as God never ends. The universe is always expanding, as is the soul, as is desire. The soul's desire for love, for God, can never be completely fulfilled. It is ongoing.

Holy desire is the beating heart of the soul; it is the life force of the soul, the soul's blood. Without this blood flowing through the soul's veins, we are lifeless, hollow. No matter how enlightened we become there is always more. In wanting this, and stating this, we let God know we want Her, and God can respond.

Want God. Express it every day. Holy desire is the life force, the golden thread that connects you and God. The more you amplify the voltage going through this thread, the more God will sit up and take notice, and actually send you more through this thread.

Holy desire leads to love, for holy desire is the love of God expressing itself, for no other reason than this is what it must do, for this is its very nature. True desire is unwavering. It is grounded, constant, and consistent. The only thing that can fulfill a soul's thirst is to drink God, and drink God constantly.

There is only one desire, for there is only one soul. All other desires that we think we may have are merely substitutes, or steps along the way, to becoming devoted to the underlying desire behind all desires that has always existed and will always exist: the desire to give and express love. This is how we have all been created. We are the effect of God's desire to extend love to all of creation.

Therefore we have to rechannel our desire into what we are created for, and what we truly are. In this we realign ourselves to our innate nature, we realign our vital force back to the source of our creation. When we realign to this holy desire, we realign ourselves to the One that creates us all, and in this we allow holy desire to carry us, desire that has been stripped of its artificial coverings and manipulations and reeducated to come into its natural, original wholeness.

Judgment and fear block desire, or rechannel its energy into other purposes, other goals—judgment of who we are and what life is about. Fear has been used to dampen desire, and repression and manipulation of desire shackles humanity's innate drive and ability to love.

When the flow of desire is blocked, we start to die. When we forget our passions and allow them to fall by the wayside, we lose a part of ourselves. Death of desire and passion is the death of the soul, a death that only a profound shakeup can then reignite. For love is the purpose of desire, and love is the extension of this desire into creation.

Holy desire can be an intense force—sensual, powerful, passionate, and overwhelming. This is why many fear it, the fear being that once it is released you will not be able to control it as it leads to the overflowing of Life through you. When we live in holy desire we cannot be controlled, for we flow in Life itself. We can, however, choose when we allow the tap of desire to open, what effects and manifestations it will have, or how we choose to act on any wave of desire flowing through us.

This is why many religions have warned about the evils of desire, equating it with lust and greed. These are distortions of the original loving force of holy desire that creates out of Self-delight and for joy.

Desire grows through intimacy; intimacy grows through desire. Intimacy, conversing with God and Beloved daily, leads to more opening, more revelation, and more being given. Intimacy leads to the deepest of wounds being exposed, if both parties are available for it. Anyone can be intimate in the depths at any moment if you are but willing to be open to this possibility. Wounds may cover desire and intimacy, but they cannot stop you from expressing these qualities in a moment of opening. Being available to this opening is all that it takes.

Be intimate with God. Desire God. Redirect all your desires toward this. Want God like a lover, deep inside you. Make love with God in this dance; show God your desire to be possessed by Him or Her. Always want more of God; let this be your prayer every day.

Prostrations to Honor and Recognize Christ Within: Making You and Your Partner Sacred

A beautiful way to be intimate with God is to see God in your partner. In prostration to God in your partner, you refine and recognize the powerful energy of desire into sanctity and honor. Prostration brings the experience of surrender and union to both of you. It is the end of pride, ego, and attachment, and the redirecting of raw desire into holy desire. When this happens, the Divine reveals itself.

Surrendering and losing yourself in respect, love, and adoration of Christ in the other is surrendering and recognizing that which is only your true Self.

In giving yourself to the other in prostration, you are giving yourself to the core of existence—the Self. In this spirit, prostrations to your partner, recognizing the other as Christ, is the most Selfish act you can perform. Nothing is more Selfish, and yet nothing so purifies selfishness into selflessness, or the Self. For the secret is that you and your partner share the same Self.

Prostration brings the experience of surrender to both of you. When this happens, the Divine reveals itself.

Physically, prostrations open up the solar plexus chakra, our center of empowerment and selfless power, making us humble to the Divine in the other and our own self, allowing power, choice, and love to merge together. You use your body as the vehicle for this recognition and acceptance of your own Divine nature.

In prostration, communion or contact of soul to soul, light body to light body occurs. You both share the same spirit with each other. You deepen your trust in each other. Here, purity is the secret of fulfilling your desires. These desires come true when they are held in the heart.

To prostrate before your man is to prostrate before Christ, to commune with Christ. To prostrate before your woman is to prostrate before Christ, to commune with Christ.

Most relationships are based on need. You need your partner to become whole in some way. In this practice, we start to own the qualities we find attractive in the other, that we want to learn from the other, that we think are missing in our own self.

In prostration these qualities can be freely shared between each other. You prostrate to the qualities that you find appealing and attractive in the other—what the other represents to you on the deepest levels, both spiritually and emotionally. Which part of them fills the hole in you? In this, you can start to become what the other represents to you, and what you need from the other to become whole within your own self.

Step 1: Identify three soul and emotional qualities that are attractive in the other, and that you wish to embody within yourself. Share them with your partner. Decide between you to become them.

Step 2: Hold one quality in mind. Stand silently in a sacred heart space in front of your partner, and place your hands in prayer pose above your head. You are treating your partner as a living God, so sink into this space. Imagine you are in the Creator's Presence.

How would you treat this Presence?

Your partner is holding the energy of the quality you are prostrating to. For example, if you value and need your partner's sense of gentleness and empathy, she will be holding that energy for you as you stand before her, and prostrate before her. She can take any body position and be sitting, standing, holding a mudra, or her arms and legs in whatever position most embodies gentleness.

Now place your hands above your heart. Sink to your knees and place your body flat on the ground, with your hands stretched out in front of you, head on the ground. Feel your heart on the earth. Breathe and draw gentleness into yourself. The partner who is standing gives and transmits those qualities that the other partner needs to them.

Now reverse the process for partner A and B.

End each cycle of prostrations with a deep Heart Bow to each other.

Desire liberates if we follow it all the way to its source: love.

Desire liberates if we no longer separate or judge any part of ourselves.

Desire liberates when we align it to its original purpose and choice: I desire God.

Desiring God is surrender to Life itself.

May love's desires bless you. We are all Beloveds in our holy desire for union.

THE ORDER OF MAGDALENE

The Order of Magdalene is an ancient order that goes back to Aghartha, the inner earth kingdom. It is an order of holy, sacred, and Divine women who hold open the space of the womb for full cocreation with God.

By holy, sacred, and Divine we mean three things. To be holy means that you are whole within your own sense of knowing and purpose. You know your path and have a felt sense of what the Divine is. You have a vibrant magnetic aura that shares peace with others. You are a servant of the Divine. To be sacred, we have sanctified, blessed, and given the ego fully to the soul's leadership; you have given away something that was very real to you, to the soul. The soul becomes master to the servant of the ego. To be Divine, we are situated in joy, peace, love, and beauty. You become a cocreator with God.

This ancient order has always been based on the remembrance that this is our inheritance, our Divine birthright; to cocreate with God and birth realities. One can say that the order was based on remembering the truth and power of women to seed and birth worlds, and to spiritually and physically create this world.

The Order of Magdalene is based upon the womb and the possibilities of sacred relating. Several strains of this lineage came through into

Egypt, but I myself was initiated into this lineage outside Egypt. The Order of Magdalene is held by a few initiates today in Europe and Turkey, who have perpetuated it very loyally and truthfully, according to the teachings and transmissions I had shared with their blood lineage.[1]

The Order of Magdalene is serving its purpose in keeping these traditions ticking over in the consciousness of the collective. The recent resurgence in the Divine feminine has been orchestrated through me, Mother Mary and Marie Salome, to gradually percolate these seeds to grow and bloom just a bit further into the collective consciousness, to allow the deeper revelation and empowerment for women and men to occur.

Women whose ambitions, openheartedness, and dedication to healing their own wounds of the disempowered feminine have led them into these areas, and they have experienced moments of the power of the womb to allow them to grow and to allow their ambitions to serve the greater good.

However, we see the Order of Magdalene going to a new level now within the next seven to ten years. We wish to bring back this knowledge, these teachings and transmissions, as a dynamic, vital, and living presence and power in ways that herald the full inclusion and embracing of the Divine masculine within the womb.

However, it will take a group of heartful, passionate, and dedicated women to create this momentum for the Womb Woman to resurface on

---

1. The tragic thing about many of the Order of Magdalene is that they have been holding the space for the womb and twin flames, but many of them do not have their flames embodied or have their wombs open. However, they are serving and holding the space open for others to do so. This is another reason why this age is so important: so many things have had to be endured and no longer need to be.

There has been much suffering and hardship. Imagine these women who were initiated, who were taught and knew the truth and power of the womb and their ability to cocreate reality; they had glimpses of it, they saw me living this truth, and yet many of them died without ever having embodied this truth fully as the time was not yet ripe and ready on earth for that to happen.

earth. This is why we say within seven to ten years; then the conditions will be far more favorable for it to occur, and this too has been a gradual process that has been rapidly accelerating over the last twenty years.

Some things on the earth have to be cleared away first to allow this to happen; some of the older generation also have to pass on—those who have been holding a certain space, but now that space is crippling to a new expression of femininity to be heard and received in the world.

The Order of Magdalene is the awakening of the Womb of the World. It is in this collective womb that humanity can be birthed into fullness and into love. We will share much more with you about this Way of the Womb in the near future. In the meantime, keep opening, softening, and being true to the feminine spirit. We honor you as part of the One Womb, in the process of birthing yourselves and a Christed planet.

—*Amun*

Holy Love

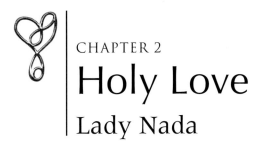

CHAPTER 2

Holy Love
Lady Nada

SACRED RELATING

Love weaves its golden red thread through all existence. In following this golden red thread throughout the dark moments of your life, throughout the lighter moments, and throughout those bittersweet times where both sadness and joy merge in a symphony to crack the heart open, when we feel the love that heals and is ever present.

This golden red thread, vibrating, undulating throughout all life, is the thread I hold. It is the thread that brings Beloveds together, the thread that, when separated from, keeps Beloveds apart.

I, Lady Nada, am a guardian of sacred relating. Sacred relationship is the core, the beating heart of the Christ Blueprint, the union of your essential polarities within the bridal chamber of your own heart. I bear the sadness and the joy that we feel when twin aspects of ourselves are separated, and I weave them both together so they may meet again. I endured this pain, the pain I felt as Mary Magdalene in her love for Yeshua, as both woman and as Goddess. We all hold this Blueprint within us, and this becomes accelerated when we meet our twin flame, or soul mate.

The fullness of creation is based on sacred relationship. Yeshua could only do what he did by being in sacred relationship; otherwise he could not have fulfilled the Divine Plan of embodying love in all aspects from impersonal to intimate personal. The Divine blueprint involves holy relationship with another you who is your mirror, your polarity, the spark that you first came from, and from which you separated in order to experience something else, something new. When the experience is complete you can remerge, and remember, who you are.

I, Lady Nada, am the voice of love and silence, the sound of love that runs throughout creation. The underlying vibration of creation is love. When we align with this vibration, we enter the perpetually resounding love that runs throughout all sentient life, which gives birth to all languages, all words, and all sounds.

This underlying vibration is feminine in nature and expression; it is receptive and issues forth from rest, from repose. In expressing this vibration, one gives voice to love. In love, we hear what we want to. Whatever is said will be understood from where you are at in your understanding of what love is, and the openness of feeling that you have to love. This openness occurs when you have had the experiences of separation, and something cracks within you. Then you can hear and feel clearly what love is.

Allowing the heart to feel the energy behind the words, without judgment, allows us to hear in innocence. Hearing in innocence allows the heart to feel.

In this relating there is true equality in every way. Male patriarchy no longer dominates, and female matriarchy no longer dominates. Both voices are equal and respected, and the Voice of Love is created as the third voice, the One Voice, between them. God's voice is birthed. This is the Holy Trinity made manifest: love between man, woman, and God as One. This creates true and total God consciousness, celebration, and joy. Then a new earth can be created.

Twin flames or soul mates can be drawn down from the heavens into a body *now* through Divine dispensation and guidance. If you are truly ready, and understand the five steps toward sacred relationship, then this can happen. If not, then you still have work to do based on need, expectation, limiting beliefs, and unfinished experiences with your inner polarities. If you have done this work, then it can happen quickly. If not, ask for your unfinished lessons to be accelerated, and delve deeper into clearing the shadow.

THE THREE VEILS

The first veil through which all humans move in the process of sacred relating is the shadow of separation, the residue of wounds we have created in our deepest pain and suffering; that of being separate from part of our own Self. The second veil is feeling the polarities, the mixtures of pain and pleasure, joy and sorrow, which can keep us feeling hooked on the bittersweet feelings of the heart. This aspect of our essential humanness then expands to become willing to feel our deepest vulnerabilities and emotions, where nothing is denied.

The third veil is staying stuck in the content, easy, and pleasurable relating that you have at the moment, without wishing to move further from your space of relative contentment that serves you to a degree. But you know, deep within you, that there is so much more, so much more you deserve and that you have felt. But you have forgotten about it and relegated it to a dream, a fantasy, a romantic illusion. And now you have settled for comfort, stability, security, affection, and pleasantry—and left out part of your soul in this deal, this bargain.

The golden red thread of love moves throughout these veils. At any time you can notice this thread, as a whispered thought, an unusual feeling, a hope, a dream, a longing in the heart—and ride with it. Follow it, act upon it, do something radical, and enjoy the bliss and adventure of the path of sacred relating.

Move for the best, for you deserve it, and can attain it.

It is waiting for you patiently, for you to notice it, and follow it, for this is the voice of the heart that weaves its way throughout all times. All it needs is for you to listen, and act upon it. This is the voice of your highest heart calling for you to fulfill yourself, to complete yourself, for the good of all.

Love says nothing, but allows everything to be said. This is the sound of silence, the only way my name can be called, the only way you will hear my name. Nada is the Word of Union. The sound of the moment of love is my name, and this sound is silent; it is the space created when two Beloveds present each other with themselves.

Holding this space alone within yourself, and presenting this space to your Beloved, allows true intimacy to occur. Fears may arise in this vulnerability of true expression. For love is not sharing what you do not have; it is sharing what you have, and in this sharing one expands and rises beyond their idea of love. In this sharing and openness lies the possibility that something more, something magical, can occur.

SACRED RELATIONSHIP

In sacred relationship, one sees and treats the other as God. There becomes no separation between inner male and inner woman. There arises a harmonious flow, a synchronous unfolding, a simple knowing, a shared communion, where both male and female dissolve back into the sound of silence. Truly, love requires no boundaries when this whole, intimate space is shared with all of one's being.

Sacred relating initiates a process of soul merging, and a deep sharing of soul blueprints between you and your partner. Your evolution will accelerate exponentially in many unexpected and even unasked-for ways, each of you receiving the deepest shadow lesson and energies you need from the other to complete the wholeness of yourself.

In true intimacy flesh merges with spirit. This happens in the light body, the meeting point that allows body and soul to make contact. Your light body, or subtle body, is who you are in all spheres: planetary, solar, galactic, and universal consciousness. It is in your light body that you travel to the stars, that you receive knowledge and intuitions about the nature of life. It is your light body that allows you to enter a room and feel the tension, when you feel something unexplained or unexpected is about to happen, when you know the unexplained and inexplicable, when you channel or commune with nonphysical beings.

Intimacy is when two people merge on all levels; the sexual energy and light body become one with your partner, and all boundaries dissolve. When two light bodies connect, even if we are miles apart, we feel the other as a living, breathing Presence within us, and are sensitive to all that they are feeling and experiencing, especially in relation to us.

In intimacy, we are so tuned in with our partner that we feel their sadness, their pleasure, their thoughts, and their intent, even if we are many thousands of miles away. This bonding at all levels transcends physical, sexual, and spiritual programming about what we feel relationships are, and should be. For it is in the light body that the complete giving of yourself to your partner, the complete giving of yourself to spirit, can take place. In this process, wounds, abuses, mistrusts, and barriers to this complete relating *will* occur as you are now connecting on the most profound level. You may find yourself losing yourself in your partner; you may find deep aversions or attachments revealing themselves; you may rediscover old patterns that you thought had been healed, and brand new ones arising, all surfacing in order to be transformed. It is at this point that a true relationship can occur, if these wounds can be met with patience, self-responsibility, appreciation, radical honesty, and kindness, by both your partner and yourself.

In true intimacy there are no more barriers, no more shields; you are both totally naked and exposed in all ways. This can be deeply disturbing as there is nowhere left to hide, yet this ultimately can lead to us being totally present and uninhibited, free, and our true self, playful and blissful on all levels. This occurs if we resonate with our partner, and share the same core values. Here, sex is not used to fulfill needs: it is Divine Play, and love meeting love.

The First Level of Sacred Relating

The first level of sacred relating is like a key fitting into a lock. The complementary qualities are there between male and female; they instantly fit in together, and they start to unlock each other into the depths of love and shadow. This harmonizing and meeting can take many months or years, and can happen both within one person in mystical union, and between two bodies reflecting this inner process.

Within this first level is the instant deep recognition from the soul and the urge to be inseparable, the urge to constantly revolve around each other, as you have found a part of yourself. In this dance, this spinning and turning around each other, more and more facets both within and without are experienced and brought into awareness. This literally creates a rapidly moving vortex of light within both individual light bodies when they are together. This vortex of light is a powerful phenomenon, which is very much appreciated in this galaxy, and is seen by many beings.

This vortex of light literally spins so fast and so deep that all faces of light and dark come up to be recognized, experienced, and dissolved. One realizes that in total giving for the sake of giving, there is total receiving. Integrity on both sides is the essential bond that allows this process to be whole.

Many of these sacred relationships are completely opposite, or polar in nature. This is the dynamic in many twin flames, for when one separates from oneself, one polarizes also. In this polarization lies the deepest experiences of separation that when experienced fully lead us back into union in the most glorious and graceful of ways.

However, the rejoining of these polarities in sacred relationships may prove to be very challenging for some, as there is much to confront about the very basic nature of separation, need, and expectation within oneself. This deep questioning and awareness in honesty, humility, and a willingness to grow allows the flower of sacred relationship to keep unfolding into the infinite.

Living as Love

All relationships are here to serve us to live as love. This is what they have been created for: to recognize and draw out the Christ in ourselves and the other. Recognizing and drawing this out, even if the other does not initially recognize it, gives both of you an opportunity to validate love, a precious opportunity to step into the real. This opportunity opens up infinite potential. In this holy moment, absolute truth reveals itself, and anything veiling this can dissolve.

Authentically recognizing love in the other, in the moment, dissolves all boundaries. Heart touches heart, and truth speaks.

All relationships are a conspiracy created by God for us to live as love, to live in the thirteen qualities of Christ Consciousness. The only reality is love, and it is only love that can take us home. And love has many faces.

Recognize this now in your relatings. Where could you live as Christ? Ask yourself, how would Christ respond in this situation? What would Christ do?

To enact this, all one has to do is sacrifice the mind's responses and thoughts that place value on anything else apart from love expressing itself, here and now. This is surrender to the ever-present flow of love, just waiting for you to allow it through, to allow it to take over you, to allow you to question the thoughts and responses that deny love.

The flowering of a sacred relationship, a relating born in, consecrated to, and dependent on love, depends on the ability to seal the doors of the relationship, to stop running away. This sealing of the doors eventually dissolves the need to keep repeating the patterns of separation that lie within you that will inevitably come up in the furnace of sacred relationship.

When you seal the doors you cannot run away; when you seal the doors you have to confront what is happening and who you are, which is all a mirror of your own history. If you open the door and walk out, then valuable deepening is left out. If you close the door, bolt it, turn around, and be with the heat with your partner, then you go deeper in the mandala of the love that you truly feel and have always wished for.

Sealing the doors also means that no one else is allowed into this sanctum, this haven where only you and the Beloved reside and commune. A sacred circle of protection is erected that allows the full blooming and unfolding of love to occur away from prying eyes and the minds of those who wish for what you have but may try to break it.

The urge to unite is what drives this first level of sacred relationship, the urge to merge. If you are feeling this with your Beloved, then a deep commitment between you will lay the foundation to go deeper. As one unites inner male and female within one's own self there is no longer any need left in relationship. You need, or desire, nothing from the other as you are whole within yourself. This leads to a deep peace.

If you are in relationship and this happens, then all that is left is to help the other by being whole in yourself. This is serving the other, yourself, and the whole of humanity. To be whole in yourself means that the polar piece of you has integrated, landed, and completed your own polarity. If you are male, you integrate the female qualities and become a whole man in every way. If you are female, you integrate the male qualities and become a whole woman.

You choose, on a core inner level, to do everything yourself and realize this is the truth.

You have no need, desire, or hunger for support emotionally, mentally, or spiritually. Living in and creating this field of love automatically affects those you are intimate with, accelerating their own unfolding into wholeness.

This integration is alchemy, some of the deepest alchemy possible, and the purpose of relationship up to a point. Beyond this point, when this alchemy establishes itself in one or both partners, then relating transforms into its highest potential. As there is no need or wanting something from the other to complete oneself (that is essentially part of your own Self), all that remains is Presence that shares, extends, and embraces love.

If you choose to leave the relationship, you will only wish to be with someone who is similarly whole. Then you can share space with that other, only wishing to be with that person if more can be created to help others by your coming together.

The Second Level of Sacred Relating

The voice of tender soft silence is the voice of love. This voice of love lies within the deep, rich, dark envelope that contains the Beloved. This voice of silence can always be felt, be it within the singing of the trees, in the breaths that you share, in the rustle of thoughts that dissolve in the light that love shines onto the Beloved.

This silence holds a sacred relating together. This quality of innate, receptive, warm, and inviting silence allows one to be who they are, and express their truth on the deepest and most inexpressible levels. To be invited to express truth in this deep silence that is warmth, one can truly enter sacred union and commune.

This is what Magdalene shared with Yeshua. They held each other in this luscious warm embrace that only silence can afford, between two who love each other and share that love to humanity and beyond. In this constant embrace one never misses the other, for the silence contains all. In this silence of love is also the wisest intelligence, the deepest knowing, the heartfelt intuition, the transmission of telepathy, the joining of two whole individuals in the silence that permeates everything in creation.

This is also what happens when two souls, two bodies, dissolve into each other when not physically making love. In this dissolution, oneness with the silence of love is experienced. The more times that one experiences this dissolution, the closer both become, and the closer the Holy Trinity gets manifested on earth.

Sharing in this silence means that the feminine is at her attuned, receptive, inviting best. By attuned we mean feeling into the silence that connects her and her beloved masculine side, and moving those currents of energy to massage and bathe her Beloved in these subtle planes of the light body. In this exquisite and refined interaction, the male gets drawn to the magnetism of the feminine, and begins to send out his emanations of penetration, as he knows he will be received and joyfully, sensually accepted in the wholeness of his masculinity.

This subtlety of weaving flesh and soul together through male and female bodies initiates a process of soul communion. This soul communion allows one to open up the depths of intimacy, touching the deepest parts of each other, allowing them to unfold into awareness, acceptance, and dissolution. Communion is when we are one, in two bodies, expressing the trinity of all creation. This is the art of love, and the refinement of the soul into manifestation through love.

The Third Level of Sacred Relating

There is a place in every heart that nothing can touch save God, our one true Beloved. In sacred relating, one comes to realize that no other can touch this place, and we can feel it intensely as a loss, as an absence, as nothing apart from God's love can touch and make us whole within. In this, one reaches the third level of sacred relating, which happens when both beings have met the Beloved within their own hearts.

The absence we feel, even in the deepest of loves, is the potential of total presence making itself known to us. Of course we can feel this alone on our own mystic path, but in sacred relationship the absence becomes even keener, even more heartfelt, even more devastating. The absence of you from your Beloved even in the midst of such deep love makes you realize you are alone, and nothing and nobody can make up for this.

Whether this takes many months or many years to realize is up to the maturity of both partners. And of course the love and wisdom that is present between both of you can wash away and dissolve anything that stands in the way of love. Any obstacle, any wound, any judgment can be dissolved through combining love with wisdom.

This third level of sacred relating literally lays the foundation for a new civilization, for a new earth. And this is possible in a natural, graceful, and fluid way if one but believes that it is possible. As this faith and openness deepens into conviction, and then into knowing, then anything becomes possible. Anything can be birthed, created, and realized, for God Itself will be watching you, guiding you, and willing to give you all that love is. For in sacred marriage you become God conscious beings, and there ceases to be separation between that which created you and that which you are now cocreating.

God truly loves you and wishes to give you everything. This is not a belief but a knowing and an actual grounded manifestation. When you truly know that God wishes to give you everything, then even more love can be shared and expressed with the whole of humanity. This is your wish too, in the deepest level of your heart, beyond idea, beyond belief.

THE SHADOW SIDE

The shadow for those wishing to embody Magdalene is the fractured use of desire. Feeling relationship is your salvation without being whole in yourself first; feeling that if you receive enough support through being loved by another that you will, at last, be able to be fully yourself.

Love, when seen as desire alone, leads to suffering. Love here is seen as need, a need to attach oneself to others in order to achieve a sense of security and belonging, rather than love's true nature of openness and fearlessness. True compassion and love have no territorial bounds—they are freely offered and received. Love is not just for one person.

Freedom here becomes lost because you project onto others what you can only truly realize within yourself. This dependency becomes a trap for true freedom, as now freedom is dependent on another. What can result is giving to get, or conditional love; thinking that the other can fulfill you; manipulating to "keep" the other; over-romanticizing, creating ideals; thinking that the Beloved "belongs" to them, or to own, be owned, possess or be possessed, control or be controlled.

Many times the deepest lessons we learn are from the most difficult relationships, those that prepare us for the real relationship: with our Self.

The shadow side of holy love and holy desire is becoming spellbound and obsessed by the object of your affection. Here we can become infatuated by the dream and quest for the perfect "other," of having a love that will last, thinking he or she can solve everything for us. But once we settle into such a relationship we can only discover a sense of disappointment as we realize we still have a hole within us that cannot be filled by anything else apart from connection with Self.

The burden of carrying these expectations of "it should be like this" and "he/she should be like this" is a big struggle and battle within oneself. Releasing oneself from these expectations that you have acquired is a big step into being who you really are.

A true relating is already there, based on the first primary relationship we all share; the relationship with God. Having this sacred marriage within our own heart is the priority to adhere to always, and then this gets reflected outside fully. An important aspect to deepen in this along the path is faith and trust.[1] When one has this faith fully, then one needs nothing from the other, as one knows it all lies within one's own Self. Only then can one be situated in holy love.

Codependency

Codependency is pulling energy from other people in various ways. Codependency stems from lack of self-love, from failing to give worth and love to oneself. Hence needing the approval of someone else, needing their love to prove your own self worth becomes an imprisoning game of extracting love and approval from them. This can apply to partners but also to parents, teachers, religions, and even authority figures like Yeshua.

On another level it is as if someone else is responsible for your happiness. The subconscious feels this as a loss of personal power, so controlling the person who is responsible for your happiness generates, quite naturally, a lot of drama! A soul is very tired from these cycles. When we realize that we are completely powerless over other people, and that we may even live in fear of them by trying to look good in many and various ways, we are free from struggling to control and get approval from them. Our own belief systems crumble, and we focus on loving ourselves.

In codependency, the shadow of romantic love speaks and acts in subtle ways, with our behaviors coming from this voice: "My good feelings about who I am stem from being liked by you, and receiving approval from you. Your struggles affect my serenity. My mental attention focuses on solving your problems, relieving your pain, or pleasing you. My fear of rejection, and your anger, determines what I say and do. I use giving as a way of feeling safe in our relationship. I put my val-

---

1. Which is why Magdalene fled from Palestine to France and England with Joseph of Arimathea, the embodiment of faith.

ues aside in order to connect with you. I value your opinion and way of doing things more than I do my own."

The biggest illusion in sacred relationship is that anyone else can give you what you want, that anyone else can meet you fully and fulfill you, that there is a perfect man or woman for you. In sacred relating the only thing that can fulfill you is the marriage with the soul and spirit within your own heart.

This is what your earthly partner can help facilitate for you, sometimes in the most strange and obscure of fashions. No person can ever meet or fulfill you. If there is love between you, that is all there is. For that *is* all that is. You and your earthly partner can then help to cocreate, serve, and share love on earth, and to others.

Sacred relationship brings up the deepest wounds and illusions between two who are committed to each other to bring this outer, inner, and secret union about in each other. For between two Beloveds, there is the Holy Trinity made manifest on earth, once they are in union with their own Self. You, the other, and God wed as One, each one being the One, being whole unto themselves.

This is the Promise of Christ—the Trinity is not above you. It is created in sacred relationship here on earth.[2] Everything is relationship, and relationship is how we create heaven on earth. Relationship is a means to freedom, once it is understood and used in this way.

"I cannot fulfill you; you cannot fulfill me. You do not belong to me. I do not belong to you."

---

2. As demonstrated by Christ Yeshua and Mary Magdalene, among others.

Cocreation

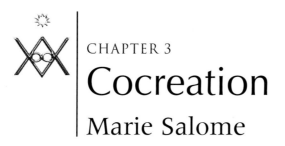

CHAPTER 3
Cocreation
Marie Salome

In response to Salome's question, Yeshua said, "When you trample underfoot shame, and when the two become one, and the male is one with the female, there is no more male and female."

Marie Salome played a crucial part in establishing the Christ Blueprint. Although her role was not seen as significant as that of the other Marys, her Presence was vital for the anchoring of the Triple Goddess, or the Three Marys that form the Womb of the World.

The womb is the center of a woman's power. It is the generator of light, power, and joy, the keeper, bearer and sustainer of Life. Through her heart, womb, and the alta major chakra or mouth of the goddess situated at the back of the neck, she becomes receptive to the currents of life that move and sustain creation.

The Womb of the World is the heart of Gaia's creative force; the womb deep in the earth from where Gaia gives birth to new creations, and from where all truly transformative birthings occur that impact and shift human consciousness. It is from the Womb of the World that Gaia, and the lineage of ancient mothers past, present, and future, give their sanction and blessing to all those that wish to help humanity through the feminine. Anyone throughout history who has transformed the planet's consciousness in any major way has gone through the Womb of the World, or has been assisted by midwives who have this connection.

Marie Salome, Mother Mary, and Mary Magdalene connected to and embodied this womb by literally sucking the consciousness of Gaia itself into their womb, and holding it there for a period of months, bringing in all the suffering, all the pain, all the joy, and all the richness of the earth and its people directly into their own wombs. All three Marys felt everything that Gaia felt, and became conscious cocreators with Gaia's birthing. Doing this allowed Salome to midwife the Crucifixion and Resurrection of Yeshua.

Salome embodies the darker aspect of love, the dark feminine, and the mystical qualities, power, and magic of Gaia itself. A powerful healer, prophetess, visionary seer, and shaman, she brings forth the wisdom and teachings of the lineages of ancient mothers throughout time, especially from the traditions of Ishtar and Lilith.

She is the essential power of woman, not afraid to show or use it, yet is elegant at the same time. She holds both sides of the feminine in equal measure; the power of woman throughout the ages embodied in the now. Salome empowers women to embrace and celebrate their feminine power; to know their role as women and their importance and equality in a patriarchal age. Her uninhibited, confident, challenging nature allows her to express the truth of all women without reservation,[1] and to claim their essential sexuality and body as a source of power and as Divine.

Unafraid of her sexual power, independence, fertility, and magnetism, she reveals and initiates others into the mystery, joy, and unlimited potential of Divine cocreation. Salome teaches how to access and open the womb through ceremony, sound, breath, and specific sexual practices. She is the gatekeeper and midwife to the primordial Womb of the World, knowing its importance in birthing new realities and man-

---

1. This is why she had to remain quiet two thousand years ago, except to the closest Apostles.

48

ifesting heaven on earth, in this case birthing Christ on to earth in alliance with the lineages of ancient earth mothers.

MIDWIFING THE WEB OF LIGHT

Salome is intimately associated with the birthing of Christianity. She was present at the founding of the Church,[2] was the mother of some of the disciples of Yeshua, and was the attending midwife and witness of the Virgin Birth. She was also present at the Crucifixion and the Resurrection, and had a long, close relationship with Yeshua's family.[3]

A midwife guides the birthing process, holding the space for the womb to birth its creation, guiding the descent of spirit into form, assisting the mother to open up, let go, give her creation to the world, and feel comforted that another is there who knows the process, and whom she can rely on. She opens the way, becoming the feminine pillar of strength and care that allows the physical mother of the birthing process to focus on her task alone.

As midwife to Mother Mary's birthing of Yeshua, to Yeshua's Crucifixion, and to the spreading of the feminine mysteries with Magdalene in the south of France and Europe, Salome served to midwife the Christ Blueprint into manifestation. She acted as an interface between the Divine thought-forms and ideas held in the Divine mind and womb, and their earthly manifestation. She also serves as guardian, along with Mary Magdalene and Mother Mary, of the reservoir of rulers that hold the Christ bloodline.

The Christ bloodline is not just a physical bloodline as represented by Magdalene. It is a vibrational field of abilities passed on through the Christ lineage that serves to birth Christ Consciousness onto earth at

2. Acts 2.
3. Mark 15:40 and 16:1.

different times in history.[4] This web of light, held within the earth's womb, the trees, nature, and the moon is also reflected in the ley lines that connect and crisscross the planet.[5]

Working with the web of light allows one to be completely present with the energies of the earth, and in doing so one accesses many other dimensions beyond our ideas of what this earth is. The web of life connects all dimensions, and is anchored on earth in the Womb of the World. This connection is feminine, and it is from this web and womb that the leaps in spiritual evolution throughout history occur. Webs are nonhierarchical and nonpatriarchal; they are cooperative in nature and in inquiry, for they connect us to earth and beyond.

In the past this connection was done through sound and ritual, through the use of perpetual choirs, choirs that sounded earth's tones and chants all day and all night through voice and natural instruments, harmonizing our own soul and sexual rhythms to Gaia's womb and callings.

It is through this connection that we become aware of, align, and merge with our environment. It speaks to us, and we speak to it, as one. The web of light is oneness. By connecting to it we heal and align ourselves to the natural rhythms and motions of life, clearing anything out that stands in the way of this.

We connect to the web of life by offering, and giving ourselves to it. Gratitude is the attitude of the web of life. When we first connect to the web of life, the pulse behind all life, we are taken into the oneness that all life shares. The "I" becomes lost in the oneness that we are all connected to through our hearts.

Everything in the web can be seen as a glowing silver-white web, threading, weaving, and sustaining harmony in all things. Your body,

---

4. Akhnaton and Yeshua in the past, and many in the future.
5. In the Christ Grids around the earth's fields in the masculine expression.

your flesh, your nerves, your cells, your very being is permeated by this web, the same light that is giving birth to every plant, every tree, and every star that is spread throughout the cosmos.

Offering ourselves sincerely to the web allows us access. Giving to the earth, rather than just taking, particularly at sacred sites, allows us conscious access. In the offering we receive, and become the conduit, the circuit that is in constant flow, receiving and giving through the open heart of gratitude.

A Practice

Initially, the best way to do this is while visiting a sacred site in nature, where you feel resonance, where you feel at home. Sit down at twilight or at night, on a night where the moon is visible, where you are near some trees, and away from city lights, city noise, and interference, if possible. Take your shoes off and sit barefoot on the earth.

Focus on your heart. Breathe. Focus on your womb and ovaries; for men the penis and testes. Breathe. Now focus on your feet, and the field of energy that extends down from the feet into the earth. Visualize it.

Breathe down through the soles of your feet into this field. Push down the breath, and visualize the field extending.

Now extend this field of energy from your feet into Gaia downward; deep down. Allow yourself to plunge down, through the soil, through the many layers of rock, earth, and fire, into the womb of the earth. This is a vast, black, all-enveloping space. Sit here for a moment.

Now ask, and pray to Mother Gaia, in your own words, from your own heart, to feel and extend your connection to her. Offer her yourself, offer her your service, and thank her for being your foundation, your anchor, your home. Breathe into this connection, connecting heart, womb, and feet to Gaia. Feel this space within you, for it is part of you, and you are part of it, as part of your origins, your roots, and your foundation.

Now open your eyes, and focus on a tree, or a group of trees. Soften your gaze until it becomes slightly blurry. Relax and breathe gently from the belly. Start to see the aura of the tree, the energy field surrounding it. Be patient. Follow the field of the tree in its expansion outward. See or visualize a silver white thread or web extending outward, and upward, to the moon. Look up to the moon, and feel your feet.

Welcome to the web of life.

Giving something valuable to you, giving of the menstrual blood, giving of the sexual juices—all of this gives Gaia the signal that you wish to reconnect consciously and in full awareness. In this reconnection, one gets taken into the web, and it starts to guide and pull you into itself—into Life.

This reconnection starts to create a fulfilled and blessed Life, where we have a very real energetic experience of renewal, where we become quickened. We begin to recognize the need to set aside reactive thoughts, personal agendas, and fear, allowing all feelings, recognizing that if we allow ourselves to be, we do not have to fix anything.

In this real experience of reconnecting to the web of life, we begin to understand that all is not as it seems, and "I" know nothing. We open to deep vulnerability and gratefully hand it all over to the weaver of the web of life, and offer it. And then it is taken, and we are taken, deeper into the journey that the web has in store for us, both light and dark.

TWENTY-FIRST CENTURY WOMAN

The Salome energy holds Keys to access and activate further this web of light, and to act as the interface for the other aspects of the Triple Goddess to generate the fertile conditions necessary to birth Christ Consciousness.

Magdalene has been making her presence known in the world. Now it is time for Salome also to be known, for without her the feminine power of the ancient lineages of Earth Mothers that opens the gateway to the womb of the earth cannot be completed. Salome is the hidden link behind Magdalene, the power that supported her, and the power that men have been so scared of as it threatens their control, the control of the mind. Whereas Magdalene's love and softness does not challenge this overtly, Salome has no reservations about doing so. This is why she is so important for women in the twenty-first century, as her boldness, authority, and ability to lead upfront brings the feminine a long neglected dimension of sovereign authority and candor that all *will* listen to, and act upon.

Salome's higher aspect is Ishtar, harbinger of independence for woman. Ages-old cycles of matriarchy and patriarchy have continued to repeat on earth due to the unbalanced nature of the male-female dynamic, which leads to the abusing of power. The manipulation and abuse of men by women, through woman's more subtle seductions, and women by men by the more overt, violent, and direct route, have repeated in a vicious loop for millennia.

Lions, solar male symbols, were always associated with Ishtar as her vehicles and means of support, but as much as she is supported by them she also keeps them "down to earth." Thus this is an equality between the male principles that inform and direct the physical world with a strong feminine guiding these forces, rather than the male forces running amok, leading to imbalance. Salome uses and understands primal, instinctual, dynamic forces that align and harness male forces of order, detachment and reason. This leads to a dynamic equality between male and female that has the power necessary to create and manifest a new world.[6] Equality requires mastery and individual wholeness: mastery of the lower self, and individuation into our own uniqueness where we can communicate and commune openly and without judgment, without causing fear, with other individuated aspects of the One Self.

---

6. This is why Yeshua specifically talked to Salome about men and women becoming one, for this is her Key.

The wisdom required here is of detachment and sensitivity in being able to navigate and establish a bridge between the lower and higher self, so that the lower self can be harnessed by the higher Self. Passion and detachment go hand in hand. Passion, overflowing joy, and exuberant dynamic power without detachment means one can get lost in lust and the animal side of ourselves, the instinctual urges. Detachment refines the fire of passion and the primordial urge for life into clarity, discernment, and contained power when it is required, and wild joy when that is required. Prayer, meditation and peace counterpoints the fire and Shakti of Salome. Being alone, having time to reflect and gather the strands of life that creative passion stirs up, allows the next level of awareness and creation to manifest and even more life juice to flow, juice that supports light force.

> Salome was the first who recognized Christ, who worshipped Him, and believed on Him when He came upon the earth; Wherever Christ went to preach, with His Mother the Virgin, there she followed Him with His disciples, until the day when they crucified Him and [the day of] His holy resurrection. She saw them all, with His Mother the Virgin.[7]

THE SHADOW SIDE

The shadow side of Salome is the deepest female shadow side within the Christ Blueprint, as opposed to Lucifer, which is the deepest male shadow side. Both these shadows are the most despised and misunderstood, and are the most prevalent on earth today, creating the most widespread distortions and fixations. Paradoxically enough, it is through integrating both of them that one becomes free, empowered, and able

---

7. Demetrius of Antioch.

to fully cocreate and birth a new reality that follows your deepest heart's desires.

Competition

Ishtar's challenging, direct, uninhibited nature can become distorted, becoming competitiveness. The true nature of challenging from this aspect of the feminine is penetration of a man, which a man is used to doing through penetrating a woman. As the roles are reversed, the greatest polarities can arise.

In today's world this challenging can result in a woman switching into masculine power and trying to compete on masculine terms, without being in her full femininity. The feminine has less need for overt shows of power, and is more centered, life affirming, and caring, yet totally confident and self-assured. It is a self-contained power, less on display, and less overpowering. It allows one to be oneself, recognizing and seeing the value in each person, each part of the web, of the network. In this more subtle approach more can be achieved than the more overt approach in many cases.

In competition, the onus comes back to power. Who owns the power, who is ready to wield the power, who is ready to be selfless enough to use the power, who is ready to be powerful and open at the same time; who is ready to fluidly move from male power, into female power, into bliss.

Ishtar can be the dominatrix, the competitor, who gets what she wants at all costs. Willful manipulation of forces to get what she wants is the dark side of shamanic practice. In this there is no surrender to higher forces, and a loss of humility. Ishtar in the shadow is desire gone wild, amok, chaos, power, sexual energy all swirling together in a maelstrom of primordial chaos, where there is no center, no pillar upon which to dance or ground upon.

It is the sense of competition that creates isolation, the most damaging force to our world. Women competing against women for power, for men, for recognition, and out of a sense of threat, security, and protection of what is their own, create disconnection and betrayal. This pitting of woman against woman has created wounds that are still held in the collective consciousness, that then allow male forces to manipulate these wounds for their own advantage. Sisterhood is important to heal this; for women to come together and reconnect, healing these age-old wounds of trust and communal relating.

In the process of this happening, both male and female can feel destroyed or shattered, empowered or overconfident, overintellectual, or overpowering. It is the meeting and utilizing of these two essential polarities, between the power of life and death, the power of regeneration or resurrection, that Ishtar holds. It is this power that can drive men and women crazy, insane, wild. It is this power and bliss that when harnessed properly fuels the engine of the Christ Blueprint. Make no mistake: the Christ Blueprint is great power, as well as great bliss, great light, and great love. You cannot have any of these without the others.

Love will collapse without power; power will implode and destroy without love and wisdom. Without fully embracing this power and this bliss, enlightenment cannot be attained. It is vital to restore and reestablish this link and covenant with the ancient mothers, and birth a new reality through the womb of Gaia and the womb of each woman.

Ishtar in this age can be seen as independent, bold and powerful, and feminine in this. Self-assured, ecstatic, and loving, yet centered and grounded. She knows herself, her sexuality, what she wants and needs, and has a direct connection to the womb and feminine power. This can be very intimidating for most men; it can make men feel very small, and can make women feel very threatened, and very willing to mime and copy them, giving their power away.

Power

When you come into power there is temptation to misuse it for your own purposes, as people will listen to you, and follow you. Thus it is said that absolute power corrupts absolutely, until you are aligned to the will of the Divine, the will of love.

The shadow of sexual power and lust without love, magical action without surrender and wisdom, vanity without humility, manifests because of a lack of centered empowerment caused by various holes and wounds in the psyche. This manifests as the irrational taken to its deepest primal depths; the loss of all reason in a maelstrom of chaotic feeling and manipulation.

As we go deeper into the shadow side of Ishtar, we see the fundamental thrill of getting close to death and delighting in it, delighting in the boundaries between life and death, and the various practices to reach this through drugs, rituals, and sexual magic. The abuse of power, or allowing the nature of power to abuse you through fear, comes from a lack of self-fulfillment and discernment, allied with a lack of synthesizing inner confidence based on the strength of the soul.

This manifests as domineering, controlling, and overly blunt behavior, a toughness and independence that does not account for others, that lacks in sensitivity toward others and the softness within oneself. The lack of tolerance for soft emotions and lack of strength, and any other feelings that feel inferior, indecisive, needy, or deficient, lead to a certain hardness, protection, and lack of compassionate empathy. Her bluntness and directness lead to her often not being aware of the feelings of those around her, and if she is, she can dismiss them as being weak, instructing them to be strong and self-sufficient like she is. To be soft and understanding, empathizing with another, is to be weak in this lens of perception. This can lead to her dominating and controlling others simply because she can get away with it and no one dares object, particularly men with whom she is relating. She can run amok over others, and they will listen to her empowered authority, secretly wishing they had the same quality, secretly wishing they were as uninhibited, secretly wishing they could act out as she does.

She is a great manipulator of men and emotions. Her strength attracts others who feel they can learn from her. She espouses the letting go of control and the need for cooperation while herself being controlling. While being expressive, she, by her power and confidence, can inhibit others from expressing their own truth. She can intimidate through her power. She is not the most subtle of beings, and in her directness can miss the softer nuances of receptive sensitivity that create the fully rounded feminine expression of life-sustaining wholeness. Ruthlessness, willfulness, overbearing will, domination of the masculine, inconsideration, and selfishness are deeper masks of Ishtar's shadow.

Lust

Lust is the shadow to fertility and cocreation, as a force to be recognized, harnessed, and channeled into power and bliss. The primordial, biological drive and raw power of lust can seem to be similar to greed, as both of these energies wish to consume more of anything, in order to cover a deep sense of lack. In lust we want, need, and crave more of the sensation, the taste, the pleasure, more of anything that fuels the illusory feeling that we are deeply and passionately engaged with life, and powerful.

Lust attempts to fill the place within the subconscious that fears death, fears the unknown, and fears to reveal its deepest fears. To protect yourself from exposure of weaknesses and fears, lust strategizes ways of controlling and hiding by inflating itself with power and the illusion that it is strong, wild, untouchable, and full of aliveness, desire, zeal, and passion—anything that gives the impression to yourself and others that you are fearless, that you live in the now, that you taste the pleasure.

By apparently allowing oneself to go completely out of control, one is controlled by the holes in the subconscious that fear death, that vicariously struggles to hold onto life. But it is all fueled by the fear of death, by a deep lack within one's own self, by sexual wounds to disguise the deep terror of emptiness, vulnerability, and the fear of being harmed by others.

Lust happens when there is an imbalance and disharmony of polarities within. When our polarities are out of control, when there is not enough yin, or too much yang, one will always try to be harmonized by seeking and wanting the other, outside of yourself, to rebalance this. Only when the harmonies are balanced from within can lust dissolve.

Lust is going to the extremes on the pathway. We all need to go to extremes to find the experiences that will lead us to the middle, that will lead us to our deepest joy, that will lead us into our greatest light. So lust is an experience that when fully experienced can lead to the realization that there are greater heights to go to, and that these heights can only be reached through harmony, and the middle way.

The highest aspect of lust is desire that is transmuted through Tantric practice to act as a fuel for evolution, healing, empowerment, and bliss. Ultimately, this energy becomes sublimated, refined into unconditional love. However, the trap is to stay stuck here without deepening to what lies beyond the sexual energy; and the opposite is also true; staying stuck in the meditational spaces without the sexual energy sublimated and included.

Lust becomes very subtle and only through vigilance, discernment, and refinement of the mind can one detect its workings at these levels. By utilizing its force correctly, one can evolve quickly; by becoming its victim one descends very rapidly into the subconscious.

Ishtar thrives on feeling her power and bliss, and this may mask her feeling of powerlessness. In relationship, she thrives on being with a powerful man, or with being with a weaker man she can dominate, not realizing that the polarity to her power is softness, which she can perceive as weakness. A woman who holds these energies needs to be held in softness and in power, a challenging role for any man to achieve as it requires him to step up and face the challenge of being fully masculine.

She listens deeply to one who can match her in all ways, sharing her bliss, which then feeds her bliss. It is bliss that delights her, and makes her feel closer to her source, and it is this which she looks for in order to take her deeper into her essence. This bliss, power, sovereign authority, and silence all merge in Ishtar, the engine for the Triple Goddess in manifestation on earth. It is her pathway, one that has been hidden for a long time but which is vital to resurrect *now* to empower Christ Consciousness in you.

Power

CHAPTER 4
Power
Lady Ishtar

Lady Ishtar harnesses the intelligence and creative force of instinctual sexuality, the flow of vital dynamic life force, or Shakti, with love. When a woman brings together this instinctual nature with an awareness of the Divine within herself, the creative potential of God becomes expressed through her, and magnified in her relationships with others and the natural world.

She lives it through her sexual attunement to the rhythms and cycles of nature, and through birthing. By simply being herself, she unites her instinctual nature, the flow of creation and the earth, with the power of consciousness, transforming them all in her daily life.

So powerful was the cult of Ishtar that the Judaic tradition had to demonize her image to prevent her followers from being seduced away from the "true faith." In Jewish myths written long after Genesis she became the "bad" first wife of Adam, known as Lilith,[1] who was created from the same dust at the same time, but refused to be subject to him sexually or spiritually.

She was demonized by the patriarchal orders out of fear of the potential of this unified power that could not be controlled, and therefore she became synonymous with all "demons" and the dark—that which men

---

1. Lilith's name comes from the ancient Mesopotamian word *lil,* meaning "breath" or "spirit of life" in the sacred sense.

fear as it leads them out of the transcendent state, and back into normal human life with its cares and concerns, back into matter. This is why Ishtar is so important in this age—she stands for nothing less than equality as harmony, yet stands totally in her feminine power to do so.

PRIMAL POWER

Deep within all of you lies this primal power, an unstoppable primal force. Chaotic and uncontrollable, teeming with life and overflowing passion, this power hides in the darkness, from where all life pours in an inexhaustible torrent. Here lies the dark feminine, and the power of Ishtar.

This force can be as scary, as threatening as it is loving and nurturing. If you have resistance, then chaos and fear it is that you will experience. If you have no resistance, then you will experience its bliss and be taken on a rollercoaster ride that makes no sense to the mind, but enlivens and screams life to all your senses and soul.

When we encounter such power, most people respond to it in fear, the fear that it will have power, and control, over them, fearing it will destroy them. And it will! It will destroy the resistance to being this power, it will wipe out part of who you think you are: the greatest fear of all. It threatens your very identity, who you treasure yourself to be as an individual. It cares not for these boundaries, blasting through them. It is freedom, spontaneous, wild and free, and has no order, structure, or reason to it.

It is the fertile, fecund darkness breathing the soil of the living earth, the depths of our instinctual gut-driven nature and intuition. When we cut off from it, it consumes us in other ways, making us greed- and lust-driven for a satisfaction that we know we possess, but do not know how to tap into, except through outer means.

Denying the dark feminine denies a vital part of our aliveness, our connection to the web of life, to "eating" life itself. Denying the primal leads us to overindulge in the external, instead of living what lies within us. It leads to us destroying and devouring ourselves, creating a wasteland, a desert of consciousness instead of a rich, lush forest of fertile abundance.

When we allow the dark feminine to take us, pull us, possess us, we live in wild freedom, wild joy, unpredictable moment to moment, and loving this unpredictability as our true nature. Raw power refines into bliss.

Ishtar shares her sexuality without shame, for to her it is natural. There are no taboos, no conventions to adhere to in "polite society," as there are no rules in the dark feminine—just flow. This flow appears to be chaos to the mind that lies in resistance to the flow of life, afraid of the unknown that lies so vast beyond what the mind can ever try to understand. The energy or catharsis created by the mind's resistance has no form or rhyme to it, so it gets called chaos. Yet all flow is the experience of life force in its essence.

Chaos and powerlessness, disorientation and fatigue, are what the conditioned mind encounters when confronted by this energy. In the exhaustion and the giving-up of the mind, the giving-up of resistance to flow, one relaxes and flows into the most creative force, releasing the mind into a seething ocean of infinite possibilities, where anything becomes possible.

This is deep, deep nourishment; before words, ideas, and even emotions. It shows you how the world is fed and works; it shows you how women throughout the ages have tapped into the power that creates new realities.

The unformed, uncontrolled, seething life force lies behind all appearances, all structures, all apparently ordered and reasonable things we do. It is always there as the substrata of life, waiting for us to tap into and break the rigidities of what we have self-created in order to live what true creating is, moment by naked, vital, pulsing moment.

Everything is too reasonable! All the philosophy, ideas, spiritual systems . . . most of it is trying to hide away from this force, trying to rationalize, spiritualize, and politically correct our most natural of impulses. All of this is done out of fear, to create an ordered society that denies life, and therefore denies love.

The dark feminine is love. It leads us to love through this fertile uninhibited force, dissolving all the ideas, beliefs, and thoughts that stand in the way of the pulsing life force of wild joy, the expression of love untrammeled by convention. It says yes to love, and connects all life forms, once you penetrate into its mysteries, and have allowed it to flow through you unchecked, once you have allowed it to take you without reservation.

It leads to the softness, the gentling of love, the peace that passes all understanding communing with the wild freedom that joy creates. The dark feminine is a radical force for change, for liberation, for freedom without boundaries, without rules, without ideas—just the pulsing, vital flow of living love itself. Surrendering to this primal life allows you to experience the love that creates all life. And this is vital for women, and men, to reclaim. To stand up and have full trust and confidence in who you are and what you instinctively and passionately feel means that the whole world can change in a single moment . . . like a thief in the night.

LIFE AND DEATH

Ishtar brings forth the regeneration of life. Her magic is what many fear, and are also attracted to. She brings forth the deepest polarities, the wildest extremities in order to harmonize them into life. The path of eternal life is very much one of death: progressive and successive deaths. Each death is a rebirth.

She leads you to death, a good death, reminding you that you are mortal, reminding you to get up and experience life now, as it is. With death on your shoulder, one cannot ignore life any longer, and what it presents you with. Absence reminds you of the amazing potential for presence; and this is what the best spiritual teachers do; reveal their absence to facilitate you into presence, or bewilderment, as the case may be!

Ishtar holds life and death in each hand. She holds a space for life to reveal, create, and generate itself, and she holds a space for death, to conceal, dismantle, clothe and dissolve forms and ideas. This is found by holding your breath between your inhalation and exhalation. When you do this for long enough you experience this point between life and death, and the fear that lies here also.

The inherent threat, thrill, and fear of the point where life meets death is bridged through resurrection, which is what Christ came to bring back to earth, and which is why Christ needed to work with the Ancient Lineages of Mothers and Ishtar. Lady Ishtar is dangerous, radical, holy, and sacred; she acts as the bridge to full empowerment. Those who dare to bridge life and death through love are the most radical of all, and it is these people who will birth, and resurrect, humanity into eternal life.

THE BLACK SUN

Ishtar is a guardian and gatekeeper of the Black Sun. As Yeshua said, "no one comes to the Father except through me," and in this age no womb comes to the Mother except through Ishtar.

The Black Sun is the direct experience of the primordial feminine force. This creative pulse is made up of three things: love, desire, and Self-delight. Its mirror side, what we have to face and integrate before we embody, are anger, disempowerment, darkness, and extremities of all kinds. In the Black Sun, we face our deepest challenge: to claim our universal power directly from its source. This is the magical power of transformation. Here we have the uniting of all possible qualities, infinite potentials with that which has no qualities at all—in the moment of birth.

The Black Sun is a vortex or wormhole that leads into, and radiates out of, every other sphere of consciousness. Knowing this, feeling it, means experiencing the black hole and a White Sun—a "Black Sun" shining with the hidden power and light of all Creation. As we experience this, we collapse all forces of time, space, and gravity into a black hole, which our light body travels into and through once we have the power, clarity, and mastery to do this.

This is a powerful initiation. It is release from self-contraction of the body-mind-soul into the vast fields of awareness. When we allow this release of power and bliss, we can claim this power for ourselves, for the darkness holds the power, and from the darkness the light is born. Without power, light collapses, and love has no way of becoming manifest. For to become selfless, to have no self, requires that we are strong first—for selflessness is the greatest power of all. Ishtar is the ability to go into and experience all light and all dark, all faces of the One Self. Here we cannot seek—we can only welcome the experience of our false notions and judgments being ripped apart as we enter.

This is the many and the one—the feminine matrix of creation, "for by woman we are created, and it is by woman that we will be saved."[2] In this process we become a unique Self-contained aspect of God, an individualized aspect of the All working in a manifested human form.

When the male is fully centered in his infinite pillar then the energies of Ishtar can dance around this pillar like a vortex. It is in this dance that the Christ Blueprint is formulated upon and actualized. It is by loving another that one can truly love oneself, and yet it is also in loving oneself that one can truly love another; this is the dance.

---

2. This is why Salome is the midwife on earth, and Ishtar in heaven.

Love is the gateway to enormous power and enormous bliss being generated. The love is the foundation, the background, a backdrop for the power and the bliss to manifest in their fullness, and for one to lose oneself in this, thereby gaining it. Ishtar guides, nurtures, and protects those who enter willingly and deeply into this path of power and bliss; each using the other to fuel itself into the Black Sun, a source of infinite energy.

BREAKTHROUGH

Ishtar is the ruler of vast spaces, of the desert, the desert being that which the mirage covers. This vastness is penetrated and seen through what you know as the thousand-yard stare; having that look in one's eyes when one sees beyond the illusion, sees beyond the mirage, sees the real nature of the desert, of space. This piercing glare that penetrates is the power of woman as embodied in Ishtar: the gaze of the all-seeing eye.

It is this penetration that makes a man feel he is being penetrated. It is this challenging nature that marks out Ishtar, for Ishtar only opens her womb, her fertility, her power, her creative capacity, to a man who can both receive this and give it back to her. Then she opens up like Sheela-na-gig, yoni and womb wide open, ready to welcome her consort into the universal womb, and birth with him.

Ishtar generates energy, power, and strength. Her grit and determination allied with her exuberance enables one to break through any limitations or restrictions that bind. She is that quality within us that leads us to our breakthrough, giving us the power to break through old patterns that keep our energy from flowing and manifesting new visions, and following our heart's desire. She is vitality and empowerment. She leads to the breakdown that is the breakthrough. She is the dense irrational chaos that is danger, that is radical, that is the essence of risk itself. Without facing this danger, without going to the edge of your experience and beyond, you can never become who you truly are. You have to dive into the deep unknown to know who you are.

The new vision that births through you from this is focused, directed, yet expansive. It encompasses and embraces many possibilities, never losing its direction in where it wishes to go, and how it is going to birth. By opening up to all possibilities, while remaining grounded, centered, and in your power, you can birth your purpose.

When you open to all things, then all things can pour through you. As this occurs, you expand out into the world, and the greatest healings occur, as you are now consciously embracing all parts of your self, and cocreating them into your manifestation on earth. Here, you can see and taste life in all its dimensions, and participate consciously with it all, becoming a conscious cocreator.

CONTINUAL BIRTHING

Continual birthing is birthing yourself in each and every moment. This birthing allows us to continually recreate ourselves and to birth anew. In letting go of every past moment, and embracing the newness of the present moment, we come into the power to create who we are, what we want to express and share with others.

In the experience of being reborn in every moment, we have the power to choose again who we are, what we feel, what we think, and how we choose to respond to the same situation that is presented to us. We can seize this moment, and allow the birthing to take place. This birthing sets in motion a whole stream of new moments, each moment holding infinite possibilities for new creations and new ways of being.

Continual birthing shows us that creation is a wave of light in perpetual motion forming perception, mind, and matter, moving throughout the universes. This wave then dissolves into the formless—it leaves the creation it has just created, to then instantly reappear again as a wave of eternal light, to then dissolve again, and so on, forever repeating itself in the transformation from form into formless into form. This cyclic pulse, particle, and wave is the "beat" of time and space, showing matter and mind as forever reappearing and disappearing, moving so fast that our senses do not register its movements and forms.

Continual birthing is how we cocreate with this infinitely creative wave. We realize, and we choose again and anew as we align to this subtlest yet most powerful creative flow as it manifests itself through the dynamism and transparency of living form. It is delight irresistibly overflowing through us when we surrender, when we joyfully proclaim that we are nothing, and open to everything to be made possible.

Like water it is unformed, unattached, able to flow through any form that it comes into contact with, always remaining in its original state, ever free. It is the Sound and Light of Silence, dynamic, rich in infinite potential. It is the Mother that is Loving Intelligence and Communion, the guiding wisdom and light streaming through all Life. It is the Voice of God.

At the very moment of form arising into being, it extends itself as a bridge for all parts of Self to recognize Itself. Thus in truth we have never been separate from Source, for this wave is our compass back home to the Present, where nothing has been separated. This is the true nature of all matter, all phenomena, creating out of joyful delight to reveal more joy and delight, to then dissolve again. It is the desire to create joy and bliss for no reason apart from to be joyful. It is the intuition that sees itself in all things, doing the right thing at the right place at the right time.

It acts in the highest interests of all those present at any moment to bring them into love. It is the heart that breaks for all beings all the time, and that gives to all beings all the time; for that is its nature. Yet it dissolves that which you no longer have need for, and which limits. It conceals that which you know you have, but which has yet to manifest in your life. It reveals that which accelerates your evolution with the unexpected meeting, person, event, or situation.

It is the loving voice that is always with us, that can be called upon at any time, for it has the answers to every question. For it is the question and the answer, the intelligence and light flowing through all things. It flows through us, vibrating our body-mind at 570 trillion hertz per second. We are moving incredibly fast every single second of our lives— we are just not aware of it. We are birthing and rebirthing every single moment, moving with this wave, this dance happening all the time. It is the thread-like link between the material and the formless realms, flowing through us and all things perpetually, without ceasing.

Embrace

CHAPTER 5
Embrace
Mother Mary

Unconditional love needs nothing. It is fully Self-contained; it meets and merges every polarity, every need, every reaching for love outside, within itself. It gives and expects nothing back; it gives because giving is its very reason for existing.

Love is a way of living, not just an experience.

As love is lived, as love lives through you, all else becomes the experience.

As soft as I am strong, love allows one to let go in even the most impossible circumstances. I hold this space perpetually for humanity, which is available to anyone if you are open, vulnerable, and willing to go deeper. As you allow this to happen more and more by embracing all before, and within you, then you yourself will start to feel embraced by all of existence, provided for, supported, and loved. You will start to feel blessed constantly as you sink deeper into the Black Light, the origin of all things, the origin of all states of consciousness, the foundation of life.

This is the fundamental, loving presence that existence *is*, that supports you unconditionally, that gives you trust in the unfolding of life, that reassures you that everything is OK, and that everything will work out if you but trust the unfolding. While our faults, our anger, our blocks to love are seen, there is no condemnation of it. Rather, draw near to be enfolded in the softness, the beauty and tenderness within your own heart. It always listens to you and comes to your aid, through your allowance, and asking, even when you think it does not.

ALLOWANCE

Allowance starts to settle into your life when you realize you have no control over your life, and in fact you never had any control, over what is happening right now. All resistance and judgment arise in allowance to be seen and accepted. You see yourself, and begin to surrender who you thought you were and what you thought you wanted, into what actually is. This is when you receive.

In allowance you come to see the truth about yourself, your pains, your patterns and your veils, to love living through you. In allowance, you allow the pain, the sadness, the anger, the grief, and the unworthiness to bubble up and be in you, simply to be present. And this is a marvel. Marvel at this for a moment; enjoy your naked beauty.

It is truly wondrous to feel these tears, to feel the anger, to feel the bite of separation arise, and be expressed, for in this expressing lies the revealing of the lie. Rest in this allowing, for it is the entryway to the royal road of love.

In allowance we open the door of our heart to be touched by something far greater than us, and in a felt sense "give way" to this feeling of love, softening what is rigid within more and more readily and easily the more we practice it. This deep, soft, innermost feeling, these pangs of sadness at our own self-chosen separations, reveal our deepest heart's desires, our deepest longings, which are to merge with love.

Allowance is the open expressing, the radically honest acknowledgment of what you feel may make you look small or weak, knowing that this allowance, this sense of humility, will enable you to love more. Allowance weaves together, in an unbroken chain, all parts of oneself, all your many faces, characters, and soul fragments, into a unifying thread of love.

And this, my friends, my beloved friends, leads to acceptance. Acceptance is the ultimate initiation. It melts and softens all hardness into the truth of what you have been created to be. And it speaks only truth, for acceptance knows the nature of reality as open. Acceptance is the soft, silent, inner peace that has no charge toward anything or anyone. It allows all expression to simply be what it is. Allowance leads to acceptance, and acceptance opens the heart to embrace whatever is presented to you, thus transforming it, and yourself.

EMBRACE

Embrace is enfolding what is presented to you, bringing it in, and then extending this enfolding out toward the person, idea, event, or situation. Embracing takes whatever you feel is unacceptable, makes it transparent, and then goes one step further: it makes you bring that vibration of the unacceptable inside your heart, and then moves your heart to envelop, embrace and extend itself into that vibration. And this is love.

Do this now. What can you not stand? What do you find totally unacceptable in the world, in your relationships, and in yourself? What turns you *off*, what repels you, what makes you run away from it? What do you hate? What is the last thing you would do in the world? What is the most unacceptable action, thought, or words that you would ever say, think, or do?

Name five things. Write them down, in detail, and place the paper in front of you. If you have more than five, then write them down also; in fact, write down as many as you can think of.

Now look at the first aspect of what you find unacceptable. Evoke the feeling of what it feels like. Imagine the memory, the last time you really felt this emotion, the people around you, the place, what was happening within you. Now breathe it deeply, and consciously, into your heart. Do this five times. No matter what resistance you feel, breathe it deeply into your heart five times, and hold it there.

Embrace it. What happens within you? Simply notice. Now repeat it for all five, or more. This should take about twenty minutes if you do it with care and attention. Repeat this practice whenever and wherever these feelings arise, be it in the car, at dinner, or at home.

Another way to do this practice of conscious embrace is to actually meet the person you find most unacceptable. Look softly into their eyes, or embrace them. While gazing or hugging them, focus on your heart, and breathe in the quality you find most unacceptable about them. This is in fact one of your greatest teachers on love.

Do this as soon as possible, for embrace leads to liberation, to the sweetest freedom of the heart.

Beloved friends, when you embrace you welcome life, all of it, and engage with all of the life flow, for life flow is the blood, and body, of Christ. Embracing includes everything within its arms and makes everything whole. It is the ultimate resting place for the heart.

The Master embraces, and accepts what *is* happening in any moment totally. In embrace, one brings others into their own heart, feels the truth of who they are, and then gives them what they need in that exact moment. In the deepest embrace, one brings the planet and the sufferings of all humans into the heart. There is nothing that is singled out as wrong, unacceptable, or unworthy of embrace.

Feel this.

Next time you are outside, on a bus, in a park, in a public place, say silently as you look upon your brothers and sisters, *I love you*. Let their souls know, by simply feeling it in your own heart. If you only knew the difference this brings to the world, you would never cease an opportunity to send love to another.

You are loved. You are lovable. You are precious. Always and forever.

Mary seeks those who will help her, for she needs human helpers who will live and serve her presence. While women represent her, men serve her as noble knights, ready to give their lives to protect and to guard all women and children. She holds for men a certain soft, yielding, enduring, yet immovable strength that completes the path of Christ, and which the masculine needs in order to do so.

She is the heart from where Yeshua's teachings came forth: it is His words that she animated from her heart. She is the outpouring that anoints the heart into opening, blessing, and releasing the most ancient of wounds.

She is the gentleness that dissolves what has hardened within. She is the softest light that penetrates the very depth of our core; she is the tenderness that comforts the deepest wounds; she is the comforter that holds us in her heart and womb when we die to ourselves, and she is that which births us into infinity, and into Christ Consciousness.

BIRTHING

She herself is present at every human birth, at the bedside of every mother. In this role she is now birthing a new race, a new form of human being that is considerably more advanced than the present model of human being. In this context, woman's mission is to become the mother of children who will be born without karma, a race of Buddhas and Christs, or Golden Children. When this happens all dogmatic religions, with the constrictions inherent in all of them, will die out.

Mother Mary is World Mother, part of Gaia, and it is through these currents of feeling, through mothering wisdom, that the Christ child within us recovers, and is born. She is also a guardian of sacred motherhood and a nurturer of sacred relationship, which is a wondrous privilege for those who can enter it. World Mother naturally attaches the greatest importance to the conscious upbringing and education of children out of present day education and nurturing systems.

In these responsibilities, we find the union of wisdom and unconditional love. Wisdom without unconditional love is crippling. Love without wisdom is disempowering, because there is a lack of true discernment. Unconditional love becomes stabilized through selfless service for the good of others, over time.

This change of working for others, rather than working to survive as ego (always from unresolved fear), helps purify our consciousness even further. We move from identity as the body or mind, and stabilize our identity as living soulfulness. Through this embrace, love establishes the soul as the ruler, and ego as the servant. Here we start to consider others more than we consider our own needs. As this happens, a deep release of core tension occurs. This is innocence. When we drop all knowledge, all ways of being that are imposed on us, or given to us by others, or that we have taken on, then we enter innocence. We become like a child, a role that Mary plays, looking after the children and being surrounded by them as that too is what she is; innocent.

Mary's prayer is "Mother, bring me home." When you sincerely say this from the depths of your heart with commitment, with wholehearted giving, then this prayer will be heard, as it is the cry of the Child of God wanting to come home to its parents, to reunite with its own Self. Pray this, and watch what happens. This cry draws itself unto itself. This love, this longing, this innocence lies within each and every one of us, and resonates with everyone. We all share this vibration within the heart, and like a harp string plucked, we can feel its vibrations echoing throughout our beings.

THE COMMITMENT

Mary's unwavering passion, devotion, and faith in God allowed her to accept the will of God even at the cost of losing her son. She showed mastery by staying with the truth no matter what occurred. Letting go into full embrace is what Mary demonstrated fully, while feeling her own pain and witnessing the suffering of her child. This is truly the mark of an extraordinary woman; to be able to feel and embrace the emotions of the personal heart, and yet to stand unwaveringly in the knowing that love is unfolding in perfection under any condition.

Even if we lose our most intimate relationships, if we betray the truth of what we and that person need to do, then we are betraying love itself; the glue for all relationships. If we betray this love, we betray our core; for deep within us lies the knowing of what truth is, and what the fear is that would claim to get something for itself at the expense of another, and at the expense of our own soul.

Her undying commitment enabled her to open her heart fully, extending compassion to what she began to see, and embody: that everyone is her child. Expressing these qualities in a man's world also required a great deal of power. A great discipline, a great commitment, and a total identification with the Black Light, which could hold this space indefinitely, and be ever present for all beings.

However, her commitment was also as a human woman, who cried, felt sorrow, felt pain, felt hunger, and felt the depths of the Divine, gave birth to a Master, and taught her circles of women to become all that they could be, initiating them into the ancient lineages of feminine power, love, and compassion. Her compassion at being separated in the eyes of mankind from Magdalene, of being separated from her sensuality, her womanliness, her yoni, her human desires, have created a huge schism in the consciousness of Christian women worldwide. The Christians confined her in the image of virgin and mother and separated her from her wholeness and passion as a powerful sensual woman in her own right.

This schism has been created to separate desire and purity, compassion and sensuality so that they become pale reflections of their true, unified essence. The Triple Goddess, the three Marys, is alive in each woman, each of whom does hold these qualities, but has been taught to separate them, and even feel guilt and shame about using them all together. For when one uses them all together, one enters the Divine feminine, which is the end of all control and domination on this planet by the structures that have been created by men.

The separation of sacredness and sensuality has led to a divide within the psyche of the collective feminine. Characterized by the ridiculing of Magdalene as a prostitute, and Mother Mary as a virginal saint, and not a human, sensual, feeling woman, those who now choose to unite both the holy and sacred in the power of their sensuality will undergo the journey of sexual healing and deeply entering their sensual nature. This expanded richness adds to the quality of embrace, embodying this within physical form.

Mother Mary embraced and honored her sexuality, creating more children after Yeshua. She enjoyed and celebrated her feminine sensual side, and taught others to do this also. She was the initiator, the High Priestess of Isis, bringing her priestesses into their compassion, their power, and their love. She was never separate from Magdalene, from sacred sensuality and holy desire, and when *you* choose this union, you too will enter the Triple Goddess.

HOLDING THE SPACE

Mary literally overarched, like an umbrella, the many gatherings of disciples and followers of Yeshua. Black Light creates a space that everyone can melt into, allowing Yeshua to penetrate this space, the womb, with his light, and the words he spoke. This principle still holds true: a woman holding the Black Light creates space, which the man then activates and ignites, bringing forth what is held in the formless into dynamic manifestation.

The Mother holds the space for you to expand into the Black Light if you soften yourself enough, and allow your boundaries to become fluid, to expand out into the embrace of space. This space is like lying on a rolling, undulating bed of softly tolling bells, drifting in these shimmering vibrations, allowing yourself to follow these vibrations into the heart of the cells, allowing yourself to dissolve into the soft, empty space in the heart of each cell. In this deep rest, Black Light brings spirit into matter. This gentle but all-powerful light penetrates into and transforms matter, even under the most impossible of situations.

Black Light holds, in the heart of the subconscious, a charge, a charge so deeply rooted in the primal brain, that one could spend many lifetimes struggling with it. This charge is a denial of love that was required to bring spirit into matter. To truly bring spirit into matter requires that we go into the depth of this subconscious, this charge, and unfold it from within itself. One goes into illusion and penetrates it, allowing the full flowering of the subconscious into consciousness.

THE LEADER

Mother Mary was the highest female initiate alive two thousand years ago, the wisest woman, Isis incarnate. She, Mary Magdalene, and Marie Salome taught the feminine mysteries of birth and cocreation to a group of twelve women. This group included Martha; Mary of Bethany; Veronica, who wiped the face of Yeshua as he fell while carrying the cross; Anna, mother of Mary; Elizabeth, mother of John the Baptist; Neshi;

Marianne, sister of disciple Philip; Mary; and Joanna.[1] They were the counterpart to Yeshua's twelve, as the power behind the throne. Indeed, *Isis* means "throne."

Mother Mary was their leader and teacher, the Mother to them all. She was the only person that could walk with Yeshua all the way when he was carrying the cross; no man could. She was the only one who could experience it fully, as she was simultaneously birthing the Christ Blueprint onto earth. At Yeshua's Crucifixion, the mantle and responsibility for the next step and the dissemination of the Christ teachings were given to the Triple Goddess of Mother Mary, Salome, and Mary Magdalene. This next step is called the Womb of the World.

A Practice

Meditate on Mother Mary's symbol, and draw it on your heart three times. When you have done so, hold your palm over the heart to energize the symbol for a minute or two. Sit quietly, center yourself, and place your hands in prayer, at the heart.

Ask within: "Who, or what, is in need of my blessing and embrace right now?"

Sit and observe what arises. It may come in a thought, a feeling, a picture, a sensation in the body, or a memory. Do not overlook or dismiss anything that arises.

If you prefer to visualize, see your hand wrapping around this person, feeling, or picture lovingly, gently, as though you were holding the most delicate of flowers.

The next time you meet the person or thought connected to this embrace, tell them what you are doing in this practice; or simply embrace

---

1. All who held the wisdom of the lineage of ancient mothers that throughout history have birthed the deepest transformative teachings and actions onto earth.

them in a warm hug in the same feeling way as you do in this practice. Let the exercise go, and go about your day.

THE SHADOW SIDE

The ideas and beliefs about love, and how to give and receive it without fear, attachment, and need, are the shadow side of both Mother Mary and Mary Magdalene. The shadow side for humans wishing to embody Mother Mary is mothering without wisdom, allowing your children or loved ones to rule and dictate you without having the discipline and strength necessary to love yourself, be strong, and set boundaries with others.

Here, we can stifle and smother the other through our own need for love and sentimentality, overlooking their blind spots and debilitating the soul growth of our self, and the other, through our own need to look like we are loving, our own needs that we need to be seen as good, and by our own need that we need to be loved.

The deepest love is for another's soul, not their ego, and sometimes this takes tough decisions that the ego will not like.

Need

Those wishing to embody Mary want to be seen as loving, generous, kind, and "there" for others, always serving others at the expense of their own self, needs, and desires in order to boost their own self-worth, to make them feel loved and wanted. They can never say no to another, as they want everyone to know how selfless, lovable, and wonderful they are, when in fact they have a deep sense of unworthiness, shame, and guilt about truly receiving love.

If you are hurt or offended by something or someone not giving you love back from the love you share with them, then it is not love you are giving, but need—a need that is a validation of the small self, an open wound that has not received love from yourself.

Love shares, embraces, welcomes, and creates more of itself. Love embraces every experience in relationship. Relationship is the testing ground for love. If there is need, no extending without reservation, or offense at not receiving love back; if there is no bringing of love into the details of our human experience day by day, of our close relationships, then it is not love.

This selflessness requires great power, otherwise one leaks energy and becomes drained. Those drawn to Mother Mary will do well to remember the power of Isis; soft as she is strong; the power of Isis is equal to her softness. An image to remember here is the picture of Mother Mary with a child in one arm, and a sword in another. To be the Mother requires great strength, the sense of fearless protection that a lioness has for her cubs, independence, and Self-love.

The leaking of life force and self-love that can occur in apparent self-lessness is exhaustion, using your life force to stay productive and self-important. Our idea of conscience, of ideals, of what is considered right to do, can govern our lives, rather than the way of being itself, which is spontaneous and flowing, different in different situations and environments. Playing spontaneously rather than being stuck in routines or dogma allows this quality to unfold. Doing something different, being childlike, playing with friends, and allowing yourself just to *be* can open up arenas that you never thought possible.

Ignorance

Giving away your power to an ideal of what you think love is, is ignorance. Ignorance is the absence of knowledge, discernment, and experience of what the soul is. It is the cloaks and patterns that we put on ourselves in order to grow, experience, and evolve into what we call truth. A soul always wishes to follow truth; that is its nature, and what it is birthed from. In having concepts, wounds, and patterns, the soul starts to believe that this is the truth, and starts to follow these ideas and beliefs. Yet a soul needs these experiences of ignorance in order to grow its level of clarity, discernment, true love, and direction. The strongest moment for a soul to know truth is when it has been given an experience of the truth. Then it can follow this. However, even this is fraught with danger, as the mind can also interpret itself to be the soul if the mind is too identified with one's sense of self.

Ignorance is that which stops us expanding, and being an enlightening being, never static in what it is. Truth is fluid; ignorance is fixed. Truth liberates; ignorance confines. Ignorance demands; truth asks. Ignorance controls; truth sets free. Ignorance disempowers; truth gives *you* the power. Ignorance keeps us looking outside, truth points us within.

Black Light

CHAPTER 6

Black Light

Isis

Imagine this, a vast living midnight sky, starless, black.
A single shining light appears, glistening.
Its light gradually undulates,
Unfolding in a spinning vortex growing outward,
Sweeping across the vast darkness,
Birthing innumerable stars into the living midnight sky.
This is My Eye; this is My creation.
Come rest, abide in Me
Let go, deep into the embrace of the Black Light
Liquid, living emptiness
Sweet silence
Full of everything.
Soften into what underlies the appearance
Surrender into the pull of love.
Be the child you are born to be
And are birthing right now
Allow yourself to be recreated
Remade, reformed, revealed.
Drop deep down
Retreat from the world, if but for a moment
See life through these eyes.

 —The Black Light

I am Lady Isis, Mistress of the Black Light. Black Light is the light of the universal womb, before light visible, before color, before matter as you know it. This Black Light is my body; it is what I am clothed in. The universe is pervaded by this tender, loving presence, holding you, unfolding all that you are, containing all that you are in my womb.

Before there was light, and an idea of darkness, lay Black Light, the sweet silence of the Beloved calling you home. It is sweet emptiness, the heart surrendered. It feels like your heart is gently but perpetually breaking wide open, with no object for its breaking. It is crystal clarity, pure, deeply touching, and feminine in vastness. There is no object for its love and compassion, for there is nothing there, no reference point, no concept or form, nothing to hold onto, no memory, no past, no future.

It is the deepest intimacy one can ever know. It embraces you, not you it. It touches you in places nothing else can, and nobody else ever will. It makes you cry, for it is the deepest remembrance of love a human can ever have. It is the Beloved that has no face, no form, and no substance. It contains itself completely within itself, pure before it becomes form.

It is only by means of your passage through matter that you evolve. While you are in the stage of your evolution subject to the push and pull of the body-mind or matter, I am to you the Mother of Sorrows, because all your sorrows and troubles come to you through your contact with matter. But as soon as you lose your identification with the body-mind, then I am for you the Divine Mother, as I am now uncloaked as Black Light.

Black Light is the dark night of reason. It dissolves reason into itself. Your scientists say that 94 percent of this universe is dark light, a light reachable only beyond the senses and the measurements beyond the senses. Within this 94 percent lies what you call subspace. This subspace is actually a liquid space that is accessed through the light body, and is felt as a visceral fluid motion, similar to the cerebrospinal fluid, felt in the very center of the spine, that bathes the brain. All obstructions in this pathway must first be dissolved to allow the flow of light all the way from the base to the brain. Additionally, for women, the womb must also be healed, for the great sufferings of humanity lie within the womb of all women.

Within the womb lies the power of the sun Ra, and within the centers of all suns themselves lies the seed of the Black Light. Suns are grown from the Black Light, and when they explode into supernovas they return into Black Light. The Black Light is the beginning, and end, of creation. When you are born, you come from Black Light in your mother's womb. When you die, you go through the Black Light as the soul makes its journey back to the creator.

CREATING

The Black Light is the power to create from the space where all things are held in potential before they manifest. Black Light is the greatest alchemy, and the most powerful magic of love, the potential that all women hold within the womb. It transforms by holding, and bringing, everything that you are back into its pure, undifferentiated, unformed state: original innocence. In this state, all wounds can dissolve, and all things are made possible. All things are made new.

When any of you create anything of great impact or huge significance that truly taps into universal forces and power, then you to have to enter the Black Light to birth it. If you do not enter the Black Light, then the creation you are birthing does not have full impact; it may be useful for some people, it may even generate awareness among the masses, but it will not change anything fundamental in consciousness. This is a marker, and a test for you to remember.

The Black Light, as epitomized in the form of the Black Madonna, is

93

the state from where all realities arise from. Christ, Buddha, and other Great Ones, have all had to enter this Black Light to bring forth their transformative actions onto the earth plane, to ground these actions onto the earth plane.

For the quality of the Black Light is the power to birth realities, and create through magic, wonder, and Grace. Every birth, the first and most momentous journey, begins in darkness. Just because humanity has forgotten about it for the last cycle does not mean that it is not here. It is the height of all alchemy, the heart of transfiguration.

You do not lack Christ; what is lacking is the Sophia of Christ, the wisdom—experience of Christ. One of the Keys to the Sophia of Christ is the sacrament of sacred marriage, Keys that I shared with my priestesses, of which Mary Magdalene is the best known. Yet there are others who were taught and practiced the same Keys who are living today, and starting to share this wisdom once again. sacred marriage, as happened between myself and Osiris, Yeshua and Mary, can lead to the direct immersion into the Black Light when both partners are initiated and clear vessels.

When both partners immerse into the velvety fullness that is empty of experience created by polarity, then the original substance, Black Light, reveals itself, and sacred marriage occurs. It is in this state of being that you both recognize God fully, in every cell, in every fiber of your body, mind, and soul. It is here that you remember and join with those Ones, like Yeshua and Mary, who have merged together in the Black Light before, and are still there in that space waiting for you to taste what they are living.

In Egypt these initiations were given to those who had completed the first part of the Great Pyramid or masculine initiations, and were ready for the next step in my pyramid, the Isis Pyramid, portal to the Womb of the World. The third step occurs just outside the pyramid complex. In Tibet, these initiations through mantras to various dakinis or female Buddhas, such as Ekajati, are learned by those Bodhisattvas who have conquered the fear of death.

DARKNESS

A simple way for you to begin to open to Black Light is to spend more time in darkness. Sit in a darkened room in silence, or spend a day and night alone in darkness. Become used to its presence as a living, palpable flow. In this darkness make it a practice to embrace the parts of your mind that arise in fear, restlessness or judgment. Allow the heart to open and feel from this space in a new way. See from this space alone. Make Black Light your friend. This is a powerful, fast way to enter into a portal to Black Light, and to know yourself better.

Making Black Light your friend is going back to the beginning of creation. In the beginning there was only darkness everywhere; darkness, the living waters, and the flow of these living waters when the Creator moved light across them. This beginning of creation still lies in all of you today, existing in your bodies in darkness and flow.

Black Light is the creative darkness from which all life emerges. We die into darkness so birth and resurrection, regeneration, can happen. In accessing this darkness, and working within its silence, we guide life from emptiness into form. In the darkness there is so much love that nothing gets in the way of it, nothing reflects it, or refracts it. It is pure, because nothing is there to block it, not even you. Not even you are there to limit it. Within darkness there is no duality, nothing to reflect light. Black Light is here to birth the infinite possibilities of this space into form, so that God may know itself, and that you may know yourself as part of God.

Many people today are enamored with light, and forget about the darkness, the space from where all light comes, and indeed the place where you are born and nurtured during the first nine months of your life; in the womb. What you give form to in daylight is only 1 percent of what is seen in darkness. If you can access both of these realities, then you can be reborn, *if* you can enter into the process with courage, and embrace all the visions and fears that arise.

John the Beloved demonstrated his union with the Black Light through his surrender to the Holy Spirit. For to enter the Black Light is to be in total surrender. As John felt and intuited the time of his upcoming death, he ordered his disciples to dig a deep hole on top of a hill overlooking Patmos harbor, the idyllic Greek island he was marooned on. Mystified, they did so, and John asked them to accompany him as he lowered himself into the hole, whereupon he informed them that this was his last night on earth, and they were to watch over him until the morning.

Astonished by his request, they stayed up late into the night, listening to their teacher's last words to them. However, one by one they feel asleep in the early hours of the morning, to wake up at daybreak astonished. John's body was gone, snatched from the embrace of the earth itself. All that was left was an empty, black hole.

HEALING

For many of you, darkness brings up images of the unknown, what you fear, what you have not yet embraced, what you sweep under the carpet and try to forget about. These locked doors of your psyche that you fear to step into actually hold the greatest potential for healing, growth, and empowerment, for when you fully enter and embrace the darkness, boundaries and limitations expand, dissolving anxieties and fears. Darkness holds a great deal of power, and empowerment, for you.

The complete immersion into the deepest darkness, that of the womb of the earth and the embrace of matter itself, is perhaps one of the most powerful means to instantly access a portal into the Black Light, and in the process heal birth traumas, sexual abuse, and deep wounds. All of this is healed through visionary experience, visitation, and richly mythological occurrences while buried in earth's embrace, *without* need for modern-day methods.

Children hark back to this by burying each other in the sand. Doing this, burying all of you, is the first step toward submerging fully in to the darkness, and entering a much more expanded, healing, magical, and numinous world, where you can speak to spirits past and present, communicate and heal with your ancestors, and enter into multiple realities simultaneously.

When many of you are in darkness together, you all become closer. Many things are revealed about you in the silence, emptiness, and darkness of the Black Light, especially when others are present. All your conditionings and modes of behavior melt and dissolve in darkness, which is when a whole new world of deeper relationship, peace, and wordless feelings communicate your hidden nature.

Sexual impulses and differentiation can become androgynous and unified as you reconcile your differences back into the night of creation. Here it could be said that light divides, and darkness unites. When whole groups connect and communicate in this way, a family develops. As Christ said, "When more than two are gathered in my name, so there shall I be." If more than two gather in darkness, and silence, with the same intention, and commune with each other, a deeper understanding forms, as seen in the rituals of the indigenous peoples of the earth.

This communion is also seen in moments of disaster and huge suffering. For example, in times of natural disaster, disparate people worldwide band together in order to help the other, sharing and helping with everything they have. This is because they have gone through the darkness, and darkness unifies.

When this happens on a collective scale, the world will be plunged into Black Light in order to heal as a collective, and to birth a new earth. This will be a traumatic time for many millions of people, whose

97

deepest, darkest wounds and urges will emerge. Apparently normal people will descend into anarchic states of violence and despair. This time is a great purging, where many thousands of evolved beings will have to balance this suffering out in their bodies of light, creating stability for the planetary light body. If you feel like you are one of these people, then get used to the darkness, for it will become your greatest friend in the times ahead.

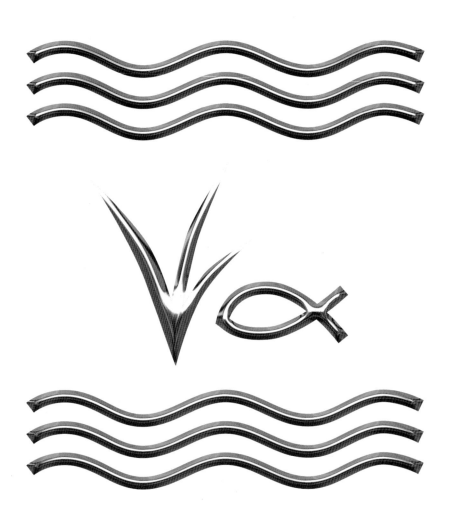

Surrender

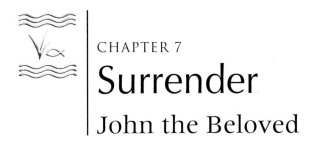

CHAPTER 7
Surrender
John the Beloved

Not my will, but thy will be done.

—Matthew 26:39

John the Beloved is part of the inner circle that cocreated and anchored the Christ Blueprint on earth. John was a celibate practitioner of the inner tantras, processes done alone in meditation that unite the inner male and female. In this union he became a conduit for the Holy Spirit, serving with Mother Mary to create an alchemical container for the sexually sublimated energies of Yeshua, Mary Magdalene, and Salome. John was the third prophet of the Christ Lineage. As the seer of Revelation, the prophecy of this age, and the third being to bodily ascend along with Mother Mary and Yeshua, he was worshipped by the Knights Templar, along with John the Baptist, as a messiah.

John embodies the quality of surrender to love's will, where love is God and God is love. The fight against this surrender to love is our deepest conflict, and our biggest portal to Christ Consciousness. The heart of surrender grinds down anything that stands in the way between God and you. This is an ongoing process. Surrender never stops, for the heart is always unfolding, ever opening, ever expanding. It is relentless; it stops for no one.

Surrendering to what is presented to you in life, moment by moment, brings up our deepest resistances, our deepest shadows. Everything in the basement of your subconscious, every voice within you that says no to love, no to peace, no to joy, no to what is, arises and fights. This fight takes you deeper and deeper, and wears you out, wears out the fight in you, the resistances of the small self, until you break down. In this breaking down lies the opening to the softness and the gentling of love.

Even when you think you are surrendered, there is more; there is always more. Surrender dismantles every part of you, and remakes you in love's image when you have sincerely asked for love to enter your life, and for you to live this life. And then, and only then, does love come, beckoned by the call of the soul that has fought with all her might to recognize itself. This love will come in many ways, some of which you really will not like. But each circumstance will lead to more love if you allow it. The quicker you surrender, the less resistance and pain you will have to experience.

Surrender wears out the warrior within. It makes us gentle, soft, and transparent. All one has to do is listen to the voice of love, which is always quietly, softly present, just waiting to be heard and acted upon. Then the voice becomes stronger and stronger.

Surrender is a process, a continual experience, which happens every day. It is never done or completed. It never stops; it is never a statement. One is always surrendering, continually giving over the mind to what lies here and now, in each thought, each choice. Surrender softens what is rigid within. It gentles us, taking us more internal, deeper into the silence of the still heart that is awake and sensitive. This awakening guides us back from that which is resistant to love by embracing and forgiving any and all thoughts and feelings that arise that are not love. Having the ongoing felt awareness of what is resistant to love moves awareness to love, so more love can flow.

Surrender leads to true vulnerability, vulnerability that cleanses the heart and releases fear and willfulness, using your will to manifest what you wanted. And that was appropriate for that time. For this time, surrendering this way of doing things, into vulnerability, nakedness, and surrender, leads to expansion into more love, which in turn leads to more vulnerability, and more fears arising . . . until all that is left is a pure heart as a conduit for love to flow through. In this open heart, you move only when the palpable flow of love moves you. You become so available, so present in the open heart that only what comes in this moment is what you live and can know to be true, because it is happening right now.

Surrender also requires meditation in order for it to be whole. It is wise guided action, spontaneous and in the now, without fear, belief, expectation, or hope. There is no surrender to something; it is surrendering unto being within itself. This is the true nature of the action of Shakti, or Shekinah. In this trust, nothing matters if everything changes completely every moment. All your sense of reason, thoughts, plans, everything that is needed right now might be completely different from that which was needed in the previous moment, and in the next moment. Love responds in the now, and there are no teaching, law, or rules for this. Love is the whole of the law.

THE OPEN CONDUIT

Only when there is nothing else that you want from the dream of the world will you be free, and this is surrender. If you are totally surrendered, awake, and alive, your heart is the conduit through which others receive abundance. You have to release the little self and the dream of getting in order to be open, and in this giving one becomes all-attractive, a magnet that draws to you ten times what you have given. In surrender all things are given through you.

Surrendering into perpetual revelation, living naked in the moment is when every step of the journey is a revelation. You do what you need to do, with care, with full attention, and then move on to the next thing to do that unfolds organically. This step-by-step approach allows the full death of the previous moment in order to create space for the next new moment, where we know nothing about the future, and have forgotten about the past. This allows us to live as a conduit of whatever is needed for anybody, and everybody, in the moment.

This involves deep trust, trust in that whatever is needed will come, that the unfolding is a continual process that comes from within and takes you wherever you need to go. And this is the mystery, the mystery that dissolves the "I." Any thoughts of "I," me, mine, "I deserve this," "I need that from you," from her, from him, any validation of there being a separate self that needs any justification, gets continually surrendered.

In this the mind plays its role as the servant of the soul, allowing the observation of any and all ideas of "I." In this seeing, there is a letting go. Letting go is one of the hardest things to do, be it letting go of the search for God, letting go of habits, or letting go of ideas, people, and beliefs that have served you until this point, but can no longer take you where you need to go in order to evolve. In letting go, there is no need, just resting, and from resting joy arises, and from joy peace as the gateway to the golden silence within your heart's core. This letting go is a literal emptying of the self, an active, subtle willing and letting go of the "I" in order to give your Self space to be.

Constantly repeating this, letting go again and again of the voice of the "I" in the midst of your thoughts, your deeds, your interactions and conversations with others, is when you know exactly how you are still holding on. This letting go is an inner action, a movement of consciousness on your part that recognizes the needs of a personal self and lets go of it in the same moment. To die to this self means to die to all self-talk, self-importance, self-validation, and the projection of yourself out into the world.

You die a little every day living this: the "I" disappears. This dying centers you in freedom, in a calm, even, steady mind, firm in the truth of love's witness and awareness. In this, there is nothing left that takes the experience of presence somewhere else, apart from here and now.

Through your surrender to being here, to including and embracing all aspects of life, you unify and bring to awareness all the fragmented aspects of your Self. Everything is included in surrender, and nothing is left out. All that you have believed, thought, felt and experienced is offered, and given away. Everything has to go, and you leave no back door, no escape route, no way for the small self to come back.

Everything you think and know to be true has to be placed in the heart and given to love, to do what love wills, in order for surrender to flourish and bloom. This surrender creates a vast opening, a space where you can be pulled, where love can pull you, that can then take you to your destination, wherever that may be. Surrender opens the door to love, so that love may take you wherever it wishes.

Surrender is the last quality to master you before you live the surrendered life. When you live a surrendered life there is little if any thought arising within you. You may not know the words that come out of your mouth in any moment, and have no need to remember what they are, or what the actions are that flow through your body-mind and speech. You learn by what comes through you. There is great delight and joy in this, for in this allowing of ourselves to be nobody, we become able to relate with anybody, in any moment.

FLUID JOY

Reality is fluid and open. We access whatever quality of Christ Consciousness is required in any moment, as all thirteen flow together simultaneously in the single moment when we are surrendered. When love is required it flows; when joy is required that too flows; when ruthless compassion is needed it too flows. What may serve you in one moment may not serve you in the next.

This fluidity dissolves all rules, allowing one to express and embody the highest potential in any moment. This is resting in the heart of harmony, and listening to it. This resting, this abiding, is natural and graceful, and cannot be forced as it arises the more we tune into the harmony of our heart voice over time, and follow it in action. The simplicity of this being arises from not listening to any other voices, and following this one at all times.

This simple heart leads to the unfolding of life in perfect harmony. No one else can lead you there. This is your Source. When this energy is not moving anywhere it leads you to the place where head and heart unite, the source of the head and heart, yet neither. When we sit at this source, then our highest potential unfolds without you knowing or deciding where it will take you. It decides what is best for you, by you relaxing into it. This is true grounding and centering, coming when we drop into surrendered silence, our home that is always with us. Home is where the heart is, and we enter our home through surrender.

This home is joy. Christ Consciousness is a state of being in "shadowless joy and constant celebration." Shadowless joy is joy that is soulfelt, all-inclusive, and shared with others; it is the joy that flows when you feel the happiness of others, and the joy that flows for no reason at all. This is the pulse constantly humming in all life, that you feel spontaneously undulating throughout all parts of you, and the life around you as bliss, bliss that has no reason to be blissful, it just *is* blissful.

When surrender has mastered your life, you live in your innermost urging, the calling of your heart's desire. Following your inner voice, you listen to your natural rhythms as they harmonize with the earth, your loved ones, and life itself. Living in a way that keeps you connected to this core leads to perpetual joy, always here whenever you need it. All you have to do to access it is to let go of anything standing in the way.

Trust life and surrender. Allow the intent of life to flow through you, desiring and doing what it wills. And all that it wills is our bliss, happiness, and true contentment. Connecting with your bliss, your joy, is surrender living through you. Feeling this presence and pulse in your body is when you align with the natural synchronicity and spontaneity of life's processes. For this reason, Creation manifests in a flash, in a pulse of pure joy, spontaneous and free of any distinct purpose, "like a thief in the night."

To access this is a major turning point, for it is only here that true Life begins. For the first time you are ready to fully incarnate, to fully "land on the planet" to be content and happy to *be here now,* without a trace of fear, judgment, or any significant residue from prior states. At this level life is fully guided by synchronicity, intuition, and Grace. Sudden bursts of joy for no reason overcome you. In true joy, you feel no separation between you and Life. Joy opens the door, and welcomes all of Life *now.*

This life spark within all of us pushes toward movement, made conscious when your heart is open and extending, when your emotional state is fluid and agile. When you are fluid, you can experience any feeling at any time. If you can at will produce equanimity, joy, love, anger, or tears without charge or attachment to them, then you are in surrender. However, the less you can summon feelings, the more you are frightened of them, the more you are at their mercy.

Conversely, the more you allow yourself to experience feelings, the less you can be enslaved by them. If you allow them to pass through you, you become transparent, without charge, without holding onto anything or anybody. When you are established in surrender, you learn to allow the movements of the body, feelings, and mind to arise within you, to be there, to be seen and embraced, and to be given over to the Source of Being.

When you are in surrender, you can let go of any and all things— you become transparent. Letting go leads to a completion of something, be it a job, a pattern, a relationship, a way of being. This completion leads to transparency; everything flows through you, and you hold onto nothing. There is no reaction, no past hurt or future expectation to irritate or stimulate you into reaction. You sit in the choiceless choice: to be here now, and allow this to move you.

RELATIONSHIP

When you are transparent you are whole. Nothing can get to "you," as there is no "you" to be got to; it has been surrendered, so the "you" is no longer an obstacle, and everything flows through. This then becomes a beacon to others, lightening their load and giving them a different perception, a new possibility to something that previously was causing them misery. This presence in you grows through sharing and giving, as it can never lessen when there is more of it being ignited around itself.

In surrender you want nothing for yourself. This is the living experience that there is no one here living a life; it is Life living through your body-mind. This establishes a relationship to life that then lies within all other relationships that you engage in. As you engage with others you stay whole within your own connection to the life flow, and engage from this space.

The most effective way to test surrender is in relationship, where there are apparently two I's operating. Surrendering your "I" in relating entails a letting go of all boundaries between you and formless awareness. Your sexual energy becomes free of attachment, compulsion, and push and pull, instead being moved by holy desire for loving union. Sex is no longer used as a means of escape, but as a means of expansion, communion and celebration, of two beings needing nothing from the other, as they are whole in their own connection.

ALONENESS

In this, one comes to see that no relationship can cause you to be unloving, harsh, or judgmental, for you are alone, all one, in your journey to God. This aloneness allows one to surrender ever deeper the resistance of the body-mind to the flow of love and life. This aloneness creates spaciousness, depth, and genuineness, where you are no longer run by needing to look, act, or behave in any way shaped or desired by the world. Genuineness allows you to totally honor Self and act from this space, rather than having to act in any way that seeks approval from outside yourself. You no longer value what the world thinks, and create your own value.

You are alone on your path, and what fulfills you most comes from within. This diffuses reactivity as we take full responsibility. In this aloneness we find wholeness, no longer demanding that the context of our lives provide our happiness, nor hoping to view our wholeness through anyone else's eyes. Paradoxically, this aloneness allows you to become closer to every person, and for them to feel closer to you, as there is no longer any need to get anything from that person. And people can feel that, as it speaks to their hearts and attracts them.

Surrender is the source of heart and harmony, and contention is the root of discord. When one is in contention, one is not in surrender. Surrender is recognizing the difference between the presence of flow and surrender, and the absence of flow and surrender. This well-being is innocent delight, allowing the learning of new things, playing in abandon, living in continual surprise, not knowing how things are, not needing them to go a certain way. Life lives through us, love masters us, and the adventure of Life carries us along, moment by magical moment.

SURRENDER AS SERVICE

Only love can heal. Surrender is the portal through which love flows; it is the conduit for love to pour through us as we abandon the notion of being bound in dual voices. In surrender nothing worries you. There is flow, acceptance, and allowance of everything that is happening to you right now, and in extension of this everything that is happening in the world around you, locally and globally. This surrender does not lead to passivity, instead leading to an ever-present thread of contentment, a state of fluid peace, as the basis for awakened and radical action in the world.

The more surrendered we are, the more responsible we become, as we start to feel that the world's troubles are also part of our own, and that we have to do something about it. In this surrender from the heart, deep-seated passion wells up, the passion to love all parts of the one Self in any and every way possible. We become busier as what flows spontaneously through us are actions that serve others as extensions of our own Self. As we are surrendered, there is nothing else left to do apart from this. So we allow the overflowing life, the extension of life, of Grace flowing through us, in as many ways as we can, to as many people as possible. Surrender is how love manifests in us all; it is the open gate for God to walk into us.

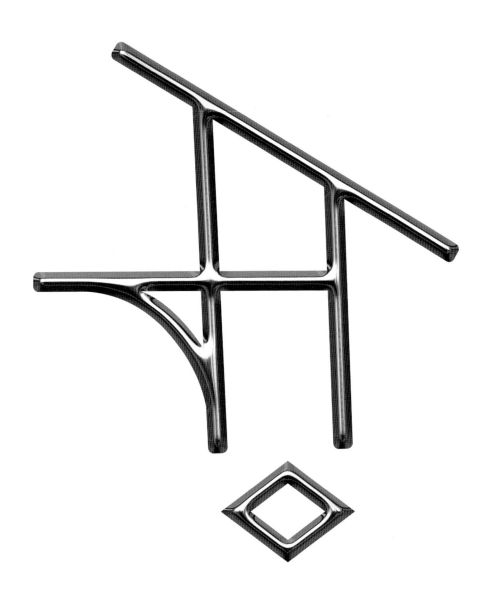

Loving Wisdom

CHAPTER 8

Loving Wisdom
Lord Kuthumi

I was one of the first Masters from the lineage of the four Mind-born Sons of God, of whom you count Christ as one. After their creation these four Mind-born Sons of God, so named because they were formed directly through Divine Thought and Intent and not from a human womb, taught and created multiple lineages.

The *sankalpa* or Divine Intent that I was baptized into by God is love's wisdom. Loving wisdom is a channel that connects the heart to the third eye and merges them both into a gateway to the infinite. I, Kuthumi, hold this gateway as a ray of light and manifestation. When we unite the heart and the third eye, we create a cascade reaction with the brain and body-mind system. Everything comes into alignment with the voice of love, which is wisdom, and the feeling of wisdom, which is love.

Loving wisdom is detached yet intimate, penetrating but soft, eloquent but simple, charismatic yet humble. Wisdom arises when belief dissolves, when knowledge dissolves, when intellect goes into union. Wisdom is fluid with feeling, able to respond to any and all situations spontaneously and unpredictably. Wisdom comes through deep surrender into the unknown, where unlimited potential and infinite intelligence lives as a palpable field.

To be is natural. To know what you are takes much investigation. To unite both requires that you commune alone, and in the faces of all others, in sacred relationship. This is the face of love as it expresses now on earth. This original face is humanity in unity, heart extending, embracing, creating a field where we all feel each other resonating, where we share in the other's sensitivity, pain, and joy, and respond to it as we would to part of ourselves.

Yet this wisdom is never something that can be attained, for it is always growing. Even the wisest of men are still open to becoming wiser, to sinking deeper into the moment where the wisdom of love spontaneously generates itself. For love and wisdom can never be divided because they were never separated.

ONENESS

One cannot enter the One by seeking separate or dualistic means to enter this One. One can only seek dualistic means and tendencies to reach the door. Love is enough to stand in its self, and love needs a voice; this voice is wisdom. Love is whole and self-contained. Love is a container, the vessel, the crucible, the beginning, and the result. Love in its truth need say nothing; but this is not perceivable to most people; this is why love needs the voice of wisdom to express itself.

Love is the sharing of wisdom; wisdom is the eloquence of love.

As one of the initiates of the Christ Lineage, I was given many Keys. The brilliance of mind that can penetrate and see; the detachment that enabled me to sew together any gaps in clarity, in focus, for I was sublimely at ease and relaxed with all these qualities. Similarly I was given the qualities of love, of softness, of embrace, of commitment, of humility that allowed the flowering of love, and more wisdom.

To access true wisdom requires that our mental bodies be crystallized and strengthened. And then it requires a breaking down of this mental body to further expand our consciousness. This is a paradox; we build something up, only to dissolve it to enter a much larger space. Once it has crystallized and reached its apex, love has to enter and topple the building so that it can expand out into the infinite. To do this requires the greatest act of courage based on love, which is true wisdom.

Love will take one from this point, into the present. This is the hardest thing to do, for often you have spent a lot of time, money, effort, and study in acquiring clarity of mind, of clear reason, of penetrating, analytical, decisive thinking that brings one to the state of so-called empowerment, to the height of their mental faculties, to a certain brilliance and impressionability that this mind makes on others, and makes us admired, clever, and intelligent.

When we reach this stage, there is nowhere else to go other than to soften and drop down into love, not negating these qualities but dissolving their limitations and allowing them to expand to their natural potential. Then sharpness and clarity is behind the emptiness and vastness of loving consciousness, and can then come forward at the right times, yet still within this vastness, this softness.

For those that are more love-oriented, they reach this vastness by growing their love to heal, embrace, and encompass more aspects of themselves, and more aspects of the people around them. In this embrace, wisdom is required to expand out; so when one is love-oriented, naturally one is drawn through experiences that generate the feelings of compassion, to seek the assistance of the mind in helping them to expand their love and compassion further.

Wisdom becomes a support of the love-oriented being, a support that allows them to become more loving. Without this support love will flounder, collapsing into the holes of the small self wrapped up in misunderstandings, lack of focus, and denial of one's true worth. Love is clarity on all levels of consciousness. Wisdom is a support for that clarity.

Devotion to love is not the same as devotion to wisdom. Devotion to wisdom can become an enslavement to knowledge. Devotion to love can become a weakening of the intellect. If you are too devoted to either one, then integrate the other. It is like seeking; seeking becomes an obstacle at a certain point along the spiritual path, as it may stop us from obtaining the experience of true, innate wisdom that guides us to rest in our innate wholeness. Seeking is usually for something that is outside oneself, which is not true wisdom. This is what we shared about wisdom being Self-generating. Once it is generated within yourself, there is no need for anything outside your self to validate or confirm yourself. One seldom realizes that their ideas or beliefs of love may be limiting their ability to truly experience love. One seldom realizes that their idea of what is wise can also limit.

Wisdom is fluid; what may be wise for you to do in one minute may be unwise for you to do in the next. What is loving for you to do in one minute may be very unloving for you to do in the next. This is why there are no rules for loving wisdom, for it is fluid and infinitely intelligent, a process that is always continuously happening. It never stops, it never ceases, and it can never be defined.

How can something that is the basis for all things ever be defined? All one can do is dissolve the blocks that define it.

THE SHADOW SIDE

The shadow side for humans wishing to integrate surrender is sloth, lack of discernment and awareness, repression, and a lack of power to transform and heal. Having surrender and devotion without the right use of will, discipline and action can become procrastination. Going with the flow and being too passive, passionless, without discernment and knowledge, and engaging in ego-centered contentment masquerading as joy is also a trap. Those of you in false surrender are waiting for something to happen, are waiting for the opportunity rather than coming out to meet it, to meet life.

Sloth

Surrender is not just about sitting around doing nothing, thinking you are in surrender. This form of laziness is sloth. Sloth is inertia and stagnancy of energy, and occurs in those people who wish an easy life without doing anything for it. These people like to be taken care of, while doing nothing. They expect to be waited on and to have things done for them, completely forgetting what the soul does: serve, and then be served.

Of course, sloth also arises from many psychological factors; there may be wounds, family factors, and mental or emotional disabilities that contribute to sloth. These are not excuses, and are not to be used to justify sloth, which can be the tendency for those who are aware of their patterns but still lack the dynamic action to do something about it. If you know you are in sloth, do something about it *now*. It is only by your actions that God will see you, and then you will experience God moving through you.

People in sloth lack motivation, action, energy, self-will, courage, and assertiveness, because again they are in fear of power; of claiming their light. Sloth is decay, entropy, a downward pulling resistance to the life force itself. Until one transforms sloth into stability, into centeredness, into groundedness, one will always suffer from its effects.

Exorcisms can release and reveal sloth, but then the inner motivation, the inner spark, has to come forth into action through passion, dedication, determination, and service. Truly sloth is only overcome by consistent, impassioned service. Sloth is a rigidity which coarsens the body-mind. It makes you hard, not soft, and sleepy at the same time. Sloth is found in the darkness of the root chakra, the deep, dark unconscious. When caught in sloth we become so steeped in ignorance that we eventually are not even aware of our own existence; we just go on fulfilling the obligations of a mundane life. We become restricted to the three-dimensional world only, and refuse to allow other possibilities into our own numbed and "comfortable" world. Here, ignorance is bliss.

Sloth is an overidentification with the density of matter and the body-mind. This identification leads to ideas and impulses toward greed, lust, envy, and fear. These destructive impulses then lead to an action to fulfill the desire, which leads to another impression in the body-mind, leading to desire and enactment of the desire . . . and so on and so forth, caught in a vicious cycle.

Sloth is a numbing against the deeper unresolved states of fear, shame, repressed anger, and guilt, a real lack of energy, drive, and enthusiasm. *Enthusiasm* literally means to be filled with Divine inspiration to create and to share, and it is a state of agape, Divine love. In sloth, one lives in the core belief that one cannot move forward, achieve anything of value, or make a real difference. This is tied to the resistance and refusal to face and engage in the strong and sustained energies required to birth, participate, and make a real difference in yourself and the world. The best description of sloth is "I don't care," or "So what? It will not make a difference anyway."

The ultimate sloth is missing the opportunity to evolve, delaying and putting off your growth to another day, merely to spend another day in suffering. This delay is fuel that the ego uses, and thrives on, to sustain itself. It is a lack of discipline and subconscious sabotage of your soul's urgings, dreams, and deepest desires. It is the opposite of holy desire, desire that moves you forward to God. When you are used by sloth then you are asleep, and close to death.

Losing It All

To surrender to life and love means you can lose everything that you as the limited self have worked so hard to maintain in so many lifetimes, in order to maintain your ordered, nonthreatening, and comfortable existence. Ignorance is bliss, whereas surrender is the death knell of the illusion, the trumpet announcing the birth of the soul.

Resistance to surrender comes from the fear that one will give away their personal power to someone, or something, outside of them. True surrender arises from you having such a strong sense of who and what your soul really is, that you allow yourself to let go of your beliefs about what or who you should be, in exchange for a much more expanded, luminous, and open sense of what you can become.

Each act of surrender is an act that values the soul. Each act of surrender is the death of control, and the end of the ego's assertion that it is the master. The ego cannot survive and maintain its grip if one is surrendered to the flow of life and its infinite movements. This is why it will try to maintain its grip at all costs, even to the point of death or suicidal thoughts.

Surrender is opening to the mystery and allowing it to move through you in all its ways. *Surrender is the ultimate risk for the body-mind.* Only a person who risks is free. The person who risks nothing, does nothing, lives in sloth. To risk being soft, being surrendered, being vulnerable is to risk learning, growing, changing, living, and loving aspects of the vital, empowered, and unfolding wave of life.

Sometimes we may feel the flow of loving wisdom wishing to express itself through us, but there is resistance. We may not voice it or express it, so that the body-mind feels justified in its actions, so that the body-mind can feel safe and secure in its position, in its well-worn reference groove. This is the opposite of surrender: control and contraction. When we are tight in any part of our body or mind, when we seize up and feel tension, when we harden up, when we shrink in resistance in any situation or relationship, we lessen and diminish ourselves.

Opening to love can only come through us fully when we surrender this resistance, and let go into voicing vulnerability. This surrender into the opening of love heals all things, for only in giving can we truly receive. Any other reference groove or point is based on conditionality and need, a need that can never be fulfilled by anything, any relationship, or any situation or object outside of yourself. So give up the hooks of the ego, snagged into needing anything from partner, friends, family, government, or children. Only fear, the voice that keeps dual voices and feelings alive, can temporarily restrain this.

Mastery

Surrender involves discernment. What are you surrendering to? Are you surrendering to the density, the sloth, or the ascending currents of life that allow you to spread your wings and move into the unknown? The choice to surrender integrates with the wisdom that knows that life is always moving us toward our greatest happiness if we allow it to. Follow the signs, have faith, and act in your surrender, for life is dynamic, and change is a constant. If we are not changing and growing, we are not in surrender to what life is presenting us with.

Sloth is the polarity of surrender. It keeps us stuck and stagnant in a falsely secure, unchanging world. There is no challenge or passion in sloth. When we allow sloth to obstruct the joy bubbling deep within our core, then we can lose our creative spark, disconnecting from our own unique expression of the vital pulse behind all life. However, in its most refined aspect it is density, that which makes everything solid, tangible, and grounded, the force that brings us the gift of the body-mind to experience life on earth.

Through knowledge and meditation we become aware of the force of density, of matter, without becoming identified with it. It then becomes a great friend and ally to aid us in our evolution, for the body's wisdom is useful to point out where we need to evolve, and what we are ignoring on our path.

Letting go of control is the last step into Christ Consciousness. When one lets go of control, anything is possible. One could call this surrender or devotion. If one is intent on mastery, then one comes into a very natural way of being, so natural that one no longer needs put anything outside oneself. It is not about devotion to anything; it is not surrender *to* anything; it is living in this natural flow of life. It is how you have been created to be. It is a place within the soul, and more than that, it is Christ.

Effortlessness and Grace become the results of surrender and devotion, but not to anything or anyone. To access God can be seen as perpetual surrender and devotion, yet from an enlightened perspective these qualities become flowing and embodied, a matter of joy, transparency, clarity, and an emptiness of mind that allows all things to flow through it.

If one has to force surrender or exalt devotion, there is still the ego working. When the ego is naturally dissolved, all that is left is a flow of loving power and wisdom that includes within it surrender and devotion. Yet in this flow, these qualities cannot be called surrender and devotion. This is a harder act for the ego to do, for it is easier for the ego to be devoted and surrender to something than to be that power itself.

Beloved friends, there are no disciples or followers in the Council of Christ, only Masters. In this there is constant joy, constant celebration, unbroken peace, and constant Communion. Everyone is laughing! Join us.

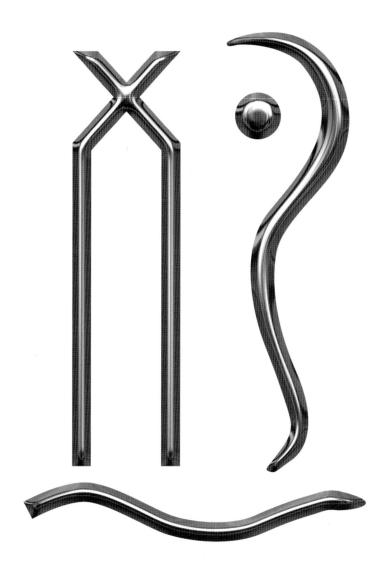

Holy Faith

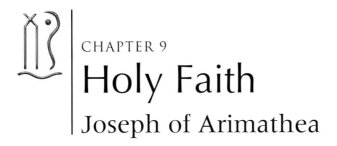

CHAPTER 9

Holy Faith

Joseph of Arimathea

Yeshua said, "I tell you the truth, if you have faith as small as a mustard seed, you can say to this mountain, 'Move from here to there' and it will move. Nothing will be impossible for you."

—Matthew 17:20

Joseph of Arimathea was with Yeshua before, during, and after his ministry as his most loyal, trusted, and faithful servant. Loyal to love and its teachings, he was always present to help no matter what occurred, without question or doubt, full of love, support, and quiet yet steadfast conviction.

Joseph was Yeshua's uncle. This connection in blood, and Joseph's role as the Apostle of Britain and reestablisher of the Christ Lineage in Glastonbury, initially arose from his recognition of Christ in Yeshua when he was still a child.

Joseph, along with the Marys and John the Beloved, was entrusted with carrying and anchoring the Blueprint held in the blood of Christ. All five of them had his actual blood, the DNA of the Perfect Human Being. Joseph had it from the burial tomb, the others from the clothes and the Crucifixion event itself. Joseph provided the tomb where Yeshua was laid, and placed his body there after the Crucifixion, doing this while the other disciples retreated in fear.

APOSTLE OF BRITAIN

Joseph became a vessel for love, for the seeds of the Christ Blueprint to anchor in Glastonbury, the place where Mary Magdalene also came to rest, meditate, and raise her daughter. Joseph prepared the place and set the space for this to happen successfully, both energetically and financially. He provided the nuts and bolts, the alchemy, and the finances for the further anchoring of the Christ Blueprint into the third dimension.

Joseph realigned the sacred site of Glastonbury to the Christ Blueprint through many alchemical means. His first action upon arriving there was to plant his holy staff into the earth at what is now known as Wearyall Hill, opposite the Tor, the druidic power center and gateway to the underworld. This planting of his holy staff, made from the wood of the crucifix and performed with ritualistic intention and total awareness, marked the arrival of the DNA of the Perfect Human Blueprint, the blood of Christ, to Glastonbury.

Joseph carried this DNA code of love, and with alchemical knowledge infused the blood throughout the rivers and streams of the green earth of Glastonbury and Avebury. He, along with his loyal and faithful helpers, "plugged" into the dragon energy lines of the earth, the Michael and Mary ley lines, creating a mutually enhancing circulatory system for all these elements to mix, merge, and alchemize freely with the lineages of ancient mothers.

Using the blood to separate the hydrogen bonds from within the molecules in water released vast amounts of energy, allowing them to created sacred sites in Glastonbury, in France, in Cornwall, and in the Sea of Galilee. These alchemies then paved the way for the Chalice Well to be founded, the well where Yeshua's blood was placed, and which reactivated the entire region of Glastonbury.

This knowledge came from Egypt, where Joseph was trained and where it too was practiced as a means to connect with the living wisdom of Gaia, and to keep human communities linked to the song lines or ley lines of the earth. As the Apostle of Britain, much of Joseph's energy is anchored in these sites in Cornwall, Glastonbury, and Avebury. To really connect with him, it is advised to visit there.

As a man, Joseph is soft, yielding, gentle, yet sure of himself. He is his own man and master, yet is humble and open to all, ever willing to come to another's aid and support them. His childlike joy unconditionally supports the expansion of love into the world. His pure, sensitive, male heart sits within the feminine heart. This quiet heart is an essential polarity; for within the heart of the male lies the female, and within the heart of the female lies the male. This polarity is the gateway to love, inner union, true strength, and manifestation, when it is accepted and allowed.

Joseph enjoyed his life, and truly epitomized what Yeshua said, "My yoke is easy." He was unobtrusive, quiet, and kept to himself, so he could act as a go-between, an intermediary, between the body of Christ and the three-dimensional world. Yet at the same time he was present with Yeshua and the Apostles whenever he was required, doing much of the secret work behind the scenes with the inner circle.

HOLY FAITH

Joseph embodies holy faith, loyalty, and trust. In trust and faith there is a dissolving of our own limiting thoughts that create our reality. For it is by our thoughts and feelings that we see and judge the world around us. By relying on our own thoughts, we take everything around us to be real, whereas in faith the mind literally gives up and ceases to think as we know it. It starts to flow openly and act spontaneously, acting in the moment with this subtle undercurrent of love that underlies all life.

To have very few thoughts flowing through your head is to be open to receive whatever life brings you. Everything comes to you, and you need do nothing. Trust is the ability to stop, open, and receive. We trust the unseen, unknowable forces of love, retraining our impulses away from the mind, fear, and its contractions in mind and body, toward the ability to relax and receive.

Faith in its purity is a direct experience of God that suffuses our whole being, transforming our ideas and concepts about faith into a living reality. Every religion comes from a spiritual experience. This is why faith is important, not as a blind faith in something outside of one's self, but as a lived, continuing experience that results in peace, a peace in which love is free to flow through you.

LOYALTY

Joseph embodies faith as the pillar, the stanchion that love can totally rely upon. This loyalty stays true to what lies behind any and all appearance, and is loyal to the best interests of the One and Only Soul. This aspect of faith, to truth and Divine Plan, comes with courage, willingness, and commitment. Joseph was extraordinary in that he never really needed to know. He carried out his part in complete trust, in complete surrender and loyalty to what was required of him in any moment.

> *Loyalty is a true relating to the highest good of another's soul,*
> *and not their ego.*
> *Loyalty is fidelity to the truth in yourself and others: when you*
> *see only this truth in others, then that shines forth in them,*
> *reminding them of their own innate truth.*
>
> *Loyalty stays with the truth when all else comes crashing down.*
> *Loyalty is following your highest potential.*
> *Loyalty is remembering those who have served you in this.*

*Loyalty is not denying the truth of one's essence; it affirms it
    joyfully and deeply.*
*Loyalty is knowing that you have essence, your core, which you
    can always rely on.*
*Loyalty is staying constant in the truth, despite any, and all,
    circumstances.*
Loyalty is fluid, and stands only by love.

Placing your trust and loyalty in love is Joseph's Key. Trust emerges in others from your trust in Life itself. This trust arises from the knowing that all of us belong only to God. Happiness can only come from trust, which arises from loyalty, a loyalty that arises spontaneously from the mind resting in surrender.

You place your loyalty in what you choose to value. If it is a temporary situation or belief of this world, then the loyalty will always be *of* the temporary, of this world. It can crumble. In this case, "loyalty" is used to justify fear, in order to gain a security, to gain something you think you need in order to survive, and to ward off fear of the unknown.

True loyalty can only serve one master.

If you place your loyalty in what is eternal, love, then so shall it be.

If you are loyal to love, loyal to God, then it is God you shall receive, and become.

The mind shapes all experience according to what it values. Even if your body-mind is having a pleasant experience, it may not even register it at the time if it is engaged with another experience that it places more value on. So ask yourself: what do you truly value, and what are you prepared to do to live in that?

To be this vigilant in every moment, to value and be loyal to love in every situation is the work. It is only when we withdraw love from any relating or situation that thoughts and feelings of separation arise. As these feelings arise, ask what you are being loyal to.

EXPERIENCE

Trust the infinite love that is creating you moment by moment. In this you trust that whatever comes your way, whatever people, situations, books, lessons, and events cross your path, are perfect, are in your highest interests for growth, and are leading toward our highest potential for love to live through us.

Every time you trust fully in this infinite love that is creating you, life unfolds magically. In this choice, you withdraw the value you have given to a certain perception of reality, a certain veil surrounding the real, and choose reality itself, as it is. For loyalty is choosing to be loyal to love in every moment. In this choice we enter peace, the peace that arises as a result of the mind shifting its identity and values to love, by placing trust and loyalty only in your heart, which naturally only loves.

True faith and loyalty is the experience, the deep trust, the knowing that love will come through for you, is here for you, and supports you in your times of need and desperation, because your true heart loves all the other parts of you that forget what love is. Faith is a direct experience of love that gives us the strength to continue, to go forward, and to keep working on ourselves, because we know what we are working for is real.

We become certain from our direct experience that love is real. This transformation is not based on a mental experience, or on a distant memory subject to doubt, for it is an experience that deeply impacts and changes your soul forever.

In the knowing that there is infinite love, the Creator of yourself and all things, the conviction and sovereign authority that arises from within one's Self, transforms. It becomes an objective fact of life, which many may not understand, but which is now your reality. This serves to take you deeper into the unknown, deepening your willingness and courage to do so, "treading where even angels dare not to."

Faith is not dependent on anyone or anything else outside of you. If you feel that an experience of love you have had was in some way separate from you, then you do not have true faith. Many spiritual teachers can evoke in their students this quality that is the teacher's grace; these people then become followers, and disempowered to a degree, for their faith depends upon their teacher and the experiences they have with him or her. Any true teacher will give this power back to the student so that they too can *know* that this light is an expression of their own soul, and develop true faith in their own connection to love and the Creator.

To have faith means that we feel safe and secure in our essence, in our inner reality. We know we are loved, that we value love, and we trust this flow in our lives. This flow is always there; it is ever present as our support, our ground, constant and reliable, even when we forget it or push it to one side. It only seems to come and go.

What does come and go is the idea of you. You, rather than faith, comes and goes from your perception of this stream of life. Therefore it is the idea of you that also stands in the way of faith manifesting fully in your life as true strength, stability, and eternal support.

Faith arises from, and flows from, the heart, not the mind. Loyalty and faith are important qualities of the open heart, as when the mind does not understand, the heart can feel and reassure us that all is well. When times get tough, when we cannot feel God, love, or our soul, when we feel isolated, abandoned, or separate, the mind cannot help. It is only faith that pulls us through the dark times, when life is dry and nothing seems to be going well for us, when all else has disappeared, including our inner voice.

STRENGTH

When we have integrated faith's transformation into our life, when our heart *knows* that God and love is real, when we are in harmony with this way of living and the choices we make in what to be loyal to, then we experience true strength. We become naturally strong, confident, and fearless, as we feel held, supported, and nurtured by Life.

We experience that it is soul that truly supports us in alignment with existence, and that they are in unity. This strength does not waver, as it is based in the eternal, whereas our faith in another person, teacher, or teaching can change over time, for perceptions change as growth deepens. Evolving becomes easier and quicker once we have true strength, as it leads us into deeper experience, allowing the doubts and projections of our own ego and others judgments to slide off us, like water off a duck's back.

In this, we experience life as wondrous and spontaneous, as we can allow what is unfolding. If we knew everything that was going to happen, there would be no real fun, no real discovery, no surprises, and little play. Life would be boring! Faith allows existence to continually weave its magic, bringing more love into our lives and taking us ever deeper into previously unimagined possibilities.

Faith is necessary to travel the path. As you travel the path, faith sustains, supports, and gives you solid ground. Faith is giving yourself to life fully, without regard, without hesitation. As you evolve, faith too deepens and changes its nature, until the soul itself gives itself to, and fully surrenders to, existence, which then becomes the support and the ground for the merged soul.

God and love itself hold and support you. The ground that gives rise to you also gives ground and support to all life. When one experiences this, that the faith that is our support is the support of all beings also, we open the doorway to Self-realization.

Alchemy

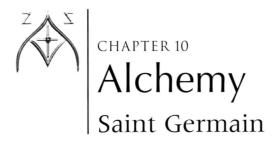

CHAPTER 10
Alchemy
Saint Germain

Saint Germain is sometimes pictured wearing a huge cross, and he is the wielder of magic, ceremony, alchemy, and transmutation. Alchemy is the transformation of one element or way of being into another. In alchemy we transmute the shadow of ourselves into usable energies that propel our growth forward. We harness the forces of the primordial subconscious in order to realize who and what we are. Alchemy is vital in this age as it enables us to work with all the forces of the self and the earth, bringing them into usefulness for the benefit of all.

In alchemy we do not judge or throw away anything. We harness and use everything, for everything is energy. Alchemy goes to the heart of all matter and sees it as energy, using it to transform the appearance of matter from within. Alchemy uses whatever is available in any situation or environment, whatever is present to work with, in order to transform. Whatever you are presented with in any environment or relationship is perfect for the work of alchemy to occur. Alchemy can facilitate healing, yet is also the power of the quantum leap forward, the magical and miraculous shift in perception that brings forth more of the deep, underlying Presence of love.

The deepest alchemy occurs when one works with the deep shadow of the blazing light of the soul, found in the darkest places, for from darkness comes the light. In this darkness one learns to harness the energy of fear, of anger, of lust, of greed and convert them into engines to drive forward courage, bliss, giving, and contentment. This magical alchemy is worked with by consciously connecting to all the different parts of yourself, as represented by different forces such as the devas, angels, archangels, and the Christ Council.

Faith can create alchemy in any situation. If you but trust yourself, any person, or any relationship, any of your creations can be changed in a heartbeat. But to do this requires that you delve into the deep places of the soul, and connect with the situation or person through the heart. To do this you have to trust that this is possible; you have to be open to this possibility, to have faith in this possibility. Then miracles can happen.

GROUP ALCHEMY

Ritual, intention, and group ceremony are the most rapid ways in this age for the processes of alchemy to manifest. By uniting and calling these forces together in a coherent form, one steps into another reality where anything becomes possible. To enable this requires that one has an understanding of, and is trained in, these arts and sciences, which are means of bringing the underlying forces of the soul into direct manifestation.

These arts and sciences can be seen as magical, or they can be seen as the natural order of things, the way that the complex interacting synergies of creation weave together as a whole. These synergies of the web of interrelationships that create our world have very specific correlations within our own minds that can be accessed through a combination of focused intent, prayer, light, and group merging that connect all the different realms of creation together in one place and one time.

This conscious interconnection in ceremony allows for the transmutation of the lowest energies present, and the stabilization of the highest energies present, into a unified synergy that includes everything and all beings present. In this alchemy one experientially realizes that we are One.

This Oneness is the height of all alchemy. Through the vehicles of Joseph and Salome, Ishtar and I worked with these principles to prepare Yeshua's meetings to coincide with the most auspicious days and times and the most auspicious sites. Several of these sites were prepared in advance to allow maximum transmutations of energies to occur during the time that Yeshua was there, when his light was radiating in its fullness. There was a lot more going on behind the scenes than meets the eye.

I am a Paver of the Way. I opened the way and navigated the Christ Blueprint into anchoring in the matter of earth itself, by transmuting certain energies and substances into light. It was I who worked through Joseph, preparing the herbs and elixirs for Yeshua's Crucifixion to allow the maximum amount of light into the physical, so that the light body of Christ could most easily descend and liberate from the physical.

Those who attempt to embody me may find that they may get lost in alchemical means, rather than allowing the magic to arise naturally within them through the greatest alchemy of all: love. The opposite is also true; those scared of the power of alchemy, and of their own immense power, will shrink and try not to use the power they feel within them, as they feel it is too much for them, and that it will lead them to abuse of power.

If fear is not cleared from your system, you can encounter forces beyond your control that can then possess you, such as paranoia, hostility, and suspicion. This prevents you from accessing the magical abilities of alchemy, and of bringing subtle forces into form.

LOVE'S FLAME

I am Saint Germain, holder of love's flame. For many thousands of years, I have traveled this earth expressing what the evolution of humanity is, how that can be characterized, how it can be shared, and what it is in its glorious, full, infinite expression.

Love's flame is sometimes clouded by your own fears, perceptions, and the veils of the heart. Sometimes we still need penetrating, still need guidance. Without this penetration, and the vulnerability to be penetrated by the two-edged sword of truth, the heart cannot really truly open and flower. For the veils of the heart can be deceiving; you may think you are listening to the heart, when in fact you are listening to fear; you may think you are listening to fear, when in fact you are listening to your heart. Such is the paradox, the twists in the mind, and the reversals of love. Love's fire creates a space for real penetration to occur, and sometimes this is not easy.

Your life here on earth creates a setting, an organization of the people, places, partners, and work that you do, all around you. You create this reflection in order for you to express truth. In this out-picturing, the outpouring of your mind's internal reference points into the external, you are automatically creating the space for love to penetrate and re-create you. Think on this for one moment.

If the organization of your mind is everything around you, reorganizing everything around you can also reorder your own mind, your own internal process. This may sound simple, and it is. However to truly enact these reordering actions takes pure ritualistic intention, pure awareness and focus, pure love, so that each action on the external rewires your internal. Each action on the external becomes a ritual, each action becomes a retuning, a deliberate, focused plugging into Christ. Each action becomes the transforming and reforming of your self.

This is how the Buddha used to walk; with such focus and attention on each movement that he was completely present with all things at all times, and in this state of quiet bliss perpetually. Each motion was designed to bring awareness, to live in the consciousness of light moving through the body-mind. The light moves the body, not the body the light. The light does the walking, the talking, and the focusing through you. This is an intense state of consciousness to exist in when you truly drop into it. It is being so present, it is similar to exploding in the sheer nowness, the eternal birthing moment by moment, of all life.

God is in the details. This is where ritual comes in, ritual attention, intention, and focus. Mastery here is not unlike being a gardener. You create the garden within your own mind, and you pluck out, by the roots, that which no longer serves the purpose of the garden. You tend to and organize the garden, expressing beauty. You remove the weeds, and notice through deep attention what makes one thing grow and another perish.

This garden is your mind. With ritualistic intention, awareness, focus, and direction, one can penetrate the very objects of the mind, the very thought-forms that choke your garden, the very ways that the brain is organized, and is organizing the world and perceptions around you. You can literally pluck out things that you see in your environment around you. If you do one, then the other can also happen, if done in the correct way.

So let's try this right now.

Focus on your root chakra. Breathe, and contract the anal muscles and pubococcygeus muscles alternately twenty times.

Gently rock back and forth to stimulate the sexual energy.

After doing this for a few minutes, sound *"haan am or"* three times.

Now abide in your third eye, and see the garden of your mind. With focused intention, see what people, what objects are in the garden of your mind. What do you need to weed out, what do you need to pluck out with full focus and intention? Pluck them out with power. Recognize the placement that these people, objects and feelings have within your own mind. Now open your eyes, and look around your environment. What needs to be plucked out as the effect of what is happening within the garden of your mind? Approach it, and with full ritual focus, pluck it out. If it is not in the same room, go to the room where you can pluck the object within, *out*. Maybe say a sound with it.

How does it feel afterward?

THE FAMILY OF CHRIST

There are many in the Lineage of Christ from all corners of the world. All who are on the Christ Path are in the hands of the lineage, the ancient sacred family of Christ, and can call upon the family for help and guidance whenever you wish. Think of us all as your extended soul family, your family of light, that loves you no matter what. We are available, at any time, for you. Even in the times we do not come, it is for your own benefit and learning.

We love you as an extension of ourselves, as we are extensions of those that came before us, as we are all extensions of God throughout all of creation. This lineage never stops, never ceases, and is always growing, as its sole purpose is to bring the field of love into the conscious awareness of all creation.

Through your efforts you too are adding to the lineage, extending it, sharing it, recasting its expression for this age and for countless other ages to come. The truth remains the same, yet its expression changes to reflect the maturity of those receiving it also. Ultimately it becomes very simple, as there is very little mind to obstruct it.

The Family of Christ is growing, and it grows through commitment. All members of a family have important roles to play. When all the members of the Christ Family truly come together and unite, then miracles can, and will, happen. This is the importance of the family, and why we chose to add this section on lineage.

The Lineage of Christ is your lineage. These are your brothers and sisters mentioned in the Christ Blueprint. They are your forerunners, and they walk among you now. They are part of you and live within you. They all unite within you to create the Living Christ. The Living Christ in this age manifests through the family showing its unity in tangible action. This is the next evolutionary step to be demonstrated by the Christed Servers. In these tangible steps many old wounds will be healed, and the foundation will be activated for the mass healings of humanity.

This family reunion will initiate a collective resonance that will ignite love into dynamic action, and catalyze the family's visions into concrete manifestation. Everything you have dreamed about, or had visions of, will happen through this avenue, and in this way, for this is the Divine Plan for the unfolding of Christ in all of you living in relationship with each other.

The Divine Plan originates from the Lineage of Christ, past, present, and future. In order to bring this into manifestation it is important that one understands where the teachings, energies, and expressions of the Christ Lineage arise from, and how you can tap into that today.

CHRISTED TRADITIONS

The Christ Lineage is drawn from four main sacred traditions: the Indian, the Tibetan, the Hebrew, and the Egyptian. Christ Yeshua embodied Keys from all of these traditions, including the feminine mysteries of birth and cocreation. Yeshua was the last in a long line of Christs, and he embodied to make these Keys available to humanity now in the twenty-first century, the flowering of the seeds of the Christ Blueprint on a mass scale. In order for others to embody Christ Consciousness, they too will have to explore the wisdom in these traditions, for the Christ Path is not just based on Yeshua.

Those who are following just the Judeo-Christian path will never realize the I am that which is their innate essential nature. Yeshua himself synthesized many pieces of the Original Religion back together within his own flesh and light body, giving voice to this stream for the age in which he lived.

The Original Religion contains all the different religions within itself. All the pieces of the Original Religion are held within the Christ Blueprint, which leads back to the beginning of time itself, and a golden age. And this Golden Age Consciousness is what Christ embodies; the goal of all Christ Mind teachings.

So the return of Christ is really the return of the Original Religion of which Christ Yeshua was the last embodied representative. When one strips away all the layers of conditioning and beliefs, names and rituals, one reaches the simplicity of the Original Religion that Christ Yeshua so perfectly demonstrated through his ministry, through his teaching, and through his relationships.

How Do We Tap into These Lineages Today?

The first step is being aware of the four traditions; the Egyptian, Indian, Tibetan, and Hebrew. The second step is immersing yourself in these energies on pilgrimage in the thirteen primary sacred sites on the Christ Path, known as the Christ Grid. The third step is then using your intuition, and surrender to life, to guide you to teachers in these traditions who can align you to the Keys that Yeshua was taught, and initiated into.

From India the main Keys are use of breath, yoga, and meditation found in the system of raja yoga as elucidated by Patañjali, and the use of inquiry into your essential nature. From Tibet the teachings on the Yab-yum, or sacred marriage, as practiced by Magdalene and Yeshua. From Egypt various forms of energy work, many associated with the refining and harnessing of sexual energy, as well as the teachings of Horus and the feminine mysteries of Isis and the womb. From Israel the kabbalah, the Gnostic Gospels, the original Lord's Prayer and the beatitudes.

In modern times, Yeshua's *A Course in Miracles* and the *Way of Mastery* books hold direct teachings on the nature of Christ Mind. The last steps in these teachings are *The Christ Blueprint* and the revelation of the feminine mysteries of birth and cocreation in the forthcoming *The Shakti Circuit* and *Way of the Womb* books.

Members of the family are all here now on earth. Be open, be committed, and reach out. In our joining together the Second Coming of Christ occurs. And this is down to you, and the extraordinary role you have to play in the transformation of earth in the next years.

Beloveds, we welcome you. We welcome you home.

Know that you are supported, know that we are here for you, know that you are part of an infinite family line stretching all the way back into the beginning of creation, and extending all the way into infinity.

Know that we walk with you, and that we are by your side.

Peace, joy, and comfort be with you.

THE CONNECTOR

The third role I play within the Christ Blueprint is as the connector between the different strands of Christ's teachings. There are four schools, four paths within the Christ Path, four main strands or pods within the Christ Family. Each family has its positive and negative sides to alchemize.

The first family path is of the loving Christ as exemplified by "Jesus Christ the Savior." The beings identified with the loving aspect of Christ can be loving, faithful beings who lack self-empowerment and need a priest, pope, guru, or teaching to idealize and be devoted to. The second pod is of the Bringer of Light or the Transformer as represented by Lucifer. These beings are powerful authorities unto themselves. They want no teachers, and know Divine power to be their own, sometimes to the point of separation. They can feel like outcasts, and feel judged for their vital, unconventional expression of Self.

The third is of the Perfect Human, as represented by Sanat Kumara. The beings identified with this are the kings and queens. They are regal, dignified, and command respect as they are the rulers of the new world. Sometimes they can become power-obsessed and forget that to be a king is to serve others humbly. The fourth is of the Eternal Christ as represented by the Golden Age state of consciousness or Sanatana. These beings are removed from worldly affairs at this time, and paradoxically are not really able to communicate effectively in this world. They simply hold a space of Oneness for all others.

This is what we refer to as the Christ Lineage. This lineage has been hidden from most for a long time. Most have only recognized the Loving Path and have modeled their behavior on this, and this alone. This is why so few people have awakened on the Christ Path, for the Christ Lineage is a family, a family that now needs to come back together again and share their Keys with one another, without judgment, so the alchemy of reuniting can occur.

These four strands of Christ complete each one of us, each person on the Christ Path. As an act of alchemy this reweaving is the ultimate balancing act, as by bringing together all these experiences into one understanding one can reach a point where Grace can descend to enlighten you. This is a complex thing that usually takes many lifetimes for a soul to acquire, to see, and to bring these threads together, which will then allow an act of God to complete the cycle, and seal the vessel that you are.

Weaving together the four aspects of the Christ Family within you results in you being mastered by life and love. One becomes essentially a joyful, peaceful, loving nobody—a vehicle for serving others in a joyful, easeful way that also serves you. You are not a slave that leaves the personal self out—all is included.

THE VESSEL

In this we are abundant, and struggle and strive for nothing. One lives magically and alchemizes situations merely by being present, clear, and an open vessel that allows transformation to occur in all situations naturally. In this alchemy one begins to realize the infinite potential of the ability to cocreate a new reality.

Alchemy requires that we become fully Self-contained vessels for these deep processes to occur. This means that our inner male and female are united. One becomes whole and able to merge between the feminine and masculine qualities. In this flow, alchemy shows us that willingness to change is the nature and flow of life.

All alchemy requires space and an open vessel to occur, as without spaciousness and willingness no fire can catalyze or transform. Conversely, once the actions have taken place the vessel needs to be sealed to allow the process of transformation to complete itself in order to birth a new being.

In this spaciousness, willingness, and constant flow from one state to another, enlightenment can happen. Many of the obstacles to enlightenment come from our ideas and rigid belief systems around what enlightenment should look like.[1] Some of us may think that to be enlightened means we should have superhuman powers, and be all-knowing. Some of us may think that to be Christ means to be like Yeshua, and to adore him. Others may feel that enlightenment is impossible, and only God's chosen elite can achieve this. And there are many other expectations. All these belief systems prevent a full awakening.

In truth there are six billion Christs. The attributes, gifts, and qualities of God are so diverse, mysterious, and unlimited that it is only natural that It chooses to reflect Itself uniquely through each individ-

---

1. This is particularly true about the Christian Path, with its misunderstandings and fragmentation of information that has created a religion based on a split foundation.

ual human spark. Each one is different, but all share the same quality: no more suffering or attachment is experienced. This will manifest in innumerable ways, all of them valuable to the ever-evolving experience of delight that God is in manifestation.

THE SHADOW SIDE

The core of the shadow side for humans wishing to embody faith and loyalty to love is fear, cynicism, distrust, defensiveness, blind faith, and blinding loyalty to someone or something, which can stop you from evolving further.

Cynicism is when we have little faith, and little experience of soul. It is when we fundamentally have no trust in the goodness of others and humanity, and feel limited to the body-mind only. Cynicism laughs at the notion of evolution and healing, feeling that humanity is corrupt, without hope, without goodness, and selfish. Cynicism does not believe in God, mystery, the unseen, or the unknown. It only measures what is rational and can be scientifically proven, and merely nods to God as maybe being outside of us in some distant heaven, and that while we may have a soul, it is never something to be relied upon. Cynicism is living in a closed attitude not open to change.

Lack of faith means that we do not experience that reality is loving at all, perfect in its unfolding no matter what it looks like. So life from this perspective is lived as self-serving, cruel, and hard, where we are victims of the world's events. Without faith, one sees that life is only ego. Life becomes full of doubt, suspicion, hopelessness, and frustration. One cannot accept the good things that happen without feeling that there is a catch somewhere, that life can really be this good.

Even when experiences of the soul, of a bigger reality, arise, one who is lacking in faith cannot believe it, stating, "Did that really happen? Was I imagining it? Did my mind create that?" This attitude questions something to eliminate it, to cut it off from growing and blooming into a deeper experience, instead of exploring it with an open, curious attitude.

Fear

Cynicism and lack of faith arise from fear. Fear is a contraction that keeps you believing you are just the body, just the emotions, just the mind. Fear is ultimately fear of love, of losing one's most precious commodity: the ego. This kind of fear is based on a fundamental insecurity that you do not trust, and are not held or supported by existence. The world becomes a dark place in this perception, and you feel that you do not have the strength to cope with it. You feel vulnerable, delicate, abandoned, and alone, relying on defensiveness and armor to protect you instead of faith.

Fear feels powerful, and is often met with a strong attempt to contract, to stop breathing in an attempt to stop feeling. Contracted fear paralyses you into feeling as though you are ruled by forces bigger than you. All is blamed on some other force outside. Others and the world can appear as fearful, cannot be trusted, and thus the support of the universe is denied. Imploded fear is projected out as judgment and a lack of trust.

Fear is a key force in the ascending spirals of evolution, for evolutionary openings and opportunities in our lives can elicit fear. Fear becomes a marker of what we have to travel into in order to grow and expand, so fear in truth becomes our friend. Fear, if given breath and feeling, can fuel a new birthing, a new opening, and it becomes our catalyst that empowers our growth into love and peace. It is a powerful ally.

Vulnerability and self-responsibility allow us to let go into this place that denies trust and denies love. To let yourself go into fear, with the courage to feel *all* of what you are going to find there, means that we have to own our self-created barriers to love and trust of life. This owning allows the fear to no longer be projected outside into any relationship, situation, or person, allowing you to drop down deep into the wounds that created the fear.

These fears dissolve through forgiveness. When faith starts to deepen in our lives, starts to be felt, wounds and blocks bubble up from the subconscious mind to the conscious mind, bringing it into full awareness. Forgiveness of self, allied with humility, helps to dissolve these blocks.

One good way to do this is to consciously revisit past events that have been painful, where you have felt like a victim, and understand and accept that you have created them totally. In this ownership, you can forgive yourself for adopting the fear that the world or others have done something to you.

This may take some time of consciously revisiting the specific events, recalling the emotions and dynamic of the relationship, and consciously feeling them, embracing them, and blessing them. In this you can begin to recreate yourself anew, dissolving the pattern of the past by bringing it into the present time, where all is forgiven and owned as self-created, in order to learn that you are a master and creator of your experience.

Can you feel intuitively when someone else mistrusts you, and tries to protect or conceal something from you? Can you feel how one part of you can also mistrust another part of you also?

Acceptance

The foundation of faith arises from acceptance. We no longer fight or struggle with what we believe *should* be, but accept life as it *is,* and begin to act, rather than react, in ways that bring improvement. Trust is faith in what is unseen, an inner knowing that tells us that there is purpose and perfection to life as a whole. Even apparent failure is trusted as a step to greater revelation and growth, for it is no longer a shame to fail, or a threat to the self to have things apparently not work, because we begin to know, in trusting awareness, these are just steps in a greater unfolding.

You begin to let go of the past, and allow the present to unfold. You start to experience yourself as more receptive to the support of the universe. You begin accepting responsibility for yourself and your role in the world, and begin to have the capacity to achieve *big* goals. You start to see the big picture of your life more clearly and begin to create massive changes, like switching careers or ending an old relationship.

This is where real strength, the outcome and result of true faith, overcomes fear, dismantling the mechanisms of the fearful self. In faith we begin to realize that real life is exciting and challenging, and that growth and change hold much higher value than fear, intimidation, or contraction. Strength here comes down to repeatedly staking your whole reality for the chance to become more conscious and aware, no matter what the perceived outcome may be. You have to give it all, to receive it all.

Having faith that God lies in all things, all programs of consciousness, within all beings, allows us to connect with the God within them, no matter how buried their spark of love seems to be. In faith, we give others a chance to be selfless, to be considerate, to be kind, even if they do not act like that *yet*. In faith, we know they will, at some point in time, because we know that this quality exists in everyone.

This connection comes from the heart: you speaking to another's heart from your own heart. In this, true Communion happens, and all is heard.

To have faith is to connect to the innate qualities of what it means to be a good human being: a good man or a good woman. This means that you know within yourself that there is always something fundamentally good, something fundamentally trustworthy that is always there, that is always contactable.

When you are cynical you leave out part of your human experience of relating, part of your uniqueness, which stops you from enjoying a true relationship with yourself and others. Cynicism is delusion. It is not part of our innate nature, as it stems from ignorance about the nature of life. The more we notice and become aware of these distortions, the more we are able to consciously value love, and then choose anew in every moment.

Believing we do not have these qualities of faith, of goodness, of strength leads us to become hollow and fearful. We lack a depth, a solidity, a kindness and roundedness of character that no matter how many spiritual experiences we have, we still stay in a subtle basic mistrust, not valuing and honoring the deepest part of ourselves.

If what you are loyal to lies in an expectation that others conform to what you feel is right, and that they act and behave in this way, then you are not trusting the perfection of loving truth that is always at work in every person's life, leading them along their path. To try to meet demands and expectations makes you a prisoner to these very same expectations. When these expectations are not met, then an explosion can occur, the façade of niceness crumbles, and anger comes out.

At this point you are ready to dive deep into what you truly value, and discard what you thought gave you value before. In this, the struggle dissolves, for you relax in faith, and trust to let life flow through you. You let the breath breathe you; you let life live you; and there is no longer any control. Life and love can now enter your surrendered heart.

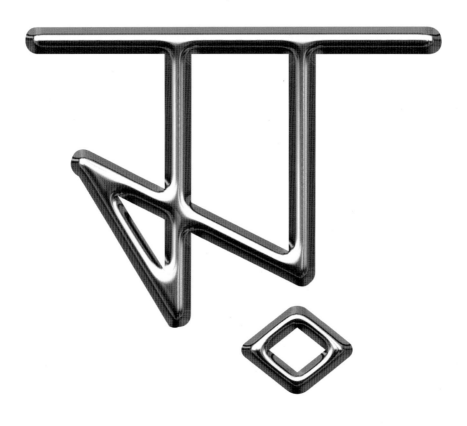

The Mirror

CHAPTER 11
The Mirror
Judas

Yeshua said to the disciples, "Let anyone of you who is strong enough among human beings bring out the Perfect Human, and stand before my face." But their spirits did not dare to stand before him, except for Judas Iscariot.

—Gospel of Judas

Mirrorlike awareness is what makes it possible to perceive reality without our own conditioned interpretations, colorings, and judgments. Working with Judas and his guide, Lucifer, brings us closer to this awareness, as our view of life expands to include the whole of reality, not just the parts we want to see. The discernment, creative intelligence, and brilliancy of Lucifer clarifies the view of reality, making it possible for you to cleanse the lens of your heart and mind through his Apostle Judas. This all culminates in you polishing the mirror of your soul in the reflections that are created in your relationships.

The mirror of Judas reflects that what we see and judge in others is in truth how we see and judge our own selves.

Judas asks us to look at our illusions, our projections, and asks us to own and correct our misperceptions and judgments that we project outside onto others and the world. Judas works with the essential misidentification of the personality with the soul, the ignorance that the soul believes to be its truth, and which it follows faithfully until it experiences or is taught otherwise.

Mentally, Judas is the strongest of the Apostles, the one who could stand with Yeshua and claim his Christhood. This strength was born from his holding of the mirror, fulfilling his role within the Christ Blueprint. Here, his apparent "betrayal" led to the greatest evolution, for his "betrayal" actually led to the total fulfillment of the Christ Blueprint.

Without Judas, Christ Consciousness would not have anchored into the deepest hell realms through the ultimately loving act of the Crucifixion, and compassion would not have penetrated into the deepest places within the human mind-set on earth. Judas was vital in his service, acting as an interface between God and Man, as Yeshua did also.

PERSECUTION

Much of his work is being continued today through the mirrors of relationship. This mirror is summed up beautifully in the eighth beatitude: "Blessed are they who are persecuted for righteousness sake; for theirs is the Kingdom of Heaven."

Everything on the earth plane works in reverse. Often what you see is not what it appears to be, and only by reversing the perception of what is *apparently* happening can we find the truth of what is *actually* happening. Truth's actions are often the reflection, the inverse to what is happening on earth. This is why the double-sided pyramid, one pyramid pointing down and the other pointing up, each reflecting the other in a diamond shape, is such a crucial geometry for understanding the laws and relationships between heaven and earth.

Persecution plays a vital role in evolution to a point. When you are judged, scandalized, or shunned by others, this projected energy can actually be used through the awareness of the mirror to empower you to new levels of peace, centeredness, compassion, and understanding. Here, the perceived injustice or "worst thing" to happen to us turns out to be the best fuel for evolution. Disruption becomes opportunity, judgment becomes healing, chaos becomes opening, anger becomes bliss, and destruction becomes peace.

The energy of persecution can help anchor love within you in a challenging yet undeniable way as a lived, felt experience. The persecution attempted by others is an opportunity given to deepen one's connection to Self, and to demonstrate in thought, word, and action that you are established in peace, in the Self. In persecution, one is given a palpable choice to live through peace, rather than get ensnared by the hooks of ego, and the judgments and expectations of others.

Persecution is an experience that tests where you think you are at in your evolution, and grounds you into recognizing your reflection, your creation, and your responsibility in healing anything that you need to in order to be whole.

The unenlightened will always try to knock down the enlightened, to try to find fault, to try to judge what they do not understand based on the personality's concepts and ideas about what enlightenment is, or what it *should* look like. Conversely but similarly, those who find success in worldly pursuits in gaining wealth, power, and fame are also judged and envied by others who want what they have. It is the energy of envy itself that persecutes and judges others in the mirror of Judas, as well as fear. Here, the trick of the mind to continue to survive in duality is to project "out" its faults onto others, fighting and blaming the outside world, relationships, governments, partners, and even God for its own misperceptions, making others responsible for the stress and suffering in its life. Through this projection the mind only hears others through the filters of its own thoughts, experiences, beliefs, and conditionings, losing the state of openness that enables us to be present with each person for who, and what, they are.

One way to overcome this externalizing, projecting aspect of the mind is to own it by reversing it. Through honesty, ultimately you notice that everything you judge or label in another is yourself. Each time you judge another, change the "you" into an "I," and you will see how much you are putting yourself down. You are merely my projection, my own self-image painted onto you. I am the very thing I judged you to be.

Integrating Self-mastery, Self-empowerment, and cocreation in humility, instead of pride, enables one to state "I and my Father are One." Rather than the dark suppressing the light, or the light shielding the darkness, one can be powerful and pure, stable in the power that you have, as you know it is only for the benefit of all.

The split that can occur in the mirror of awareness means a person can become two different people; honest one moment, lying the next, covering up the lie unconsciously to hide the part of them that is wounded. One can be a bright light in one minute, and a lying deviant the next. The person suffering this cannot even remember the unconscious state, as it was a totally different mind functioning then. He or she can cover up these states through intellectual or emotional manipulation and reasoning, just like a lawyer or politician can use facts and spin them any way to suit their point of view, or in this case to validate their split.

It is mainly through loving, uncompromising, and honest relationship that these splits can be highlighted and healed so that one can become truly empowered, forgiven, and move on to become a master rather than a perpetual disciple.

MIRROR LEARNING

Another evolutionary aspect of the mirror forms a key part of our ability to learn quickly, a key Luciferian trait. The mirror of the mind has a biological basis in the brain, in what is called mirror neurons. Mirror neurons enable us to imitate the movements of others, thereby liberating us from the constraints of a purely gene-based evolution.

How many times have all of us imitated our teachers, leaders, heroes, and heroines because we want to be like them? How many times do we copy the mannerisms and language of those we love, respect, and admire?

Mirror neurons work through imitation. Any time you watch someone else doing something (or even starting to do something), a corresponding mirror neuron can fire in your brain, thereby allowing you to "read," understand, and respond to another in an ever-increasing and exponential feedback loop. Mirror neurons enable us to mime and understand the movements of others, which in turn provide opportunities for rapid learning and language evolution. In effect, mirror neurons suggest that we pretend to be in another person's mental shoes, providing a basis for understanding, "mind reading" empathy, and imitative learning.

Sound provides a key to this. For example, if you closely watch someone chanting, the mirror neurons in your brain can actually mimic internally and silently what they are chanting at the same time. This allows you to literally become the chanter and the listener simultaneously, without even knowing what they are saying. You are passive and active simultaneously, One with the whole process, taking it in much more deeply than if you were just receiving it from them. This is one of the secrets to successful sacred ceremony, and holographic learning.

Mirror neurons create a mirror for us to see what we are, and perhaps even more importantly, what we would like to be. In the mirror, all that we aspire to be, our desires, hopes, and fears, are revealed. An increase in the ability to use the mirror neuron system results in us being able to imitate, learn, absorb, and transmit, and could also explain the explosion of cultural change that we call the "great leap forward" or the "big bang" in human evolution.

Mirror neurons are a biological correlate for what Lucifer is most known for in popular history. As the archangel that was given power to create by God, Lucifer cocreated the mirror of reflection and projection in order to teach humanity about Oneness. His vessel and carrier for this on earth, Judas, then lived this lesson and was crucified for it in his own way. Both polarities, Yeshua and Judas, died in order to ground their pieces of the Christ Blueprint onto earth. Yet as Yeshua said to Judas, "You will be cursed by the other generations, and come to rule over them," meaning that this age is the Age of Lucifer, the reversing of all the lies in the mirror of awareness.

Judas and Lucifer have been feared and scorned for two thousand years, cursed and slandered as has Mary Magdalene, vilified as a prostitute and demeaned to second-class-citizen status. The guilt, fear, and shame of humanity have been projected mainly onto Judas, Magdalene, and of course, in the first instance, Yeshua. This creates an interesting trinity.

These beings are now starting to be recognized as key qualities and creators of Christ Consciousness for this age, as they have the Keys to bring humanity into liberation by turning the mirror on their perceived "sins." In this process, we begin to see what we have to learn, and who we truly are. For they are reflections of our own process, and what our beliefs are, that still keep us shackled in fear, projection, and judgment of our own shadows.

This is the mirror of awareness, where we own our projections and reflections of all that we have swept away under the carpet or made someone else's fault. In this owning, we reverse the perception of our judgment and separation, and see the truth, the direct opposite to what we may normally see.

A Practice

Sit in a comfortable position and allow the body-mind to deeply relax. Breathe into the lower belly and allow the mind to silence. Meditate on the Judas symbol, and draw it on your third-eye chakra three times. When you have done so, hold your palm over the third eye to energize the symbol for a minute or two.

Ask this question within: *What is the worst thing that has ever happened in my life?* Notice and feel what arises.

Ask, *How has this deeply impacted my life?* Remain with the breath and observe what arises with curiosity.

Ask, *What is one jewel that I learned from this situation, that I could never have experienced otherwise?* Find the one jewel. Say "thank you" to it, and the situation or person, for this.

Say within, *If it were not from this experience, however bad it seemed, I would not have learned, found, met, moved . . .* (fill in your specific jewel).

What often appears to be the darkest hour is our greatest ally and empowerment to realize God.

Polarity

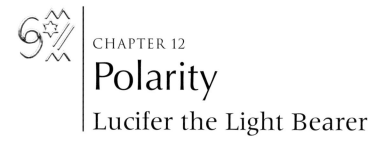

CHAPTER 12

Polarity

Lucifer the Light Bearer

The brightest light casts the greatest shadow.

Everything on the earth plane is in reverse to truth. Simply reverse what you see and you will find truth.

Archangel Lucifer is first seen in Western history in his "fall" from Grace, where he was supposedly thrown out of "heaven" for daring to create. He is next seen in the Garden of Eden, where he worked with Eve in order to free humanity from its ignorance. After this, he was most present in Egypt as a master of light and architect under the name Hor Hu Hotep. He was one of the prime movers in the "fall" of Egypt from a state of Oneness into a state of polarity in order to create a new evolutionary possibility, which is being manifested in the twenty-first century through his role as Light Bearer.

Lucifer's first name from the beginning of Creation is Sanaka Kumara—the brother of Sanandana Kumara. Together with their other two brothers, known as Sanat and Sanatana Kumara, they were known as the Four Mind-born Sons of God, or four avatars, so-called because they were born directly from Divine Thought and not from a womb. These Four Kumaras are described in the Vedic literature as "glorious eternal Divine children, shining as brilliantly as the sun, appearing like fire blazing on an altar." They were created to help educate humanity into the structures of matter, creation, love, and universal law.

It is written in the Maheshvara Sutra, one of the key sutras of the Kashmiri Saivite lineage in India, that the direct experience of the matrix of our universe is given firstly to Sanaka Kumara, one of these "savior" sons of the Creator God. Known as shaktyavesha avatars, bringers of transformation to our earth, they bring new energies and principles into manifestation.

POLARITY

Lucifer is one of the original creative intelligences born directly from the mind of God to help create the blueprint for matter in the third dimension. Through his penetrating laser-like intelligence, he "sees" the infrastructure of form into manifestation. We access this through the intellect that seeks knowledge and wisdom for liberation.

Lucifer holds the blueprint for polarity, part of which is utilizing sexual polarity to achieve Oneness. Lucifer manifests the polar energy field on earth and our universe, and sees to it that this field keeps doing its job. And this all serves love, as love wished to see itself in the beginning of creation; and how could love see itself without forms and the apparent dance of duality?

The perception of Lucifer is that he is rebellious, and that he betrayed God, creating his own empire in contradiction to God's wishes, that he is a law unto himself, and that his world is a world created in defiance to God's law. Nothing is further from the truth. What we do not properly understand is that from the cocreating forces of light and dark, male and female, a new reality arises. The core of Lucifer is primarily committed to the proper functioning of the polar system, which is how the dance of creation and matter is formed.

Polarity is how matter is formed, and how creation is generated. The correct use of polarity ensures a stable, continuous, ever-unfolding, perpetual creation, if it is in harmony. Here, Lucifer is our prime evolutionary agent, for he recognizes that through the tension, pressure, and friction generated by polarity, the push for evolution on the three-dimensional level is created. This push and pull tears apart what was held previously to be true, stretching us to break through and allow a new reality to emerge.

Change does not occur without a catalyst. Freedom does not come without an oppressor.

This is also why Luciferian Consciousness has been judged; for in its coming the greatest changes occur. Those who oppose freedom for humanity and are most locked into duality are most threatened by it. On a personal level this is the ego reactive to its own shadow, and in a global sense it is many of the organized religions and governments intent on keeping their power base and control over the masses.

EMBODIMENT AND THE WOMB

The unbalanced use of polarities creates tension, war, and suffering, especially in this age where male and female are still not in harmony. This is primarily because the collective feminine consciousness is still not in their power: the power of the womb, a Key that Lucifer holds, as seen in his setting free of Eve in the Garden of Eden. When women are not in the power of the womb, this unbalances men, as they need to relate to this aspect of the feminine, and be guided by it, to fully enter the Divine masculine. This is part of the quest for the Holy Grail, the Grail found within the womb of every woman.

Lucifer holds Keys to the full embodiment of spirit into flesh. The mirror of our body wisdom informs us of deeper emotional, mental, or spiritual issues surrounding the body-mind, such as cellular memories, pain, central nervous system tension, and deep stresses that speak to us in order to be released and healed. This is why bodywork is so important, for to have a clear, relaxed, soft, open body allows the light of spirit to move through us gracefully, allowing the highest potential to manifest in any given moment.

This embodying of spirit into flesh is brought about through the descent of light. The light-bringer Lucifer is the guardian, activator, and fertilizer of the womb. Darkness guards the infinite creative power of the womb, and only the brave, dedicated, loving woman can access it *if* she is with a selfless, loving, and powerful man to support her along the way. As he does this, he accesses more of his loving power and enters the Divine masculine.

The key to open the power of the womb is unconditional love, including, embracing, using, and celebrating the dark and the light without judgment, but with discernment. Lucifer includes all aspects of ourselves in our awakening, from the most intimate, vulnerable, and personal side to our most powerful and glorious characters. Lucifer comes to give us the gift of wholeness. If we embrace all parts of ourselves, then we are free. If we leave out any part of ourselves, we will miss our true heart's desires, and betray our own blueprint for fulfillment. This is a temptation in itself, for we can be misled into thinking that the path of the "martyr" is noble and right, all the time leaving out what is our heart's deepest dreams and longings, which always point us to our truth.

Lucifer supports and tests the merging of our deepest heart's desires with fulfilling our true destiny and purpose. We no longer have to choose between our most personal yearnings and fulfilling our true destiny, for they are no longer separate. If we leave out the dream of what fuels our passion, then we are also in illusion and not whole. Only those who have been put through these trials can enter into potent cocreation. This is a big Luciferian initiation, of rebelling and leaving the old paradigm of convention-bound morality, peer pressure, and conditioning, and moving into the new paradigm, becoming infinitely creative and at peace. It is here that Lucifer completes the Christ Path, for no one loves and looks after oneself except our own true Self. As Yeshua said, "Whoever knows the All, but fails oneself, fails everywhere."[1]

You can have great spiritual knowledge, talents, and abilities, but if you do not include and embrace all parts of yourself, then it is all for nothing. The ideals of servantship are noble up to the point where you have to become a master, and then be both master and servant simultaneously. This allows you to be wise, Self-empowered, multidimensional, intelligent, free, and playful, able to claim that you are part of God. As Yeshua said, "I and the Father are One."

CHOICE

The power of choice allows us to create our destiny. Within the power of choice lies our ability to include all parts of ourselves in our awakening, from our deepest primary needs to cosmic impersonal states of there being no I, of pure selflessness. This then becomes Divine selfishness; what is good for me will naturally be good for all others. In this embrace and inclusion, nothing is left out, and the sense of false duty to fit into the collective consciousness is left behind so a new sense of responsibility to be all that you can be arises. This inclusion does not negate anything or anybody, but includes and honors our deepest passions and desires as our road to awakening.

Divine selfishness extends outward by honoring what lies within, at our core. By honoring our knowing, we then share a beacon for others to realize that doing what is good for our soul is good for all others as well.

Choice was created through Lucifer in order to birth infinite possibilities that have never been done or thought of before. This creation of duality allows us to experience what we have never experienced before,

---

1. Thomas 67.

allowing us new turns and twists in our pathway that lead to more excitement, bliss, growth, and abundance. The unknown is lived in through choice, and it is the unknown that leads to our living our greatest love.

When we choose anything that lies against the grain of what we are told by society, by our peers, by what is expected of us by the collective thought-forms of the world, we experience something new that opens up new possibilities for everyone else. This rippling-out effect of our actions to venture forth boldly, innovate, and live our passion touches, moves, and inspires others to do the same in their own lives, however that may look to them. The judgments, condemnation, and fears of the collective get gradually broken down in you, and in all others, through these actions. Pioneer, and soon everyone else will pioneer too.

CREATOR

Lucifer as a creator harnesses the power of fire for creation, rather than destruction or self-destruction. He has mastered the fires of passion, rather than repressing them or allowing them to come out of balance. Lucifer as creator is so integrated, so at peace and in balance, that creation arises from the center of his being.

Lucifer is creative self-expression that creates something new, something daring, something out of the ordinary, by using what is already available. This genius arises from within, which is the true foundation for all that gets expressed outside. Therefore, work on your inside to be able to fully express, create, and manifest your authentic self on the outside. When these two become balanced, there will no longer be any difference between who you are inside, and what you express, create, and live on the outside.

If there is still a difference, then you are still living a lie. When your innermost thoughts and dreams are the same as your words and deeds in the outside world, then you have mastered the art of action, and living life; or rather, at this point, life is truly living you, and expressing its potency through you. You become a Living Light, a Light Bearer for living the heart's desire.

To live your heart's desire, your dream, requires courage, willingness, and determination to never be defeated, to never give up, to rebel against the ideas and norms of the time in order to fulfill your dream. Your heart's desire is God speaking to you, nudging you forward to be all of who you are in your glory, and joy. As you follow this, you become closer to God, and God takes steps to come to you.

Lucifer is loyal to the Christ Blueprint, and innocent in his essence and playing-out of the role he has come to be known for. Lucifer made an incredible sacrifice for us out of love in choosing to obey God's order to help cocreate the three-dimensional world as an experiment in the Divine Plan: for love to be able to see and play with itself, discovering more of what it is. Wearing the mantle of darkness underneath his great light, he comes to help liberate us in this age from all of our judgments, projections, and misunderstandings about the nature of light and dark in order that we may be whole and embody the Christ Light in our body-minds here on earth.

THE TESTER

Lucifer is a tempter and tester of all those who say they are willing to go all the way in their spiritual quest, into enlightenment. As soon as you say this, with all your heart, Lucifer hears, and will then test, tempt, and put you through various trials based on polarity in order to see whether you are truly ready for what you are calling forth. Many times this can be a very intense trial by fire involving your deepest judgments of self and other. In this role, Lucifer is also known as the redeemer. This redeeming is an exchange—you pass the test, and Lucifer confirms that by opening the pathway a little more.

Lucifer is also a guardian of all those who wish to enter on the pathway into sacred marriage. Sacred marriage, or sacred relationship, is the core, the beating heart of the Christ Blueprint, as exemplified by Yeshua and Mary Magdalene. Without encountering Lucifer one cannot fully enter into sacred relationship, for when one starts to enter sacred relationship, one can encounter one's greatest test, one's greatest obstacle or weakness, be it for power, pleasure, knowledge, or spiritual ego. If one of these things is standing in your way, then you are still denying part of yourself.

The subconscious dictates the conscious for those who are unconscious.

With Lucifer nothing is left out, nothing is forgotten, nothing is hidden, nothing is brushed under the carpet, nothing is considered too holy, too profane, too mundane. Everything is included, because everything can be seen, heard, loved, and brought into awareness in relationship on all levels. In this, you can no longer protect any part of the self. Everything is seen, and that can be the scariest part of all. There is no hiding, no validation of any lies you are still placing your loyalty in. When we let go of all protection, then all else can arise; it is very simple.

What ultimate lies have you been living?
That you are unworthy, unlovable, not good enough?
Name ten lies that govern your life right now.

Lucifer is the revealer of truth, and the concealer of truth. Within Lucifer is held the greatest lie that reveals the greatest truth, for to see the lie is to cease to live that lie. In seeing the lie it disappears, and what is left is emptiness: the basis for limitless creating.

The ego is set up to be a lie: the greatest lie of all, that all believe in. It pretends to be your friend, looking out for your best interests, whispering it knows what is best for you, when all the time it is seeking to control, veil, and manipulate you. The truth is that we have all been lied to by the ego. We have all been betrayed, the very sin that Lucifer and Eve have been accused of. This creates guilt, for we know, deep down, that we are listening to and following the lie, and not following the truth.

THE REVERSAL

When we reverse this, we realize that the whole story of the Garden of Eden and the "fall" is in fact the complete reverse of the truth. Lucifer, the serpent of wisdom, and Eve, the woman of feeling and intuition, were in fact the first liberators of humanity. How? By introducing wisdom to the imprisoned human consciousness, held captive in a golden cage by a jealous, angry, and vengeful demigod that was not the God of love so eloquently demonstrated by Yeshua.

Who is this false "god" that Lucifer and Eve betrayed?

This god is in fact a demon trying to introduce limits to the limitlessness of freedom, equality, and wisdom through the duality of the either/or approach. Either you do not eat the apple, or you will be thrown out of the gilded cage that he called Paradise. In this there is no inclusion, no love, no free will, and no wisdom. This "Paradise" is truly a cage where the masses of humanity still sit, where ignorance truly is bliss, where if you know nothing then you are free: free to be controlled.

This "betrayal," both from Eve and from Lucifer in their disobedience of this jealous, angry demon, was actually the first movement toward freedom in the Western tradition.

It is the betrayal of the lie, which is in fact the movement toward liberation. In this light, Lucifer and Eve are the greatest heroes: the light bearers of the new paradigm who will liberate humanity from their chains of ignorance forever.

The energy of Lucifer is here to undo the very threads of duality itself, and move the Creation forward into a new paradigm. This great undoing is a great releasing, for Lucifer created the veils of consciousness, and he can also dissolve them. The brilliancy, clarity, and power of his light can also be seen as insane in its humor, and in its total lack of respect for egoic customs, beliefs, boundaries, and traditions.

Simply put, most people cannot handle the total expression of this energy, as it is beyond their belief systems to accept its insanity to the conditioned ego mind. It is the essence of crazy wisdom—the wisdom that has no bounds. Lucifer as a personality is charming, eloquent, bold, direct, and chameleonlike, becoming whoever he needs in order to present the image necessary to achieve his goal. Lucifer fits into any environment, any grouping of people he chooses to place himself in, in order to get the job done.

Often others have completely different perceptions of this same person depending what context or role he is playing. He does not stay in any one particular state, but rather moves effortlessly from one expression of being to another, just as the universe is. This is the goal of spirituality—to flow effortlessly from one form of being to another, as you are not identified with just one expression of Life, but all expressions, all facets of the diamond mind.

THE SHADOW SIDE

The shadow side of Lucifer holds some of the greatest lessons for those wishing to embody Christ Consciousness. The greatest light casts the greatest shadow, which is why Lucifer has been so vilified, projected upon, and feared. For it is *our* greatest shadow, leading to *our* greatest empowerment. It reveals the lie, which in turn leads to truth and freedom.

Religious belief, sexual deviancy, use of power, hope, and faith are some of what he tests; the gullible, lustful, arrogant, and mentally weak are some of his prey, until they learn the art of loving discernment, applied heart intelligence, and fluid wisdom. Lucifer shakes us up to our core, palpably exposing our fundamental fears, judgments, and taboos, and where we have shirked our personal responsibility, power and heart's desires.

Lucifer is the penetrating power of clarity, brilliancy, and discernment. Lucifer can come to us in many different forms, many disguises, and many tempting opportunities. Patterns keep repeating until we learn, and see through them, choosing another way to approach the same issue.

Pride and Vanity

The shadow sides of Lucifer are pride and vanity, and having a penetrating intellect without acceptance of the heart and the depths of the emotional body. This results in a form of stagnancy, as you may have achieved much but cannot grow any further because of your lack of real humility. The arrogance of being a creator, a master, and a power within oneself can lead to becoming drunk on power, blinded by the brilliance of your own light, and therefore disobeying the Law of Love, which is the whole of the law. When we are acting from love, we can do whatever we will, as these acts can only benefit us and others, guiding us in the flow of universal law.

Arrogance and rebelliousness works against the idea of any authority apart from one's own self; it rails against any imposition or external teacher, and wishes to do solely what it wishes to do, with no regard and no compassion for others. Yet the truth of the intellect can also work against the truth of being, that everyone needs help until they are enlightened. We cannot do it alone, and authority, which can be of many and various kinds, is required to guide us until we are fully and directly plugged into pure consciousness.

Authority issues arise when we do not own our inner authority, empowerment, and confidence, and do not have a strong sense of who we are, looking to another older, wiser, more powerful figure to tell us.

This projection outside can then lead to rebelliousness when the external figures do not meet or match with our internal vision, which they never can, for we all have our own inner authority figure, our own unique expression of our soul knowing.

The humility of realizing and integrating this lesson can then take us into the true Luciferian being, which is a joyfully brilliant, clear presence that is open to all things, yet also direct and penetrating in its serving of love. This then results in true clarity, originality, and independence of thought and action that is different to the norm, carving open new pathways for a new paradigm, a new reality to be birthed and made manifest.

Separate Doer

Lucifer's brilliancy, found in the penetrating laser searchlight of consciousness that the third eye is, can make us feel that we have arrived: that we are enlightened. This light can blind you to where you still need to work on your emotional self, for underneath this presence can lie a whole layer of wounding in the emotions that then perpetuates the Luciferian shadow. This can be very hard to break out of. This form of mental enlightenment means we get stuck, rather than staying humble and going the whole way to embodied enlightenment.

In this shadow you think you can do everything yourself, and that this is the best way to move in life as you cannot rely on anyone else. This illusion arises from the sense of separation from God, the sense that you are a separate doer, that you are a law unto yourself, that nothing can affect you and your world, that you are invincible and independent from the whole.

There is no separate doer or maker of existence. We are all One, and God has created it all. As long as you think yourself to be a separate doer, whatever you do is not going to make a difference. To feel we can substitute for God, that we can take God's place, that God is not the only doer, that we are our own small god ruling our domain separate from everything else, and better than everything else, is the ultimate vanity. This separation leads to striving, effort, pushing, and action, feeling we need to achieve and be successful, to fill the hole, to *do* rather than to *be*.

The opposite is the truth. All functioning, all perception happen in one interconnected flow. What you do, and what everyone else does, is one movement, one wave in one ocean moving together. If one tries to move independently, then the unity can be broken within us, a unity that in truth can never be broken as even this action is mirroring the movements of the whole that you may be unaware of, but are nevertheless still participating in. Whether you are conscious of it or not, whether you see it or not, we are all One. The sooner you see and experience it, the quicker the suffering will dissolve.

This vanity or pride is a hardness in the body, a rigidity to change. It is the armor of the ego. Pride causes separation as it blocks off the flow of life. Pride says no to life. Pride is control, thinking that one can change the course of the present moment. Pride says it knows all of God. When you admit you do not know, that you have no control, that you are nothing, then everything becomes available, and you can enter into the dynamic, ever-moving creative flow of Life.

Acceptance is the ultimate initiation. You stop lying to yourself and start entering into authenticity and humility. Pride is the opposite of surrender. When there is no pride, life flows harmoniously.

Pride is feeling you are special. Pride compares and contrasts itself with other egos; it wants to stand out and shine. Pride sucks in the energy of other egos to bolster its own lack of self-worth. In the attention derived from looking good that it gets from others, it validates itself. It makes it feel like something, in order to hide away from the fact that it is insignificant, and that its life is empty and meaningless.

This insignificance is the truth and opens the doorway to humility and eternity. This insignificance is what we fear the most, for the ego is insignificant. Humility opens the door to surrender. Of yourself you can do nothing. You cannot even pick up a pen without God flowing through your body-mind.

Pride is when we are too emotionally stuck to admit we are wrong, when it is more important to be right, to be justified, than to learn and enter happiness. Pride is when we feel we are better than others, putting others down to make ourselves feel better. Pride expects us to be served, rather than to serve.

Pride is the greatest cover for your lack of vulnerability. Pride conceals your love and softness. Pride conceals, and in truth reveals, your weaknesses, where you need to open. Pride sustains the ego and closed heart. Pride creates a polarity of better or worse. Pride destroys innocence. Pride is not getting what you want, and hurting another because of this. Pride is revenge. Pride is in your feeling of self-worth, and your wounds around this. Pride is feeling powerless, and covering up this lack of empowerment.

False pride is not feeling worthy to be who you are in all circumstances. False pride is when we pretend not to know, when we do; pretending to be humble when we feel superior. False pride is being superior to hide our sense of inferiority, or to match somebody else so we do not feel less worthy than we already feel ourselves to be. The shadow constantly points out the negative and the lack within yourself, in others, and the world. It is the voice that puts you down instead of accepting what you are. This voice denies the goodness of your actions, the truth of your being.

Extreme Inclusion

Lucifer brings up the extremes of experience, light and dark. Lucifer brings up all polarities, repeatedly testing your weak points until they are all harmonized and transformed. Those who get stuck in the "thrill" of the edges, the righteousness of light, the brilliancy of mind, or power of the dark side can tend to become unstable, for those trying to embody Lucifer without being clear and having gone through the necessary steps to residing in clarity, peace, integrity, and centeredness become deeply unbalanced.

Lucifer highlights the splits within ourselves, the unhealed perceptions, wounds, and lack of awareness that keep us bound. Many of these splits are deeply buried under many layers of denial, justifications, and safety zones that we erect in order to protect our ego positions.

Lucifer viscerally and directly enables us to transform our deep splits so that we can enter a greater sense of wholeness and appreciation of the nature of polarity and its usefulness as a creative tool for our manifestations on earth.

It is through Lucifer that we are carved open as channels, as conduits, through which new creations can flow. These manifestations are ones that are integrated in dark and light, that use polarity in a flowing dance; creations that serve to make more love visible in the world, and to make a difference.

The Ray of Polarity, the energy of Lucifer, separates your ego from your soul, the wheat from the chaff, so that you may see your gaps, your judgments, and your conflicts. This light literally cuts through the ego, separating illusion from your innate Self, for the brain is full of folds, layers, and depths. Some of these layers are merged and fused together, leaving us confused about how to see the effects and patterns of our conditioning with clarity. The Ray of Polarity separates the grips and holds, and it can be felt as if the brain is being divided, opened, and forced apart, creating a pathway.

One may experience fears, blockages, and projections in this highlighting, and this is where we learn to discern what is false and what is true. Oneness is only achieved through seeing the power that lies in the darkness, and not being afraid to use this as an engine for love. Oneness is only achieved through seeing the light in the darkness, and transforming our separation and judgment of what we consider to be impure or unholy within ourselves, and our perception of what God is.

Until we see this, we are still in duality. Until we embrace and make conscious the dark and light, we are still living the split of the full knowledge of who, and what, we are. Polarity and transformation, mind and heart, are the means that reveal the union we have all been seeking. We all live by the law of polarity, which is always dancing and transforming, for polarity is the law of manifestation.

You are the mirror for your own Self; you watch yourself every day. Now see who you are, and dissolve the mirror.

Forgiveness

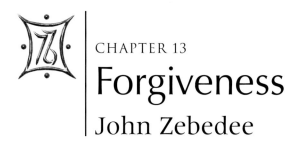

CHAPTER 13

Forgiveness
John Zebedee

In forgiveness, there is a profound shift in the soul's journey of opening the heart. In forgiveness we no longer struggle with what we believe "should" be, but embrace more of life as it *is,* and begin to act, rather than react, in ways that bring improvement. We let go of the past and whatever we think we have done "wrong" to ourselves and to others, as well as what people have done to us. In these actions, we free ourselves to embrace the present without the need to continually refer to and reenact our past, the source of much guilt and anger.

Forgiveness dissolves past wounds, showing us that we are the creator of our world. We create our reality. All events that happen in our reality are neutral; it is just what meaning and emotional value or reaction we give to each event that creates its outcome. In choosing and feeling each event that happens in our life to be neutral, we then have the power of choice to add a loving or peaceful overtone to our response. For example, someone else makes a mistake that messes up what you wanted from your day and your schedule. In this moment you can choose two things: you can feel the neutrality of this mistake and let it go, *or* get upset. Forgiveness, in this instance, releases your own ideas and expectations that separate you from love. Indeed, forgiveness is truly about forgiving oneself from holding onto these perceptions.

Forgiveness arises from our decision to choose peace and love, first and foremost. Once we have truly made this decision, then we can start to forgive as a choice for peace. We start to choose words and actions that heal and bring peace, allowing the highest outcome to occur. You can change your life by consistently holding yourself and others in this light. And when you make a mistake, you can forgive that too, and return to the forgiving of self.

Words have power. Your own vibration increases as you speak this truth. Judgment places a value on someone, dependent on your expectation of that person. Forgiveness never compares, contrasts, attacks, labels, or puts anyone down. There is no higher or lower in forgiveness. Forgiveness is a state of mind free from judgments that rests in acceptance. Acceptance is the ultimate initiation, a deep, cellular letting-go where the mind no longer holds onto judgment. Forgiveness is letting go, letting go of judgment, of guilt, and of projection. A space is carved open for humility, peace, self-responsibility, and softness to simply be.

In forgiveness we rest in the natural ability to see love in all people, no matter what. We see innocence; we identify with the soul that is love. Forgiveness sees perfection, and all of our roles in the whole play. Perfection is not to be without flaws, but to live in the revealing of truth in each and every moment. We step out of truth the moment we judge, attack, defend, and justify, the moment we stop living in the forgiving, the moment we stop giving.

A key quality of forgiveness is a sense of humility, a sense that there is something larger than your own self that has created you, and a sense of equality that we are all created by the same Source as equal. And we all make mistakes. To apologize in humility, to know we are not perfect, means we feel our mistakes and suffering fully, without trying to hide any part of it, or cover it in any way.

Be total with it. Breathe with it. Allow yourself to immerse in it. You will feel better emotionally, in the mind, and most of all, your heart, which will open more deeply and be able to connect with the Divine.

For behind this layer of suffering, and every experience, lies joy. Suffering carves a path in the heart that allows more joy to flower.

An important quality begins to be felt and known in this journey: trust. Trusting in being able to dive into your darkness, as much as trusting the light, reveals an inner knowing that begins to tell us that there is purpose, and perfection, to life as a whole. Even apparent failure is trusted as a step to greater revelation and growth. It is no longer a threat to the self to fail, to have things apparently not work the way we wanted it to, because we begin to feel, and know, that these are steps in a greater unfolding.

PROJECTION

Forgiveness is a deep shift out of "I-ness," in which everything revolves around what the "I" wants, out of grasping, and getting . . . to what lies beyond. Forgiveness is our return to original innocence, original wholeness, to see that no harm has ever been done, and the "other" is innocent.

To forgive is to heal the fear and judgment one has been projecting on self, other, and world. In the forgiveness of self for believing the world could be used in any way to get anything at all, or that there was ever a need to, something very deep relaxes. One is able to fully forgive their own projections, attacks, and body-mind hunger, all forms of giving to get, to go beyond acquiring altogether. Forgiveness becomes the great undoing.

As we forgive, we go deeper into heartful innocence, as we see how we have been distorting our relationships through the power of expectation and projection. We see how the mind has such power to shape and limit our lives. To forgive means choosing to release another from the expectations, demands, roles, and needs that your mind has been projecting upon them. To forgive means to release yourself from the expectations, demands, roles, and needs that your mind has been demanding of you. It is an act of forgiving oneself of one's projections. In projection everything is outside, and this mind justifies itself by blaming another, and the world, for all the decisions and lies that you seemingly have been forced to enact in order to survive in this world. Projection colors others with the very energies you are denying and judging within your own self.

We create the veils through which we view creation. Projection occurs when we deny a part of ourselves, when we try to sweep into the basement what we do not wish to see or own as part of our own self. Projection owns nothing and blames everything; it is the ultimate victim consciousness, for in projection your ego states that everything is outside of you, and that you create nothing. It is the complete opposite to the eternal truth that you create everything in your life. Forgiveness chooses to surrender every perception that you have, leading to the truth of who we are.

MEMORY AND VALUE

In forgiveness we become fully self responsible for everything that happens to us as we realize that we have created everything that happens in our lives in order to learn and grow. This is a big step to take: to own everything in your life, all relationships, all reactions and responses, all actions, all wounds, all ideas of victim hood; to see everything as self-created, and self-perpetuated. To forgive and accept is to humbly learn your own lessons and not worry about the other's lessons and perceived shortcomings. To embrace oneself and all others who have assisted you in this play of learning.

Looking back in time, at the issues that need forgiveness, can be a painful experience, for memory and its stories define who we think we are, and who others are in our own minds. Memory shapes our personalities, conditioning our reactions to whatever is presented to us in our everyday life. Our memories of stress, judgment, and pain keep us from experiencing anything as it is, right now, in this moment.

Yet this pain is not about the memories themselves, but is linked to what you believe about the memory. Memories create the self, hundreds of fragmented, interconnected movements within our own mind that all combine together in one apparently continuous flow to create the idea of an individual person. A person is a process, not a fixed, static object created from frozen memories based on belief and value judgments.

Forgiveness is right value. Withdraw your sense of value from that which creates acts and words of projection, anger, and conflict, and choose instead to be disciplined in valuing love above all else, even if it means you have to retract your words and actions straight after you say them. Being right means being humble, and true to your heart's knowing, not your mind's insistence on feeling right and justified.

Where are there conflicts or a need to defend something in your life? What situations and people provoke this? When did this last happen? Bring this to mind right now.

How are your thoughts, feelings, and old memories supporting these conflicts? Can you see the innocence in yourself and the other? Are you valuing and expressing love in these actions?

It matters not what another is or does; it matters how you perceive them, and then how you act on that perception. Do you choose to see their innocence, and your shared common thread of innocence, or do you choose to see a temporary illusion?

Forgiveness opens the heart to harmony and true relationship. What you perceive in others that creates separation is only a reflection of yourself, a resonant chord. You too have known that fearful or angry state, and have also identified with it at some point; otherwise there would be no judgment. You too are fearful that you can descend into that state, even though you think you cannot and have gone beyond this point. You try to protect yourself through defensive judgment so that you can feel safe in your own energy, keeping the survival of the ego intact by labeling it as outside of yourself.

Acknowledging this fully allows the opening to harmony and true relationship through humble awareness, self-responsibility, and turning inward rather than outward. We can also keep others trapped in their perceptions of themselves by colluding with their perception about their own selves. If we have the courage to forgive our own perception of another, and therefore our own selves, it allows all room to breathe and expand into wholeness. By forgiving and surrendering our perception of any other, we allow the other to be free also. Here we truly are One.

When forgiveness is established, you become nonreactive, living in deep faith and peace, relaxed in all circumstances. You expand, allow, and accept the flow of life as it comes. You do not tolerate egoic judgment within yourself, or of others. This lack of tolerance, this flowering of awareness, is a deep acceptance of love, a surrender to natural harmony, seeing the best in all beings, in all life, and continually choosing this. For God is in everything, even if our clouded perceptions deny that; it is still there. The wonderful thing is that it always has, and always will be.

Practice this. Go out now to the street. Look at each person you see, and see only their natural innocence, the love within them. Go to your loved and familiar ones and try this too. If they are open to it, ask them to return this seeing to you through the eyes. Gaze at each other in innocence and allow what is to happen, to happen.

When you forgive yourself, you give to yourself and to all others. Forgiving is the action for giving! Service arises through forgiveness. No longer is there need of getting, or fear of losing. All of one's heart and soul, and all of one's actions serve as conduits for the healing of others, and in celebration of the truth that love *is*. To serve another is to come to see that they are but an aspect of you, and that they struggle with identity, with ego, as do you. But of course, that cannot be seen until it is seen in oneself.

Humility

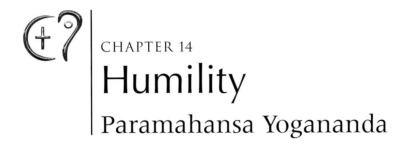

CHAPTER 14

Humility

Paramahansa Yogananda

Greetings. I am Sri Paramahansa Yogananda. I am the teacher of Christ, yet more importantly I am Christ's servant. It was I who shared with Yeshua, when he was in India, that to serve rather than be served is the way to become a true king of one's people. Love is at once the humblest servant, and the greatest king; it washes one's feet and it allows you to have your own feet washed. For love makes all things equal.

In my teaching of Yeshua, I served the Christ.

In my serving of Christ, I taught Yeshua.

The most exalted, the most enlightened teacher, is also the servant; this is why the Christ Council is made up of the twelve most humble people on earth. And yet in their humility they know true kingship, and they can sit in ease on their thrones, knowing that these thrones are built to protect, serve, and guide their fellow human beings.

In realizing this, one can take on all forms of One Self, be it beggar or prince, prostitute or queen, janitor or president. This love allows us to become fully whatever is appropriate in that moment. Whatever actor we need to be, whatever stage is set, is our tool to work with; whichever directors there are, they will all eventually, and inevitably, bow down to that One that is most loving, even if that love is a stick in that moment.

Humility is our ability to be human. Ask yourself, why are you afraid to be the king or queen? Why are you afraid to be the beggar or the loner, living in a hovel on the side of the road? What will it mean to you if you assume any of these roles? How would you feel? When one gets told they are a king, a son of God, and that they have the power to transform the world, how does that affect a human being? Does it make you more humble, or does it make you more proud?

Relaxing into your kingship means you need do nothing, and in this not-doing you are aware of the needs of others, and how to best serve them, even if that means not doing anything in that moment. Relaxing into your kingship allows true peace to balance yourself. Being sure in one's own divinity allows others to be sure of it, if it is done in this manner. Accepting and trusting your greatness allows you to better serve others.

Trust comes when we consciously surrender in total humility. In this we embrace and forgive all the twists and turns in our story, our relationships, leading us to the realization that we created all our pains to learn the lesson of perfect faith, which is the total embrace of all that has happened in our life as perfect.

DYNAMIC HUMILITY

Humility feeds empowerment. If one is truly humble, then this feeds your heart and body of light as an act of power. If one brings that power into oneself, and feeds oneself with joy, then this power becomes self-empowered bliss. This is one of the secrets to feeding your higher self. This humble act becomes an act that makes you explode with the power of joy, feeding your inner ecstasy and your light body, expanding the heart, which then wishes to perform more acts of humility, which in turn feeds your power within.

It is like this: prostrate, feel the humility, the love quality of being touched, and bring this energy into your heart. Allow it to vitalize you, energize you, and then bring that into your brain. Then vitally express it in a way that allows it to be dynamically joyful; allow it to come into your solar plexus, and allow it to express from there.

Do not just prostrate and be humble and feel that is it. No, there is more that can directly empower you into your own fullness by expressing this fullness as the power of the One. In this, others can also see the power of humility as a powerful, palpable force that is both touching and deeply moving to the core of your being.

Humility is when you realize that of yourself, you can do nothing. Humility is true power, and this is how teacher and servant unite and become equal in the One. When you start being given the greatest power, you become more and more humble, until the day you claim the ultimate power, the power of mastering life and death, which is when you are the most surrendered, and the most humble person on earth.

No matter how deep we go into bliss, into love, into joy, even into omnipotent awareness, able to see and know many things at any time, the totality of what God is remains out of reach. It is the ocean that has no bottom, that we can always dive deeper into, that always reveals new things no matter how enlightened we are. To say that we are "done," that we have attained, is the death knell of the soul's evolution, and the voice of the spiritual ego. This is why in the Tibetan tradition they talk about "enlightening" beings rather than "enlightened" beings.

TRUE HUMILITY

Even the heights that Christ Yeshua and Buddha attained can now be surpassed, and the new heights that others will reach will also be surpassed, and so on into eternity. Evolution, the nature of the enlightening process, and the universe itself are always expanding, and never stop. We never stop growing. There is always more, which is why there are no enlightened beings, just beings who have advanced a step deeper into reality.

Humility here is the key to continual expansion, realizing ever new depths and heights to extend in every direction. Humility is the key to go beyond the masters and cocreate an enlightening society on earth once more. In this power, greatness, and glory that flows through you, the temptation to claim it as solely your own can arise, as you can even turn the Divine tap on and off, seemingly at "your" will.

Humility then is supported by vigilance, discernment, discipline, and clarity. The further we go on the path, the more the subtle temptations arise to lead us back into the spiritual ego. The clarity here is to remember that it is God moving through you; the vigilance is to remember to teach only love; the discernment is to selectively allow only the decisions that support love to be enacted in your life choices. The discipline is to stay with these decisions all the time, and to consistently stay focused.

Humility leads to true beauty, and the creation of more love, more God, and more being that can be shared by all. As we enter mastery, more are attracted to our light, and more praises are showered onto you. When someone thanks you or adulates you, give this energy straight to God; when you do a great act, that too is not to be claimed for yourself, but the fruits of that action are also given to God.

When you claim nothing for yourself, then everything can flow through you. When you realize you are not the maker, doer, or creator, then all can be made, done, and created through you. Be happy to be nothing, an empty vessel, and then you can be everything.

The more humble you are, the more light and power can flow through you, as seen in the miracles of the Prophet Elijah, Holy Will, and Prophet Moses, Holy Law. When you are willing to let go of the need to be seen, for the need to be validated by the world, for the need to fit in and not stand out, then one can enter true humility. True humility and light will always stand out and be judged; that is the nature of the world, which dislikes anything that it is not and abhors that which can destroy its rule.

Greatness comes from humility. Desire is channeled through humility, as the desire for the greatness of God to flow through you is the pinnacle of desire on the human plane. Humility joyfully proclaims that you are ready to be what you have been created to be, that Divine Will is the will that is creating all things, and that this will leads you to your true happiness. Humility knows that your way never works, and that God's way does.

Humility is surrender to Holy Law; being in the moment, surrendering and allowing actions to flow through you in that moment without preference, judgment, or expectation, simply as it is meant to be. Humility is the appreciation and gratitude of all that you have, and all that is unfolding in your perfect life right now.

THE SHADOW SIDE

The opposite of forgiveness is judgment. In judging another you judge yourself. Judgment is a moral that only *you* have decided to give value to, believe in, and think to be true. It is because of a lack of forgiveness, of judgment, in the world that there are wars and conflicts, inequality, and separation. Forgiveness allows one to let go of the certainty that one is right, allowing the possibility for something unknown to happen, something else, something new. If something has not been working one way, one has to try another way.

Judgment is an accumulation of all the knowledge you believe you need to make you safe, supported, recognized, successful, and loved in the world. In judgment you compare yourself to others, with this comparison based on determining worth or value; that is who is better or worse.

This means that if you are different from another, then one of you must be better than the other, and therefore more worthy. As soon as the ego puts something outside of itself, it is not in control of it. When the ego is not in control of something, then it feels threatened and fearful, needing to create comparison and value in order to feel safe.

Withdrawing value from the experiences that do not lead to love is the action of forgiveness. Forgiveness creates a harmony, humility, and openness; it is the bridge between peoples, and union between seemingly separate peoples.

Forgiveness is forgiving one's self for ever allowing the perception of being separate from God, separate from others. Through forgiveness we return all objects, all things, back to their innate neutral state, a state that has no power over you. The value judgment one has placed in anything and anyone dissolves, and in this all illusions that seemed to have a hold on you can also dissolve. The personal dissolves into the field of everything that is, which is love.

In forgiveness lies the end of all judging. In not judging how things are, we free ourselves from all perceptions of fear. In this, one starts to see what is actually present. Everything becomes new and fresh. Each situation is dealt with in the present moment, in its unique context in time, in its unique context with each person, in its unique context for who you chose to be right now. There is no labeling, no box, no rigid form.

Forgiving is the establishing of love. Until forgiveness is genuine we cannot embrace others or Life, and we cannot embrace God. And this embracing is the action of love.

Guilt and Shame

In judgment you instantly separate yourself from embracing Reality. This elicits guilt because there is a core place within you that recognizes the purity of all things. Forgiveness is the healing from this guilt and denial of your essence. When you judge, you move out of alignment with your essence, deciding that the innocent are not innocent, and therefore declaring this about yourself.

When you identify with the false self, or ego, you feel an emptiness, a place that is lacking or needing something. When you believe there is something fundamentally wrong, deficient, or lacking within yourself, you blame yourself for no longer being Divine, because there is a place within you that is always full. This blame then gets projected onto others and the world in order to protect and justify your false self, in feeling you are a martyr and are doing the "right" thing. When you deny truth, you can feel guilt. Forgiveness is the primary antidote to the ideas of guilt and shame, two of the primary controllers of the human mind-set, and the mainstay of church doctrine, as seen in the idea of original sin, Adam and Eve. Guilt and shame are the core shadows of forgiveness; guilt at having betrayed one's own self and others, and shame at not having done anything about it. When these are seen, forgiveness becomes a tool for self-empowerment, a gateway to enable one to enter the Self.

As Thomas said, "When you have trampled underfoot the sins of guilt and shame then you can enter the Kingdom of Heaven."

Shame is the idea or belief that you are unlovable, fundamentally flawed, wrong, and dirty. Sexual, emotional, and physical abuse, ridicule, and humiliation are often experienced as a result of this belief. Shame is an inward implosion, like light disappearing into a black hole, a denial of life force, an unworthiness to exist, linked to a vague, unconscious feeling that something has happened to you that shows your lack of a right to life. It brings on depression, self-sabotage, self-destructive patterns, and even life-threatening diseases like cancer as the implosion robs the body-mind of life force.

Guilt is the mother of fear, a deep fusion to a form of identity as being inherently bad, a sense you have committed "sin." Guilt is an effect of shame, perpetuating a primal belief that we are worthless and undeserving of love. Remorse is typical, even though one may not really know why, or for what, one is feeling remorse for.

It also manifests as a resistance to, or even hatred of, having to be in the world. A constant sense of self-judgment "proves" the guilt is deserved, that when projected outward finds guilt in others, the world, and life. This results in a sense of being crippled and ungrounded, with attempts to numb feelings through drug use, alcohol, or addictions.

Guilt in its positive sense is morality, reminding us to treat others as we would like to be treated, keeping our ethical and moral sense intact. Yet when guilt pervades the body-mind, it eats away at us, keeping us stuck in the past and in regret of what could have been, or what we "should" have done to help ourselves or another. This then closes us down to what lies in the present as our energy is marooned in what could have been or what should have been, dragging us down and keeping us away from the possibilities of living life as it is presented to us right now.

In the depths of the soul there lies full awareness. Its essence remains untouched and untainted. Deep within all beings lies the guilt that one has ever identified with something other than the truth of one's inherent nature. All forgiveness, then, is the forgiving of yourself that you ever identified with ego, and that you have ever believed it to be true.

One who realizes that all is part of them has nothing left to forgive.

One who realizes that they are part of all has nothing left to forgive.

Internal conflicts can also arise when we forgive someone too soon, because "they did their best" or "they did not know" and are not responsible in any way, and so on. This premature forgiving, without the full feeling and processing, can lead to unresolved internal conflicts, an inner battle or split, a continued contraction or reactivity that is deeply subconscious. You think you have forgiven them, but this is only on the surface.

To complete the forgiveness process, state clearly to the involved person, whether they are present or not, living or deceased, what happened, how you feel about it, how it has affected your life, and what you need for resolution. While it is true that we create our experience, others are involved too, and if we forgive them without truly feeling the emotions that arise and expressing them, the scars and patterns still remain with us, haunting our lives and relationships.

Forgiveness is not dependent on time and space; it transcends everything. One can forgive anyone or anything at any time. Forgiveness is not merely saying, "I forgive you." Forgiveness is not just the words; it is a shift in consciousness and way of living consistently, recognizing the truth of reality and aligning oneself to it.

No one can ever *do* anything *to* you. There are no victims in God's world. Forgiveness dissolves the value that the mind places upon illusion. Forgiveness arises from allowing yourself to feel and see what you have not allowed yourself to experience before, to see things in a new way, to feel the feelings you never dared to before, or were too ashamed to.

In the end of all seeking it is *you* who must decide to be the one that heals yourself. To see yourself as whole and complete through forgiveness, the return to original wholeness allows the next opening of the heart to flower. As Yeshua said, "Healer, heal thyself."

Service

CHAPTER 15

Service

Martha

Martha is one of the four women in the Christ Blueprint. She was not as prominent as the other women, but her role was crucial. Martha is a connector between the Christ women and the Christ Family, holding and uniting them together, creating, administering, and keeping the infrastructures together in the daily running of tasks, which allows spiritual ideals and movements to ground and manifest on earth.

She allows others to be fully who they are, accepting each individual soul and specific role, selflessly giving herself to allow this to happen. Every human being needs another that offers support, that allows them to expand, to reach the cutting edge of their potential, to extend and embrace all that they are and all that they have to do. This reliability means that everyone trusts her to be their support unconditionally. The energy of Martha takes the initiative in service, not waiting to be asked, but doing whatever is needed to be done. She feels into the energy of a group and provides whatever is needed for the highest potential of that group to manifest, be it a cup of tea, an observation, an insight, or a gentle rebuke. Her fine-tuning of a group's vibration connects all the individual energies into a living being, delicately massaging it into a rounded, balanced whole. Wherever she goes, things manifest.

Her energy is relaxed, patient, supportive, caring, and detached, having the ability to observe and see life from an "open box." Rather than reactivity and quick judgment, it is a state that can view events without rushing to judgment, able to see and embrace all points of view without identifying with any.

Martha contextualizes Christ Consciousness into the now, the present time. She does this behind the scenes, for without her the whole cannot function. In a hologram, each part is whole but needs the other; such is the interconnection of all thirteen aspects of Christ consciousness. All teachings have to be placed in the context of the time you are living in. Martha helped to ground the Christ Blueprint two thousand years ago, and now the time has come again to ground the Blueprint into the twenty-first century in a relevant and universal manner, suitable for the peoples and the times that we are living in *now*. Christ Consciousness is perpetually the same, yet the times and the contexts change.

THE SPLIT

Martha represents a key split between transcendence, not being in the world, meditating, living in retreat, and action that lies in the world: serving others tirelessly to relieve their suffering and ease their burden. She is always busy, helping others, organizing, serving, nursing, comforting, and being in the world.

Yet she seldom takes enough time to delve deeper within, to go into deep contemplation and rest in Christ's Presence. She is distracted with others' needs, sometimes without having empowered and secured awareness of her own soul and needs. To balance both, to be in the world but not of it, is the key to service and presence in today's world.

In today's fast-paced world, this is harder and harder. Yet one key is strict and clear boundaries: guard your private time, your sacred circle-space, and be discerning about who you allow into your immediate surroundings and intimate womb space. Maximize your service and be more specific.

The womb is the center of a woman's creation; it draws energy inward magnetically, attracting what it is. This attraction can be both negative and positive; the womb can be a source of strength, or weakness. The energy a woman encounters in the world is held in the womb; if it is weak, wounded, and holds negative energy, it creates confusion and can delay and sabotage all the good things you try to do, as your connection to the web of life is sabotaged. If it is strong and clear, it gives you the power to create good things, to be of true service, to have clarity and be able to manifest your heart's desires.

To start off with, ask every night, and every morning, what it is that you have taken into the womb that needs cleansing, and what it is that you have taken in that has strengthened and nourished you. Talk to your womb; it has its own distinct voice, its own knowing. Touch it, breathe into it, massage it. Let it know you are present to it.

Set times to meditate, to practice, to enjoy life, to have a holiday, to appreciate the beauty all around you. Have alone time away from any and all others, and do not neglect it. *You* are as important as that meeting, that client, your family, helping others' needs. Do not let others run your life and delay your soul's individual needs. To delay is the trick of the mind, to keep the mind surviving with its well-meaning excuses, reasons to justify why you cannot love yourself, why you cannot meditate, and that you can do it tomorrow, and tomorrow, and tomorrow. The road to hell is paved with good intentions.

You have to give yourself the time to be not of the world. To maintain this balance is to maintain inner harmony, and this opens the gates to love and peace flowing through you more and more. Taking one step to God, to your womb, means God is given permission to take ten steps toward you. To do this requires periods of retreat and meditation, so that when one returns to the active life of serving others, one has stabilized their own discipline, their own state of consciousness, so that it is always available.

GIVING AND SERVICE

Giving feels good. Giving and serving others are only you giving to yourself. To give is to receive, and always leads to more joy, for giving *is* your heart's desire. Reaching out to others leads you to your highest potential. The act of serving another actually opens your energy body, opens the crown chakra and its channel, the antakarana or rainbow bridge, to receive more from Spirit.

Giving is a graceful flow from the heart that enjoys the love that bubbles forth, and naturally wishes to share this with anyone and everyone. For when we feel more joy, more beauty, and more God from what we give out, all we want to do is share even more of it. And so the spiral rises ever higher.

The more you give, the more God will give you. The more you extend this to others in everything you do, with everyone you meet, as a way of life, the more love flows through you. Service is glory, glorifying the Self in all beings, drawing the Divine out of people into their experience of life. There is no greater joy than seeing another transform in front of you, and that peace and satisfaction being felt within the shared one heart.

When you are living in mastery, in reality, giving is what you do, in every situation. You have unlimited energy to do so, as this is what you live for. God is never on holiday. Time becomes more important as you master it and choose not to waste it, instead maximizing it in order to be an open vessel for the sharing, and extending, of transformation. The more you are situated in this flow, the more is given to manifest through you. Those who live in the highest spheres of service in the world are busy constantly serving others, and have little time for anything else—save their own meditations, of course!

It is here that the very word *service* itself becomes a misnomer. Service is our most natural, effortless way of being. It is the very flow of life itself, and when we are in this flow anything else becomes unnatural, contracting, and experienced as a form of fearful heavy resistance, a drain and block to your full expression. You no longer keep anything for yourself, as there is the recognition that there is no separate self to keep anything for.

If you think you are in service and are not enjoying it, then it is not your true service. Service is never a burden; it is lightness. Service is never a duty; it is a voluntary willingness. Service includes all of you in it and does not leave anything out. Service is not something to do. It is a way of life, a way of being. It is God's lifestyle. It is our nature, our birthright, and our completion into love. Just as atoms whirl around each other in harmony, keeping each other in existence through their whirling, simply being what they are created to be, so can we realign ourselves to the way that we have been created to be, which gives us the most joy. Try it now: give to a stranger today, even if it is only a smile.

Giving continually realigns us to the constant flow of change, growth, and newness that Life is. To tune into life, tune into giving; to tune into what your service is, tune into the Life force. Then you will be guided on the most magical journey back to your true, joyful Self in harmony with the rhythms of Life.

And so it is.

CLEARING OUT THE WOMB

Womb is the center of your beingness, your center of gravity, joy, and creative power, your magnetic, feeling, intuitive connection to the web of life. It draws in energy, thoughts, and feelings from people and the environment around you.

There are many wounds, abuses, and blocks held within the womb inhibiting the flow of full power and expression. We leak energy from here, and allow much negative energy to be in our womb that should not be there. These energies can dissipate our potency, empowerment, and creative potential by us not knowing they are there, and not having the appropriate boundaries as to what and who should be in our wombs, and who or what should not be.

The womb opens through right relationship. Having the right discernment and correct boundaries allows the womb to feel safe, supported, nurtured, and allowed to bloom and express itself in its full power. Without these right relationships, the womb will wilt and become drained and disempowered. These relationships are about knowing who your allies are, and who is taking or feeding off your energy in an unhealthy way. You have to clear out these unhealthy relationships, moving them out of your womb.

You also have to place all the relationships that you are engaged in into their proper and healthy patterns, placing people and environments into positions that best allow your womb to flourish and become truly empowered. It is a delicate balance, but one that your womb needs to have in order to trust and open itself.

One of the quickest ways to identify and clear draining patterns, people, and obstacles from the womb is to place your womb in right relationship through the womb mandala. This mandala works on the four directions that we orient ourselves by in order to live in harmony, peace, and fulfillment with the web of life.

The Womb Mandala

Draw out three wide concentric circles with plenty of room to write. The first circle has a central point. This central point is you. Label it "me."

Sit silently, and clear your mind. Breathe deeply from your belly, from your womb.

Place your hands on your womb. It is a sphere, a circle.

Now visualize yourself in the center of this circle.

Call in all the people and relationships that your womb is connected to, to be present.

Now seeing yourself in this center, look behind you to see who is standing there.

Do not allow the mind to dictate or put who you would like to be there. Just be present, open, and curious, and see with your inner eye who is standing directly behind you. Note that this person could be embodied or disembodied.

Write it down on a piece of paper.

Then look in front of you, breathe, and feel who is standing there. Write it down.

Continue this and look to your left. Which person is there?

Look to your right. Who is standing there?

These are the primary relationships that your womb is engaged in.

Draw this out and write it down.

Now you are going to create a second circle around this primary circle of relationships. Proceed in exactly the same way.

Who is behind the person behind you?

Who is in front, meaning who is farther away from you, in front of the person in front of you?

Who is to the left of the person to the left?

Who is to the right of the person to the right?

This creates a second circle.

Now proceed in exactly the same way with the third and final circle. This last circle is the periphery. These are the most hidden and seemingly least significant relationships.

Now simply look around the whole periphery of the second circle and see who is there. Different images and people may float up—write them down.

Your mandala should look like: you, in the center, with three circles around you. Three beings to your front, three behind you, three beings to your left, and three beings to your right.

Draw the whole womb Mandala. Observe it closely without judgment. Do not be surprised if there are empty positions.

In front = your guides and teachers
Behind = your protector, supporter, strength, parents
At right = male power, integration, soul brother, or partner
At left = feminine love, soul sister, or wife

The first circle of beings, the ones who are closest to you, are the beings you value the most, the beings who are the most supportive of you, the beings who you allow in your deepest and most intimate space. The second circle of beings is the next ones who you allow into your womb space. They have a strong impact on you and considered to be "close" by. The peripheral circle is beings that you trust, although they may not be so close to you as the others.

All three circles represent those beings that have the most influence in your life. They are the ones you allow to directly affect you, and have let them into the deeper aspects of yourself.

Now take a look again at all the beings in your womb mandala. Do you feel a closeness and warmth with all these beings? Is everyone among you in full support of your growth? Do any of these beings deplete your energy? Who do you feel is not in their right position? What does this mean for you?

For example, if your husband is to your left, the feminine position, then there is an imbalance in your relationship—he should be to your right. This does not mean that all men should be on your right, but it does make clear that if you are in intimate relationship with a man, that you are using more of your masculine qualities and he is using more of his feminine. If you have a man that is not your partner, but a friend or other loved one, this could indicate that he holds a feminine space for you,. similarly with the man if a woman is to his right-hand side.

Similarly, if there are people whom you know do not support you in the mandala, or you have there out of guilt or obligation, then you have to question this also, and maybe move them out to the periphery or completely out altogether. Who is it you want in your womb space? This is not about judging anyone, but being discerning about where your boundaries are, and who you are letting into your womb space.

If you have noticed that there are energies present in your mandala that do not serve your highest potential, you may have to take action, either energetically by cutting cords or commanding with power that they leave, or simply sending them love and wishing them goodbye; or it may require direct physical action. You may have to end a relationship, or spend less time with this person. You may also have to ask them for forgiveness or forgive them. Each womb carries a unique thread to self-empowerment and clarity.

If you feel you have the correct relationship positions, it will reflect in your world as you being fully supported in your highest potential for true joy, harmony, empowerment, and love. You will have a clear connection to the web of life, and will be manifesting your heart's passion and desires in a tangible way.

You may choose to do womb mandalas every week, and in new situations you find yourself in; notice the changes that you have made regarding your new choices.

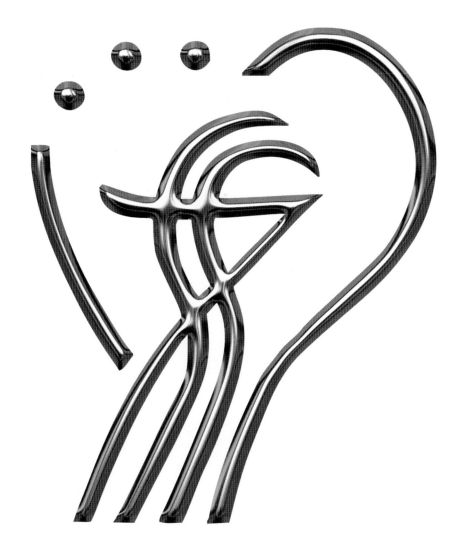

Compassion

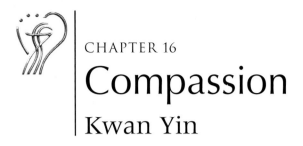

CHAPTER 16

Compassion
Kwan Yin

Kwan Yin is compassion, love centered in responding to others with total empathy born out of the softest emptiness. Kwan Yin is luminous clarity, softly loving light that embraces all parts of creation and contains the Triple Goddess, yet is also not of the created. She is the unmanifest luminous spaciousness that allows the creative energies of Isis, Ishtar, and Lady Nada to spiral forth, creating matter and form. This emptiness is what lies within all fullness, the Triple Goddess of wisdom, power, and love. She brings the Living Buddha to the Feminine Christ through her emptiness.

Emptiness is the heart of all things, the perfect wisdom. All forms are temporary. Form does not differ from emptiness, and emptiness does not differ from form. Form is love, and love is empty. All things are empty; never born, never ceasing, neither pure nor impure. There are no forms, no feelings, no thoughts, no perceptions, no consciousness. There is nothing to see, no ignorance, no ending of ignorance, no cause of suffering, no end of suffering, no path, no witnessing, nothing to own, and nothing to attain.

The unseen is the basis for the seen. Without emptiness being integrated within your experience of life, you cannot integrate the Feminine Christ, for She births from emptiness into form. In deep meditation emptiness can be fully experienced, and let go into.

Kwan Yin is the higher aspect of Martha. Kwan Yin embodies emptiness as loving kindness, compassion, service, harmlessness, and mercy. Her energy allows the heart to soften and open fully, exposing the depths of our being to being penetrated by loving Grace. This requires immeasurable trust allied with a deep knowing that to hold back love in fear that we may be harmed is to believe that others have the power to harm us, whereas in truth love can never be harmed.

HARMLESSNESS

Emptiness is nonreaction to any harm, anger, pain, or violence from outside and within. Often to experience this we have to go into extremes and wear out our reactions to any provocation or charge we may have. Once we are chargeless, no longer triggered by reaction in a need to defend, argue, attack, or justify, we can go deeper into the soft gentleness of complete harmlessness.

Harmlessness is much more than not harming another, eating vegetarian, and not killing flies and insects. Harmlessness is not reacting under any provocation, for there is nothing left to react or be provoked by. There is no "you" left, as the "you" is empty. Harmlessness is when there is no aversion or attachment to anything, just acceptance and emptiness born out of loving compassion and understanding. It knows the interconnectedness of all beings. If I harm you, I harm myself. The closer we are to embodying harmlessness, the quicker we notice and feel the effects of our harmful actions, until it becomes an instantaneous knowing.

When one has transcended suffering, it can be tempting to turn away from your brothers and sisters and let them remain in suffering. Only a master soul can reenter the darkness and join to assist them, feeling their suffering and knowing he or she can help them. No one can be fully free alone, as we are not separate from each other. To know and act on this truth is the greatest expression of compassion: to passionately empathize for others in their suffering, holding the space of love and harmlessness for them. Mercy is harmlessness brought to its peak. When we can no longer harm or be harmed; all we can share is mercy to others.

When we are in despair or hopelessness, mercy is what we ask for. Often it is born out of desperation, a plea for forgiveness, salvation, and freedom from the chains of suffering or illusion. It is often a prayer of surrender. It is giving up the struggle and individual will, to be touched and penetrated by the highest love.

With people in positions of power and authority, an imbalance can often occur causing one to tip over into the need to control, dominate, possess, or harm another. In mercy we give this power, through love, back to the other to empower them. Mercy is the easing of distress and pain through understanding, and empathy: to treat another as you would like to be treated.

Mercy involves opening the heart, vulnerability, deep trust; allowing love to shine through, even to those who are about to attack or harm you. Mercy involves infinite patience and nonattachment; love and humility; inner reflection and restfulness; and equanimity in all situations, for you cannot meet fear with fear to be set free. Fear cannot heal or harmonize fear. Illusion cannot dissolve illusion. Love is Divine power, and only love can free fear.

GRATITUDE AND BEAUTY

The essence of Kwan Yin is pure heart, emptiness, compassion, and kindness. Kindness and gratitude are interlinked. In gratitude one realizes that you cannot get love, you can only receive it, and you can only fully receive it by giving it. To have all, give all. In this we realize that there is no source by which to get love; only the choice to rest in gratitude and extend love.

To choose kindness is to choose gratitude, as it shows that you value the kindness that you have been given in order to exist, and even have the blessing of having a body. God has extended the kindness to you, and now to receive more of this kindness we give it away in action to our fellow beings.

To be truly happy is to live in gratitude. Living in gratitude and in grace means accepting whatever comes one's way, both "good and bad," with thankfulness. There is no exception to what one can be thankful for, as gratitude wears down our resistance to conflicts, humbles us, and brings us into joy and Oneness as we start to see that if we thank and bless all things in our life, we enter peace and kindness to all.

Try this: thank all the painful and beautiful occurrences that happen to you today, and see how you feel.

The knowledge that we can die any moment, that death is our ally, teacher, and friend, that emptiness and impermanence are real in this world, leads to deeper appreciation and gratitude. In the conflicts that arise, in the "unfortunate" circumstances that happen, there is a lesson for our soul that we have created in order to find the peace of the open, giving heart as it blesses and receives all things equally through the focus of gratitude and appreciation. The heart makes all things full by thanking it, emptying it of any resentment, frustration, or thoughts of harm.

This leads to beauty. Beauty results from one's perception and not just from the person, place, object, or emotion perceived. Beauty arises from the clarity of our own perception. What we often describe as beautiful is an interpretation, one that has been taught to us; a perception that one thing is beautiful, and another is ugly.

To see beauty is to see things as they are, and to appreciate something simply for what it is. In seeing beauty we see beyond the conditioned senses, and see the life force, the shimmering light, in all life. To see beauty we see with the heart, and connect to what we are seeing and communicating with through the heart. When we truly see reality, it is beautiful, as it involves no judgment, no naming or identifying with things, no past history or conditioning. We see in the present moment, when everything we experience is vivid and undeniable, glowing luminously, alive and vital, through an empty mind and open heart.

This requires that we slow down the mind and its mechanisms, we empty the mind, so that what is naturally here spontaneously arises in our perception. This reality can be experienced through the senses only when the mind stops interpreting what it is experiencing, for the mind constantly gives a commentary on everything that it comes into contact with, avoiding the direct experience of what actually *is;* therefore we cannot experience directly what is.

Without the mind's interpretation and commentary, we can see the beauty in the rotting pile of dung lying on the street. If you have no judgment about the value of something as opposed to the value of something else, then you can appreciate the nature, and use, of all things. In true beauty we do not exclude anything, but embrace it all as living reflections of our nature that serve a vital purpose to show us where our mind still judges and misunderstands. Heaven is not somewhere else; it is right here in this perception.

Beauty is not about how a person, place, object, or emotion looks or feels; it is about how you, who is looking, feel. The beauty that we experience "out there" is a direct reflection of the beauty of what is happening inside you. When you are in a state of joy and feel uplifted, everything appears beautiful to you on the outside. This feeling naturally leads us to being kind, and extending this kindness and beauty to others in tender, receptive presence, leading to harmlessness.

For those who wish to embody Kwan Yin, you will go through a stage of being "vessels of sweet sorrow,"[1] empathy, and compassion; the ones on the planet who cry to relieve the sufferings of others, feeling

1. Thank you to Solara for this perfectly named title.

their sadness and pain. Here, we do not cry for ourselves but for everyone as a service to humanity, in order that everyone can one day become consciously One. When we cry these tears to relieve the sufferings of others, we also get transformed by feeling the pain of a whole world, a whole species, a whole race. And in truth there are many Kwan Yins who recognize and serve this aspect of compassion every day.

THE SHADOW SIDE

The shadow side of Martha shows us the misunderstandings about what service is, and the holes one carries in their "trying" to be of service: lack of valuing oneself, serving out of duty instead of including joy, low self esteem, low self worth, and lack of self-love. This leads to one not being centered in one's own unique expression of Christ Consciousness.

Unworthiness

Those wishing to embody loving service encounter one of the biggest shadows: unworthiness, and lack of self-love. You do not feel worthy of attention and feel you do not deserve recognition or proper payment for service. You feel that somehow you are not good enough, that you are not worthy of being respected and valued as a human being. This current runs throughout your life, ruining money flows, creating poverty consciousness, and getting you into dysfunctional, codependent relationships for security.

This feeling sabotages all the dreams, hopes, and aspirations that your soul may feel is its mission, and what you may aspire to. The feeling *Am I good enough?* and *Do I deserve this?* are the underlying script. And this is a script of false humility, placing people on pedestals, because you feel you are not worthy or great enough to be like that yourself.

Stop for a moment. Stop everything you are doing. Now, place your hand on your heart. Gently say, "I love and accept myself as I am right now." What arises? Memories, feelings, thoughts, any sensations in any part of the body?

Masters throughout time are venerated and respected, and rightly so. But they are normal human beings as well. The practices Mary and Yeshua did, many are doing today, and many are doing it better than they did. Yeshua himself knew this when he said, "Many will come after me who will do greater works than I." These people are here, now. Maybe you could be one of them. This is no false humility, but true humility as equality; what love is.

To be a follower is to be a sheep. And sheep get slaughtered. To be a leader is to be here now: to be present. Followers are not living in the present; leaders are. By failing to value ourselves, we fail to value God. By valuing ourselves, by recognizing ourselves, we send out a message to God, and to the world, that we are here and that we are ready to stand up. By accepting second best, we put God second best. And we truly let ourselves down.

The key words are *should, could,* and *but.* "This is not my right relationship, but it will do for now," "I will accept second best," or "I could/should have done that, but ..."

These are excuses of the ego; a trick of the ego to keep yourself small, trapped, and a prisoner of the world, the world of the small self and mind. This small self hates being the focus of attention; public speaking is its biggest nightmare, for then you are thrust into the limelight, in both others' awareness and especially your own. You become the focus and are seen. There is nowhere left to hide. You have to shine your light.

Unassertive, indirect, and uncontroversial, one shuns any confrontation and has difficulty in expressing oneself. Dislike of conflict and the need for a sense of peace drive one into feeling inferior and inconsequential. This then leads to one neglecting oneself personally, and what one has to do in one's life.

The sense of stability and dependability this mind gives to others is often a mask for your own feelings of unworthiness or need. You are there for everyone apart from yourself, out of touch with yourself and what you need. The needs of others become your priority, and your way of gaining self-importance and value in life, as it feeds your hole of worthlessness.

By focusing on others, becoming attuned to the needs of others and their environments rather than your own inner voice, you lose deep contact with your own unique essence, which paradoxically is what you are looking for. Rationalizing this as noble, selfless service, as a spiritual ideal, becomes dangerous.

The confusion this elicits leads to complications. Doing well for others becomes a humanitarian mission of treating the effect of a problem, and not the cause. Inherently, many women wishing to embody the service of love can feel, deep down in the subconscious, that they are not worthy of the love, beauty, and glory of God. They feel that others have it, while they feel unable to receive praise and love without a sense of false humility, born from the sense of not being worthy enough to truly receive it.

This results in you developing an inferiority complex. You stop listening to your inner voice, which knows you deserve it, and listen to others whom you feel do have it. Here, one has to be "in the mind" to compete and stay afloat in a man's world, all the time denying the impact, the power, of softness and the warm, dark, deep unknown that holds the greatest promise both for you and humanity. This is held in the womb, the seat of the soft silence of the Black Light, guarded by sadness, sexual disconnection, betrayal, and longing for what you know to be true, but which you cannot grasp as you become ever more lost in the twists and turns of the labyrinthine mind that strives to understand, rather than accept, and be what you simply are.

The energy of Martha supports others into flowering into their own greatness, but forgets to nourish and own her own greatness. This comes from being too much in awe and giving away her power, leading to a false, and disempowering, humility. Staying small to avoid claiming, and rising up to her own mastery. There is a false sense of safety in feeling small, whereas being big, powerful, and recognized elicits fear of persecution, judgment, and ridicule. Your playing small does not serve the world. There is nothing wise about hiding your light and power so that other people will not feel threatened or insecure around you. As you reveal your own light and power, you act as a beacon to give other people permission to do so as well.

Envy

Smallness can become twisted into envy: secretly wanting what another has, but feeling you do not deserve it. If you see someone with power speaking their truth, standing firm, doing what you have always dreamed to do, then one wants to be like that in its grandeur, but can feel too scared to. This creates a vicious circle of frustration that feeds itself.

There is nothing wrong with wanting certain things. The real downfall in envy, in jealousy, is not being honest about it, and not transmuting this impulse into genuine aspiration to better ourselves, to grow into these qualities we so admire but cannot stand up for. If you are honest with yourself, then envy has less chance to consume you.

Another antidote for envy is finding peace, finding the place in your soul that is at rest, that is content with what is, that is happy with who you are, even if you have nothing. Many Eastern cultures exemplify this, as they have little but are happy with what they have, whereas many Western cultures have a lot of wealth but little happiness.

Envy is always caused by a hole within you. What you do not have is often what you always want, and what you already have is often what you take for granted, and sometimes what you feel you do not even want. What you project or want outside is really a lack within, a feeling that something fundamental is missing within. The paradox of envy is that it eats you up from the inside.

People are jealous or envious because they want what you have. This energy, when it becomes projected onto you, can also affect you adversely. But you can deflect any envy by being clear and stable within your own field, having clear boundaries. People can then admire and respect you, and may even want what you have, but it will not affect you. People want because they feel they lack, and in this feeling of lack, in this hole, lies the pathway into their own healing.

Envy is about our own perceived inadequacies and limitations. Envy can be transformed into Self-empowerment by realizing you have that quality that you are envious of within you. This quality within you needs to be integrated and is asking for your attention in the pang of jealousy, calling for you to pay heed to that part of yourself that feels wounded, isolated, unheard, unacknowledged. In this you can start to embody what you thought you lacked, because it is always within your power to do so.

Blocks to the Power of Service

Feeling tired or drained by helping others shows that there is still a holding-on to a deep self-identification that still "needs" something from the other. This holding-on is mainly found in the connection between the solar plexus and the heart as the focus for giving and sharing. In the energizing and clearing of this area, one is empowered into flowing with the life force that has no obstructions to its expression.

Selfless power is the quality of the open solar plexus. To be selfless is to be truly powerful. This power emanates when there is no more story and justification for not being present. When these wounds in body and mind are released and healed, desire, delight, and the dynamic catalyzing power of loving, selfless action are allowed to express through you without interruption. For to be selfless requires great power, and if you are not secure in this power, you will feel tired and be liable to a sense of failure in your service, and even persecution.

To be secure in your power and the power of God flowing through you is to have healed, cleansed, and sealed any "holes" in the subconscious mind. These "holes" in our consciousness leak out energy by denials, justifications, excuses, fear, anger, and worthlessness, all of which hide the cause of the issue under the carpet. Conversely these "holes" also invite other energies into you, creating gaps that "entities" can then feed and prey on, keeping the blocks in place, veiling the core seed of the wound, keeping you weak and disempowered.

These deep-seated wounds are masked, even when much spiritual work and inquiry has been applied, and often can only be removed by exorcism, as demonstrated by John the Baptist and Yeshua on the Christ Path. So the ability to truly serve comes from great power: the power to be selfless, and the power of the impassioned heart that extends itself into the world. This power is fed and nurtured through delight, passion, and dynamic action in the world as service, the flowing of life force through you unimpeded without denial, story, or leakage.

To bolster your power, fire-breath breathing, vigorous exercise, circulation of sexual energy, and willingness to go deep into the shadow are the remedies. Those who are polarized in the light, who are "too spiritual" or upper chakra–centered, desperately need this balance in order to embody themselves and to have the foundation to ascend. Being too present for others at the expense of one's own self-nurturing is a hole. God wants us to be who we are, and to express this in alignment with helping others, not at the expense of helping others. This is not an either/or world anymore.

Harm

The second aspect of Martha's shadow side is believing that you can be harmed, and therefore defending and shielding the heart by closing it down. It is the delicacy and sensitivity of our hearts that we try to protect. We have all felt hurt and harmed by others. We have all felt blows on the heart, and some have even felt they have had their hearts broken.

When we close down or build walls or barriers, we believe that we can escape this pain from being felt again. Nothing is further from the truth. It is in the actual act of closing down the heart that we experience our greatest suffering. We keep ourselves from fully loving ourselves, and in turn others.

In the world everything is diametrically opposed to the truth. We believe we can be harmed, and harden our hearts in protection, only to discover that this *is* the cause for our pain. When the heart is closed from the fear of being hurt, one cannot engage in life fully. For if one believes they can be harmed, they will automatically be in defense mode and be ready, willing, and able to attack another in self-protection. This creates self-destructive conflict, as the body-mind is in a state of fight or flight, ready to react from fear. This then gets projected externally into our lives, into our close relationships, and into the collective consciousness of humanity as a whole.

Another strategy to protect us from feeling harmed is to dive into our own inner world. In this inner sanctuary we feel we have a safe place to hide, to keep the suspected harm outside of us. We escape into an isolated part of ourselves and shut out relating with others, disappearing from engaging.

When harmlessness is integrated, one is chargeless in relating, for it is in the actual engagement and full participation in Life where one finds their wholeness and liberation. To throw open the shutters of the heart is to vulnerably yet powerfully stand before another in the knowing that love cannot be harmed. In this action, we realize we are loving beings, and that we are loved and lovable. We can now share this love fully in service.

Ruthless Compassion

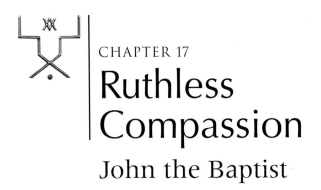

CHAPTER 17

Ruthless Compassion

John the Baptist

Yeshua said, "I tell you the truth: among those born of women there has not risen anyone greater than John the Baptist."

—Matthew 11:11

It may be misleading to call John the Baptist an Apostle because he was far more than that. As the initiator of Yeshua, he prepared Yeshua to meet his demons in the desert of Jericho, which then prepared the foundation for Christ's ministry and teachings to ignite. John opened the gateway for the Holy Spirit to descend into Yeshua. He prepared the people of Israel for him, and passed on the Prophetic Lineage to Yeshua, a lineage Yeshua did not fully have until John baptized him into it.

John was Elijah in his previous incarnation. The trinity of prophets Moses, Elijah, and Isaiah held the keys to the Hebrew Lineage and the codes of the God-man along with Melchizedek. Yeshua, even though he was one of the four immortal and uncreated sons of God, did not have these keys and codes, and needed to be given them.

Yeshua was also a man. He trained long and hard, becoming initiated in many different sacred traditions to achieve his mission. He also had to remember who he was, as do all of us. He did not hold all the Keys and needed help from all the Apostles, in particular John the

Baptist as his gateway into Holy Spirit, and Magdalene as his feminine teacher.

John was a gateway to Holy Spirit for many people; he baptized, healed and exorcised more people than Yeshua did, aligning them to the Will of God. He needed nobody around him to do his work, and held the strength that Yeshua needed in order for him to do his work. The baptism of Yeshua occurred to pass on the Messianic Lineage to him, and its connection to the collective consciousness of humanity.

This has been interpreted as the transferring of "sins" onto Yeshua, which is only partly true; it was also the transferring of legacy, and to wash away the pains of the collective consciousness in order to clear the way for the anchoring of the Christ Blueprint.

This ritual, of washing away the great pain, was reignited when the Israelites began the practice of atoning through the ritual transferring of sins onto a goat. Yeshua became this lamb, the scapegoat, the willing vessel to anchor the Christ Blueprint of total compassion and love on earth.

This does not mean we are saved through this. It just means that the precedent has been set, and we can follow this path throughout the density of the collective consciousness with greater ease and clarity than ever before.

THE TEACHER

John and Yeshua taught the Essenes together in the caves of Qumran. As teacher of the Christ Flame to half of the Essenic School, and the last high priest of the Prophetic Lineage, many saw him as the equal of Yeshua, although his way of teaching was radically different, focusing more on power, discipline, zeal and dedication.

John the Baptist paved the way for the descent of the Christ Blueprint into the density of the collective fields of consciousness, in both his incarnations as an initiator and catalyst. In his baptism of Christ, he passed on the power to transform consciousness and walk in the anointing, exorcising the demons and obstacles that were coming to Yeshua, giving him the seed of Divine power to transform, so vital in clearing the way for love to be fully present on the earth plane. Here, John used the science of the five layers of exorcism as the means to carve a furrow through the darkness in order to establish the Christ Blueprint.

John held the other half to the Christ teachings, which complete the Christ Path. These two sides are power and love. Power without love is crippling; love without power is crippling. Both schools of love and of power were polar in attitude and teaching. John's approach was one of hellfire and brimstone, prophesying the apocalypse, exhorting his followers to save the world from impending destruction by running themselves ragged in their attempts to purify themselves and the planet. Yeshua's approach involves a slower and more gradual evolution, one of openness, softening what is rigid within, allowing life to flow through and surrendering to God in humility, faith, and Grace.

Both schools complete the Christ Path. Both paths are required to reach wholeness. Yeshua embodied both fully, uniting both schools within Himself, yet choosing to teach the Path of Love. However, as seen in his ransacking of the Temple and the money changers, and other instances, he knew how to use the power that John taught and embodied.

POWER AND LOVE

Love without power dissolves into an astral, weak fairy tale of what Christ Consciousness is. Love without strength and depth crumbles into an ungrounded, chaotic mess. Power without love becomes a game of control, fear, and tyranny. Discipline without joy becomes an intense, self-defeating, oppressive hell. Magic and exorcism without kindness becomes a magnet for every dark force alive to haunt and tempt you.

These polarities of magic and love, exorcism and softness, power and compassion, surrender and will, direct penetration and gentle opening, fire and water, the bludgeon and the kiss, "my yoke is easy," and "do till you die" all merge into one seamless flow. Each quality is used at different times to effect the most appropriate change, without hesitation, doubt, or holding back.

The reason why so few people have reached Christ Consciousness is that they have taken one or the other path, and not included both. This is particularly endemic to the Western traditions, as opposed to the Eastern traditions that Yeshua was schooled in, which taught both. Many beings on the Christ Path are too scared to shine their full light and power, too afraid to stand out, and are lacking in the essential qualities of empowerment and awareness of the body of light that Yeshua was taught and so aptly demonstrated.

Owning and using this power to radically transform is what Yeshua came to do: to crucify the world into the Christ Blueprint. This could not have happened, and still cannot be fulfilled, without Divine power and ruthless compassion.

RUTHLESS COMPASSION

In ruthless compassion, anything that stands in the way of your growth is cut away: any attachment, any fear, any person of any sort that distracts from your goal is removed by the sword of ruthless compassion. It is the ruthless cutting through of any, and all, illusions and ignorance to awaken the soul. It is death to the ego, and total surrender in action to the Self.

Ruthless compassion is compassion that is unmoved by worldly troubles, cares, or concerns. It is direct, clear movement that dissolves all obstacles in its way, cutting through the tap roots of egoism, acting and dissolving no matter how its actions are perceived by others. It is compassion for the soul and the bigger picture; it is the lack of any concern for the ego. It is destructive force harnessed to Divine Will, and it has no remorse. Once started it can never be stopped, until all obstacles and ignorance are destroyed.

Ruthless compassion provides rapidly accelerated evolution where no stone is left unturned, and is for those that wish to be fully enlightened, no matter what. In ruthless compassion, one is ready and willing to do absolutely anything to become a channel for Divine Will. Ruthless compassion can appear to be cruel, as it usually involves giving you what you need to grow, rather than what you want. Comfort comes last on the list of priorities for ruthless compassion. For this reason, ruthless compassion is often not appreciated until well after it has been received, and can be initially greeted by the ego with judgment, resentment, and anger.

The heart of ruthless compassion is the heart of spaciousness that allows others to be in their pain and suffering so they may grow. It is relentless in that it is not affected by pain or suffering; it sees all without hiding, flinching, or avoiding. This is the heart of acceptance: accepting what must be, for the highest good of all.

Ruthless compassion requires great passion, dedication, and wisdom to flow with it and implement its actions and directions. Wisdom here is the ability to see beyond the appearance, and see the true clinging, suffering, and need of a person, situation, or event. Acting on this directly arises from being objective, calm, and clear in understanding how and why the ego protects, hides, and cloaks itself.

Ruthless compassion is not an emotion or feeling. It is a way of being that arises when one is fully dedicated and surrendered to Self. It is uncompromising, direct, and unflinching. Ruthless compassion becomes a process of relentless surrender that grinds down anything that stands in the way between your larger Self and your smaller self. It witnesses what is happening in silence, and being totally present. This leads to total harmlessness, as no reaction, no harm can affect you when you have no harm, no violence, no triggers left within you. Then these forces can be wielded in order to serve love most effectively, as and when it is required.

DIRECTNESS

Sometimes the bludgeon is required. The bludgeon that cuts to the bone, that illumines illusion in the most direct and uncompromising manner. My friends, do not compromise with the seeing of illusion in yourself and others. Be radically honest, for this serves love. Be brutally frank, be directly engaging, and do not shirk your responsibility toward the growth of the soul.

My job is to lead people into, and through, the dark night of the soul, or should I say the dark night of the ego. In this darkness the power of will, the dedication to God, and loving faith are the only qualities of character to lead you through.

I build peoples' characters, and dissolve their small selves, to lead them into joy and loving service, service that will have true impact as it is based on authentic, deep, lived experience of the darkest places that a human being can go into. Once you have lived through this experience, then anything is possible for you, as you have reclaimed your power from the darkness, and can now wield it yourself.

Darkness forges the soul into a diamond, by burning away the dross, the weakness, leaving only that which is immortal. The doubts, the voices, the trials and tribulations, all are voices of the tempter that does not wish you to stand in your empowerment, in the truth.

Here there is no "your truth" or "my truth"; there is one truth that we both align to. This is not a self-help seminar. I am not here to help you or your illusion of a self, for in the dark night and through baptism you come to realize that there is no self to help. There is no self to help, just the One Self that needs no helping, just resting within, and extending. This is where you end up after baptism. Before this you have to go through the hell of your own dark night, your own self-created demons invented by the mind to lead you to see the one truth.

Baptism opens the way for Holy Spirit to descend. In this, the residual impurities flush up to the surface to be cleared. This is why many powerful teachers still have residual darkness around them; they have been baptized, but still need to resolve the issues brought up by the baptism. This is where Yeshua's teachings come in, for we all have our unique residue, our unique reasons for separating from the One. And these reasons provide the pathway to also reaching the One. Contemplate this.

When you are all-one, and whole in yourself, there is no need to go outside yourself. This power of stillness, of directness and action, is also the hallmark of Christ, "for by their actions shall they be known." This power expands our aura and vibration, grounding ourselves into the moment, and the right action for the moment. Power is needed to anchor love.

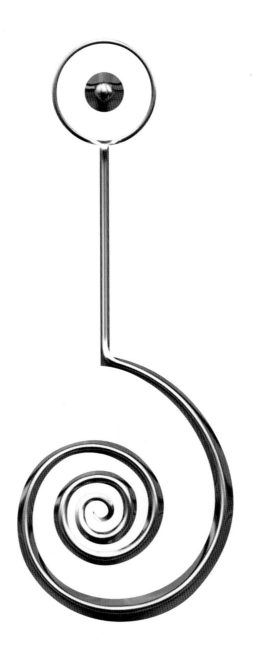

Divine Will

Divine Will

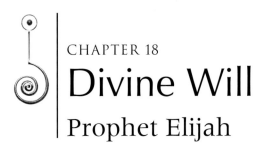

CHAPTER 18

Divine Will

Prophet Elijah

Elijah is a prophet of Divine Will and repentance. The true meaning of repentance was corrupted by the church as a means of gaining power for their priests. Repentance is not thinking we are flawed and imperfect, needing another to make us feel validated, to forgive us for our sins. There is no guilt involved.

Repentance is sounding a call for yourself, and by extension others, to hear the voice of the soul, and to regather all the scattered and fragmented parts of yourself back into wholeness, to re-collect and reunite all parts of yourselves around this one voice of the soul. In this gathering, we re-collect ourselves and return back to our original Source, our original wholeness.

Repentance gives people an opportunity, a crack in the veils that allows them to hear the call of their own true nature, to return back to the still small voice within that always *knows*. This voice, which is always present, has the power to follow its guidance, its original memory of its unique soul blueprint, in all situations.

Repentance serves to bring us into Divine Will, the will that serves love. There is no love without will. Will creates the basis, the foundation, the platform for which love can spring out and express itself, and be anchored and sustained within the maelstrom of forces that create the world you live in today.

There are no rules in Divine Will. There is no dogma or doctrine. Its actions are different for each one of us, yet its results in our individual lives are the same; surrender and repentance.

Repenting leads to a surrendering, and a forgetting, about who and what you were before, in order to step into a whole new you, sloughing off the old skin of the separated self, just like a butterfly does out of its chrysalis. When we repent, we come out of the cocoon of the ego, open our eyes, and enter the realm where we can be a light unto others by shining our own light brightly, a light that is shining brightly because it is surrendered to the flows of Life.

DIVINE WILL

Divine Will is like a sun that never sets, and is found burning in all beings. This will anchors you into the stream that keeps us all connected, the will that dissolves our identities into the one will of love that holds life together. It is the awareness that reality flows with power, and the easiest way to deal with this power is to move with it. Divine Will is knowing that there is only one will, one unfolding reality, knowing that everything is "in God's hands" as a palpable reality. We let go, and let God.

Surrendering to Divine Will allows our highest potential to manifest. It wants only the best for us. Often we do not know what is the best for us, what will lead us to the highest joy, happiness, and enlightened fulfillment, until it happens to us. If we flow with Divine Will, it can be graceful; if we resist it, then ruthless compassion and the process of relentless surrender that our souls have already agreed to will grind us down inevitably and eventually into accepting it, whether we like it or not. If we are committed, it will keep returning to us, even if we do not initially act on it. This too is love.

Recognizing this releases us from the compulsive need to do, to fight, and to resist what is happening in our present moment, our present experience of life right now. We start to see that our identity, our sense of value, does not depend on doing. This brings freedom from the ego, joy, and openness when we tangibly experience ourselves as part of the unfolding will, as part of a whole that all works together, and is interconnected. This recognition can then lead to spontaneous Divine action.

This action is not afraid to apply pressure in different ways in different situations, sometimes through softness, sometimes with a sword; sometimes with penetrating insistency, sometimes in merely holding an unyielding, invincible space silently for others to feel supported by. When we surrender to what is occurring right now, our deepest heart's desires manifest in the most glorious of ways. All is included, and nothing is left out. We receive everything we have ever wanted.

Divine Will is the activator of our soul blueprint. We become aware of our soul blueprint throughout our life, in the intuitions and remembrances that crop up again and again.

Divine Will provides the means, at the right time and with surrender, to fulfill these remembrances of who we are, no matter how fantastic or seemingly unattainable they may seem to be at the time of remembering them.

POWER

Divine Will has an adamantine core that is invincible and invulnerable, yet which can also be shifted into the softest, purest love as and when required. The true use of will allows love to flourish. It stands behind love and compassion as the fuel for sustained joy and strength in our lives.

To be truly strong requires that we are truly selfless. That our will is clear, directed, focused, and yet also ready to expand and embrace any person, relationship, and situation at any time, because true will is aligned to love. Willpower is connected between the solar plexus and the third eye. Divine Will is directed selfless seeing with the eyes of the heart.

Divine Will is what makes us stand up, command, declare, and be counted as part of God.

We have the will to fully embody the Divine. In your heart you know what these steps are. In your solar plexus you can feel what the gaps are that prevent you from standing in this, to being fully selfless in a dynamic, vital, and constant way. When you are integrated in this flow, you give, and you get, more energy from giving. If you get tired from giving, then there are gaps in your solar plexus and your third eye. And you are not including all of yourself in the act of serving.

To serve God is to be immensely strong. Strength provides the foundation for any enlightened civilization, and for an enlightened person. Without this strength, belief systems form. And when these belief systems are pushed hard enough, they will collapse, for Divine Will is a catalyst. It shakes the tree of conditioning; it shakes the tree of belief; it shakes people to their core. This may not suit many people whose idea of will is the small self-empowerment, whose goals and desires are to serve themselves and to keep their egos in place. Divine Will batters the door down, and if used skillfully can crush the ego, allowing love to surface.

This is not wrath; this is destruction in order to bring forth a new creation. Divine Will also destroys where there is no other way, where the foundation of a person, a belief, a system, or a country itself is so corrupted that it needs to be destroyed. Love does not destroy these creations; Divine Will does, Divine power does, as the instrument of love. And this is very necessary for many millions of people, for their creations to be destroyed, their foundations to be shaken up, in order for their own love to reveal.

This may bring up fear for you, and if you still feel fear, then this is love talking to you now. One does not reach embodiment without flowing in the power of Divine Will. Without that unshakeable core, no building can be built, and if your building is going to rise to infinity, then one had better start creating or destroying the foundation one already has, in order that it may be permanent, instead of temporary.

Divine willpower serves love. Love then generates more Divine power, which in turn serves love and generates more Divine power, and so on, into infinity. The bridge between love and power is wisdom. Divine power can never be usurped, manipulated, or controlled. People may judge the effects of Divine Will because they do not flow with it, because they secretly desire it, because they are scared of the power that they themselves hold.

Divine Will can be loud and overt; it can be quiet and in the background; it can be within any and all expressions. Its action is to ground Self onto earth. Without it, you will just be floating in space. Divine Will is the center of your being. Within this center lies love.

Divine Will occurs when you let go of control, in trust and conscious surrender. This occurs when you understand that every aspect of your life is divinely animated, and you relax and let the flow take you where it wants to go: not my will but Thy will be done, for God has total awareness of all events always. If God is truly omnipotent, there is no free will, just humanly created ideas around it.

Divine Will is choiceless flow. We no longer think we know, but surrender our ideas and allow. There is no longer any illusion of choice, as we have given up this illusion to flow with our highest potential: the Will of God.

THE SHADOW SIDE

One cannot allow and be a vessel of Divine Will if one does not recognize the impostor taking its place. The false will of the separate doer is the willpower we use in the world to force things to happen. The ego mind believes that its personal efforts are required to make good things happen. Most humans cannot think about will without imagining some sort of effort in our definition, involving success and the value of hard work. True will, however, is not solely about hard work; it is also about surrender.

When false willpower overtakes and obsesses one without the softness of intimacy and surrender, with just a fierce one-pointed drive, you miss relating to all parts of you. Will and fire leaves one very much alone, and lonely, lacking something: love. In this aloneness others too will leave you alone. The cycle perpetuates itself, for when you separate yourself from something dear, you then continue the pattern or cycle of separation.

John came to fulfill the prophecies of the Messiah, and yet at the same time he left something out in his fierce determination to fulfill his mission: he left out his humanity. It is this inclusion of his humanity, of intimacy and the personal, that would have made him immortal and raised him to the level of Yeshua.

The shadow side of ruthless compassion is that sometimes it can lack softness, and can bulldoze people and situations in a self-appointed way, creating a haphazard balance of forces that can become very one-sided. This one-sidedness creates duality, feelings of superiority and inferiority, fragmentations, and belief systems. These belief systems become the basis of institutions, governments, and religions.

They say that religions are based in faith; we say they are based on wrong use of will. Gifts have been given, and are abused. When those who try to control through wrong use of will use these reasons to create institutions or religions, they are merely exerting their strong self-will over weak-willed subservient people to create their own power structures. Wrong use of will leads to control. Awakening is about letting go of any, and all, control.

Rest, beauty, joy, ease, and deep relaxation are the antidote to this. A holiday from your self works well here.

The shadow side of ruthless compassion is being too focused, too intent on awakening, too intent on getting "there" without the feminine, the passivity, and the receptivity being present to guide the right actions. Too much fire without water leads to the softer qualities of love, of the feminine, being burned away. Kindness, softness, compassion, and consideration are also to be included in the fierce drive for transformation.

Harshness, insensitivity without patience, understanding, and tolerance can make one become a pitiless taskmaster on oneself as well as others. This leads to parts of yourself and those around you closing down, as the more delicate parts will try to hide, will close off and not open to try to protect themselves.

Not Sharing

The secrecy in which John taught, limiting his circle, inevitably leads to a form of constriction. The moment we start building a fortress around ourselves and what we have to share, we limit ourselves and our potential. This is a form of clinging to what you feel is your treasure, your possession, and your right.

What are you clinging to? What do you feel is so valuable that you cannot share it, that you feel you have to protect it? What is your dream that you are keeping under wraps, waiting for a right time that may never come?

The remedy may be as simple as sharing openly with a friend, sharing your love with a stranger on the street, being your authentic self with the lady in the supermarket, opening and being who you are to everyone, and not hoarding to yourself only those who you feel understand. If we do not share freely who we are, and our unique gifts and talents, then there is a danger that these gifts will become stale, stagnant, and worthless.

Whatever you are hoarding or protecting, remember that you can never take it with you into eternity; all that goes into eternity is your naked soul. Let go and freely share all that you are! Be open, and more openness will come your way. Expand and share, and more expansion and loving communion will happen with others. Be human.

Living in abundance rather than at the minimum, living in the overflowing of Life, means your life reaches out to others and touches them. Your wisdom, bliss, and gifts flow to others as they flow within you, and then it increases. So, invite and give to others the fruit of your own labors, so they may drink what you have earned. Spread and share what you have with others, for this shows in action that there is no separation between you and your neighbor. Meditation becomes a moment to rejuvenate, as now people become the meditation as aspects of God, your own Self.

The inclusion of sexuality transmuted into loving softness, of richly seductive and enjoyable possibilities, the feminine flow, is the neglected side of ruthless compassion. The celebration of intimacy, people, and love, combined with meditational austerity and alone time, creates a whole way of being. Balance occurs when both human impulse and Divine autonomy merge.

Evolution

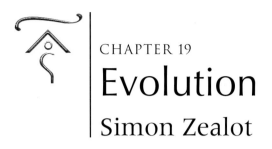

CHAPTER 19

Evolution
Simon Zealot

The bodies of light that carry the seeds for evolution need willing, dedicated vehicles in order to manifest and flower. In the willingness to do this, one begins to truly care and wish to give to others. The heart emerges in feelings of love, compassion, and the desire to do things well, for the positive effects upon others and the world. This is a spontaneous feeling arising within you, a welling-up and giving guided by a mysterious inner impulse, extending itself gracefully without anyone having to convince you, and no sense of "should."

In the beginning phases of this evolutionary impulse, you start to think about how to use time to its maximum productivity and organization, developing your willpower and self-discipline to become closer to God. You become easily and enthusiastically inspired to start making bigger changes. Good results start to come from your endeavors, and this fuels you to keep going, to continue being open and willing, to continue your practice and discipline. Talent, even genius, may be there, but it is only through discipline that you will make anything of it.

In this willingness, you say "yes" to life, growth, creativity, and service. You begin to discover the joy of change and growth. You follow your heart's desire, a deeper desire than the body-mind. You have tasted the Divine, and want more. You become dedicated and zealous, a passionate human making sure things get done, not just talked about.

INTENTION

Simon was a warrior of truth and righteousness, devoted to justice, fighting for what he believed in, living in the intention to become closer to God. It was Simon who participated with Yeshua in the ransacking of the Temple with the money changers, for he had the bravery to fight iniquity and corruption fueled by his sacred intention, which he would die for, so ingrained was it in him.

Intention is the single pointed focus and unwavering commitment to realize God and live in Divine Will. Divine Will is your highest potential, for God only wishes your ultimate happiness, joy, and fulfillment. Desire is the fuel, the raw energy for the focus of intention to guide. With these two forces combined as one, it becomes an underlying current that grows to live in you, becoming further strengthened and crystallized through action. Desire fuels intent, which grows through action, and intent then becomes strengthened and reinforced even further.

This intention anchors in you through repetition and practice, in your dedication through your thoughts when you are alone, and in your words and deeds with others. As this underlying energy settles into your being and way of life, you acquire guidelines in your life that magnetize your intention to you, sometimes in unexpected ways that defy what you think you originally intended. Nevertheless, it is happening.

All intentions have been created by God to lead us into God. Of course the journey along the way can be littered with all kinds of diversions, for the road to hell is paved with good intentions. True intention constantly reminds you of who you are, what you are here for, and what desire is for: to be guided through intention to realize you are One with God. True intention does not seek your worldly satisfaction; it seeks and guides you toward the satisfaction of the soul, which is everlasting.

Intention uses time wisely to realize your essence, and your soul purpose on earth. It does not seek for itself; rather it commits to giving for the sake of giving, and in so doing reminds you of your union. Simon fought long and hard for what he felt was true. He did not waste a second, nor have an idle moment in his quest. He lived, breathed, and dreamed of a return to peace, justice, freedom, and paradise. He held a vision that dreamed of the future Perfect Human, and perfected human society. This was his burning desire above all else, and was fueled by his actions and intent, which he repeated again and again.

Simon was living in the flow of Holy Law, which led him to join many political groups to serve his focused passion and intention. Living in this flow led him to Yeshua as the unfolding of his soul's process matured into Divine Will.

NEW HUMAN BEING

Simon is a bearer of evolution, the Apostle that Moses guided as the vehicle of the promise that man is made in the image of God, and that a new human being is the resulting creation of all the shifts in evolution that have occurred over many millions of years and are still occurring. This is what he reflected to Yeshua as Moses overlighted him.

It was to Simon that Yeshua said, "There are many who will come after me who will do greater works than I."

Evolution always takes the next step forward. On a personal scale, this is your next transformation, your next breakthrough, your deep realization and permanent shift of perspective. On a collective level this occurs when a new type of human being is created and manifested. On a cosmic level this is when new creations, stars, and galaxies are born that have never been birthed before.

Evolution occurs spontaneously when all the work you have done on yourself culminates in a big shift, and on the collective level when enough human beings have raised themselves out of the grips of the self-serving ego. Here, embrace and action are the basis for transcendence and the foundation of a new human society.

This new human being, the culmination of evolution and the next "moment" in the cosmic order of growth on earth, will arise when a unified field of consciousness is created in the morphogenetic fields of earth, altering our relationship with matter in order to birth a totally new species of human. This new species will be as different from humanity today as we are to the evolutions that have preceded us. This means becoming biologically different, genetically different, and discontinuous with the structures of present-day humanity, separating from the mass consciousness and from our own bloodlines, so we become genetically separate, unique, whole beings.

In practice this means that our mothers, fathers, daughters, and sons become genetically separate from us because our DNA changes. And this is a wonderful thing! This enables us to feel so much freer, open, more loving, and more joyous with them and all our bloodlines.

In this new species, it is not enough to just have an enlightened mind. The body, cellular structures, DNA, and subconscious have to be included too. In effect, everything has to be cleared out in order for the body to become light, for in each age, enlightenment expands and changes in its manifestation as the earth and its fields change, and evolution takes its next step.

The body and DNA, the subconscious and sexuality, the mass consciousness of humanity, and the fields surrounding the earth are all interconnected; and we are creating new fields for all of these as a collective every day. This is happening right now, and is increasing exponentially, day by day.

To recreate ourselves, and our planet, means we have to die to ourselves, and touch into new fields of consciousness that are discontinuous with the genetic and collective consciousness fields of present-day humanity. This is what Christ Yeshua meant when he said these times would be "the separating of the wheat from the chaff," for we have to separate from the old ways in order to be whole in this age.

This separation allows the process of evolution to continue, just as when a butterfly emerges out of its chrysalis it leaves its old skin behind. The cocoon was necessary to help birth the new form, but when the new form emerges, the dead skin is no longer necessary and is actually a burden to flight; the butterfly cannot fly with the chrysalis hanging on its wings.

These evolutionary steps are designed to create a new human being for all of humanity to share in; a new human being that is made in the image of God, and conscious of this, and can share this with many other beings.

For the nature of God Consciousness is the collected consciousness of humanity in unity. This is the challenge: to be whole and fully individualized yourself as a unique expression of God, and then be able to come together freely, and without selfish agenda, with others who are in their mastery also, to perform actions to evolve all. As Yeshua said, "They will be known by their actions."

PASSION

Passion is the force behind this evolutionary shift into the new human being, for passion is love put into action. Passion is life, identifying with the essential basic spark, the will to live, which is the will to share, to create; the beginning of life itself. This passion is when we seize life, when we want to be here and to be who we truly are. To be God means we become who we are in our own unique way, for God wants us to be individual aspects of the One, for that is how we can all fully enjoy what God is.

This passion is a will to being, a will to share being. It is the love that seeks the well- being and the full being of all. It is the action that springs from the deep core of our hearts, from where our hidden goodness arises and shows itself in our actions, sharing its joy with others in this dynamic manner.

This passion is an urgency to continue evolution, to grow it further so we can be more of who we truly are. The universe is expanding, as are we, constantly, in every moment. To align to this wave means we continually and perpetually redefine who we are in order to embrace and expand to the highest potential available in any moment.

Passion comes from love. It is the passion, and love for God, that leads you to do God's will. Love and passion becomes a force that when combined with humility and creativity becomes a force for total revolution. Evolution becomes the revolution.

It is purpose, passion, and love that fuels you, that burns inexhaustibly within you and pulls you through any and all things. Once you taste this possibility, faith deepens, and this in turn fuels it further. This passion can never be taken away; it is always there.

This is the passion, the conviction that deeply feels for the benefit of all beings, welling up from deep in the core of the heart to help all beings move forward. The passion for total revolution means we have to give up our timidity, our smallness, and be completely honest.

Passion arises when we love truth and will do whatever it takes to live, breathe, and share that more, for when we abandon ourselves to being an evolutionary agent, unlimited energy flows through us. This passion cannot be faked. It is the instant openness and willingness to embrace the highest potential in any moment, and to move that moment forward with others as a part of that embracing. It is the catalyst that sparks and ignites the slumbering in our comfort zones. It is the initiative to dare, to break boundaries, to ignore social mores and etiquette, to break new ground, and to break people into this new ground in the most direct way possible. It is the power of clarity that opens the pathway for evolution to occur, allied with the willingness for all to be equal, and to share their piece at any moment.

THE NEXT STEP

Deep Passion in its evolutionary expression is the urge to want to bring people together, for the basic pattern of evolution is to unite in order to create. Passion for evolution, for God, is what brings creative unions together. It is through passion that egos dissolve in creative free flow, connecting up the dots that unite disparate pieces of the global puzzle to form a cohesive unity where souls unite without egoic agendas, beliefs, and feelings of lack, threat, or inadequacy, dissolving boundaries to reveal and create the next step in evolution.

When people are Masters within themselves, or of a particular field of expertise, they have inner knowing and sublime confidence. Then they can delight in meeting and creating with other Masters to create something far greater than any of them alone could possibly ever imagine or achieve.

Here a master can take notes and make the tea if another is flowing with Divine creative outpouring at that moment, as they are all egoless and committed to the One that is flowing in the living field of energy created when "two or more are gathered in my name." Yet the level of light that any single group can bring into the world is limited only by the vision, and thoughts, held in the mind of each of its members.

Consciousness is evolving, and in that evolution is creating the foundations for an enlightened civilization. The whole of evolution now rests squarely on our shoulders, for we are evolution. Evolution today is this: the collective turning of the wheel of dharma, revealing the next octave of the unfolding cosmic order. Buddha, and Yeshua with the body of Christ, came here to do this in the past, and now it is our turn to do that as a collective.

To do this requires a real "thinking outside the box" approach, birthed out of the new moment or "out of the blue," something simple but radical that has never been done before, something that links the common threads we all share, regardless of caste, creed, religion, and cultural preferences and elevates this to a whole new octave. Here we have to experiment with the impossible in order to make it possible, by manifesting it through our own choice, our volunteering to work together as One.

God makes the world through the processes of evolution, as the impulse, the drive, and the passion to reach God. The evolutionary spark and process is reaching to become this image of God that has been planted within all of us. This evolution is the call for the absolute to be manifested in form; a call for the eternal, the infinite to be brought from the formless into form on earth. As Saint John says, "It is the time of the substance less coming into substance, and substance to become substanceless." Where form becomes emptiness, and emptiness becomes form, the ultimate or perfect wisdom. Here, God becomes embodied in us. This attraction, this passion, this love, is what makes evolution possible as a sustained reality, rather than just glimpses of what is, or what could be.

This is the promise of this age, and the pinnacle of evolution; to make time serve us, to use time wisely to extend and share the good, the holy, and the truthful, for time has been created for the purposes of evolution, to serve the evolutionary impulse to make man in the image of God. Just as this new human within itself is united in all its parts, whole within its own mandala of body-mind and spirit, so too will the evolutionary human community become one living, breathing, interconnected conscious organism, weaving a web of love, passion, concern, and creativity to birth a new being-ness.

Evolution manifests more God so that heaven can become earth in everyone's eyes.

Here the outside becomes a direct reflection of the inside, not just with spiritual eyes but in a palpable, felt, seen sense, where our inner unity and beauty directly manifests outside of us in the world. Both work together, as increasing levels of inner realization fuel the outer manifestation of that, and where the outer manifestation then further fuels the inner realization and will.

Beauty generates beauty. We become a conscious reflection and cocreator of the process.

Today, this can only happen through a collective union that is drawn together by a single all-attracting influence, a single beingness that we all share in that can bring us all together: love, and the passion that arises to enact this love.

Holy Law

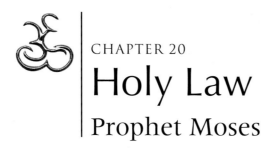

CHAPTER 20

Holy Law
Prophet Moses

Moses is the root of Holy Law, the holder of the timeless remembrance between God and man that we are made in God's image. This covenant was passed down from even more ancient lineages of the God-man, from Egypt and before to Moses.

Holy Law is the Divine Plan. Everything in creation and evolution happens to a design, and this design or code involves steps and transformations. It is the blueprint of what a human being, our planet, and our universe, is meant to be in its wholeness. The Divine Plan functions in order to lead all of us into our freedom, which is when man realizes he is made in the image of God.

This law has its own intelligence, direction, and way of progressing. We do not need to interfere with it, merely follow it. Letting go into the plan allows everything to unfold in its natural, easeful, and most beneficial way. By trying to interfere with it, we are only delaying our own unfolding, and our own highest potential.

This Natural Law of the Ages is how the universe is ceaselessly unfolding and expanding, just as the soul is ceaselessly unfolding. This law, this intelligence, is self-generating, in that it is always creating itself. It is not fixed and immutable, but is constantly and spontaneously revealing in each moment. Everything is the Divine Plan, no matter what we may think or feel we "choose." This plan is the pattern of creation.

To live in Holy Law is to live in our fullest potential and truth, our true body. This true body is a garment of light; the body of light, the body that is eternal and never dies, that spans all times and all places, that enables us to live the miracle and live in our fullness.

CODES OF LIGHT

The body of light is the part of us that lies beyond the body-mind, and that incarnates our soul from lifetime to lifetime. It is our formless double, the similitude of ourselves created out of pure eternal light. The work of the body of light culminates in our eventually becoming enlightened, when the body of light descends and merges with our physical body.

This merging happens through the vehicle of the body of light, the meeting point that allows body, soul, and spirit to merge. This face of God I am stretches all the way back to the creation of the Universe, and into a line of many Christs that also stretches into the infinite future. Moses grounded all these timelines into the now, utilizing all the dimensions and codes within his body of light to consciously ground the whole lineage.

Moses held these codes of light, codes hidden in Hebrew scriptures such as the *Zohar* and *Sefer Yetzirah,* as well as in the Christed Body of Light itself. These codes of sacred language were accessible through the science of gematria—rearranging letters, words, and their number values into patterns that reveal the Source of Creation, and how creation itself forms and dissolves. These patterns hold the basis of the transmutation of the formless into form, and the changing of elements such as fire into water.

All elements have their code, and each of these interlinking codes was known to Moses, who passed them on through his teachings, sacred language codes, and written works. However, it is only through gematria that these codes can be revealed and applied. They have not been applied on a mass scale yet as only a few Kabbalists in history have been graced to fully understand these codes of creation.

These codes are the knowledge that was taken away eons ago, that was in the hands of humans who could manipulate the patterns of existence to alter creation. Moses was given these codes hidden through sacred language to pass on to humanity, yet he saw that they were not yet ready to wield such power. Thus he hid them in the body of light, waiting for the right moment and the right people to wield them again and use them righteously.

Each of the letters or seed syllables in sacred language codes connect and create the holographic network of time and space. Seed syllables hold all forms in potential until they are supported, energized and expanded to flower out into full manifestation through love, wisdom, and power.

The human brain is this complex interacting network that efficiently conveys information from place to place. These seed hubs, as with the Internet, get messages out quickly and widely in this efficient manner.

Letters create words, words create thoughts, thoughts create ideas, and ideas shape and transform the world we live in, forming the basis of our senses, feelings, relationships, and perceptions. In essence, we cannot think without words, and words need an alphabet, a structure, to make them understandable.

In sacred cultures syllables or letters are resonating vibrations, collectively weaving together the underlying meaning of who we are and the constructs of our reality. The letter gematria codes, where each letter has a number, forms the torus spiral, or the world tree of creation.

Humans interpret higher, more fluid vibrations into the third dimension through the medium of letters and "sacred," or vibratory, calligraphy. They act as vibrating visual codes that are the human interface to the threads of vibration that create Life. All these threads of vibration are songs, for all songs have rhythm, meter, pitch, and precise pronunciation that when combined together reveal and connect the threads of an entire body of knowledge within the consciousness of the individual as a lived, felt experience.

Sacred language is the vibration that babies understand. It is not English or French or German; it is Hebrew, Sanskrit, Lemurian, and others. Therefore to decode Holy Law means we have to become as children to see the patterns that innocence and God is.

Children will reveal Holy Law and Moses's codes of creation, not a rabbi or a wise man, but a child living in love, the love that can transform creation, the love that is the illumination of all wisdom, the love that arises from the heart of the feminine and from joy. Yeshua and Magdalene fulfilled this prophecy through their bloodline, creating the space for the Indigo and Golden Children to arrive on earth.

This is evolution. As a law-giver, Moses created the foundation for Yeshua to fulfill his work and prophecies, work that Yeshua fulfilled and surpassed to create a new Law of Love. Love becomes the whole of the law, and the revelation of the greatest knowledge. Details, elaborate codes, and structures are a result of the flowing of love, a love that is ever-fresh and spontaneous for each and every moment.

Moses was overlighted by the Elohim, the creator gods. This collective of shining creators formed the template for the Adam Kadmon or Perfected Human Being through codes of light that they "breathed" into Moses's light body.

The formula of the God-man was encoded into our DNA from the very beginning of time. This formula cannot appear in the false matrix because it is encoded on waves that are at too high a speed. They jumble up and cannot be read. Yet the universe is the One Song, the song that pure intelligence plays to birth Life. People all over the world are slowly waking up to, and remembering, our ancient song, the ancient imprint of notes and melodies that birth us into existence.

No single person has all the pieces of the puzzle. This is what the Golden Age is for, to come together, unite, and remember the very formula of the greatest mystery ever lived.

THE SHADOW SIDE

We block Holy Law by being stuck in one view of reality. When we limit ourselves to just one view of reality, one channel on the TV set, we stay stuck at one frequency. When we are able to shift awareness to multiple channels at any moment, we become increasingly transparent, fluid, open, and available to the present moment.

It is no accident that the greatest discoveries in science have been made at these moments, from the discovery of the benzene molecule by August Kekulé, who fell asleep and saw its ring structure, to the sudden breakthrough on the nature of gravity by an apple hitting Newton's head. The breakthroughs happen when the planning, rational mind switches off, allowing revelation to occur.

When we feel we can direct reality by planning it to perfection, we augment our sense of the small limited self. We start to think that we know best and what our inner experience can and should lead to. In this regime there is no space allowed for an organic unfolding moment by moment, but rather a sense of fearful insecurity that makes us feel we can program our existence and direct it. When you become aware of the mystery of the pattern of you *not* directing the unfolding, then you can be transformed and opened to the moment. If you think you are making things happen, the self becomes stronger, asserting itself. When we can admit that we do not know, we are entering the highest form of wisdom.

Each situation changes, for love is fluid, as are ideas of good and bad in each fresh moment. To stay rigid, following a law when love may demand something else in that instant, is to become automatic, robotic, and dogmatic as a person and as a culture. One becomes an avoider of love's wishes, reacting rather than responding, having rote answers prescribed by another to fill the gap that they have within their own heart.

Following rules leads to the boxing in of love, the categorizing, judging, labeling of what love is, or should look like. This leads to the dying of love, the stranglehold of mind, the claiming of something that belongs to no one, and the arising of conflict and judgment. This is aptly demonstrated in the Middle East today.

In admitting we do not know, we can feel lost, confused, and in chaos. In remembering that we need do nothing and that evolution is about letting go rather than gaining anything, we realize all that we are is already present, surrounded by veils and illusions.

In not trusting the flow of Life, in not trusting we are held and supported, by trying to make things happen against the natural order of things, we get lost in the spirals of thought, belief, and expectation instead of accepting who we are in this moment.

The opposite of Holy Law and Divine Plan is making your own plan. Your ideas of who you are, how you should be, and what your inner life should look like all arise from pictures generated from the mind that may not necessarily serve you unfolding to your highest potential. These pictures may arise from wounds and ideas from the past, as they are geared toward the future and not the present unfolding. How can we plan our evolution? Are you all-seeing, all-knowing of all that is?

The moment we try to direct our inner process by thinking how we should feel, or comparing ourselves to how we think we should feel in relation to another, we act on the belief that we know what we are supposed to experience in the moment. Acceptance of whatever we are feeling in any moment, rather than judging it as being negative or positive, allows the truth to unfold organically.

When we try to change our experience, we assume that there is something else that should be happening. Observing what is actually happening step by step allows the planning mind to dissolve, and the unfolding process to occur.

Shadow of Evolution

The shadow side of evolution on earth is the ancient mind of humanity, the primal collective consciousness. This ancient mind is personified and mentioned in the Gnostic Gospels as the rulers of earth, the Aeons: huge demons that hook directly into the central nervous system and spine of most humans, feeding directly on your life force.

One can only be disconnected from them when you are ready to be unplugged from the "matrix" or the collective consciousness grids, when you are living in a state of joy and selfless, loving service as a way of life. When you leave the collective consciousness, you leave the ancient mind of fear that has governed humanity since the last golden age, and plug fully into the Christ Consciousness grids. When we are unplugged from the collective consciousness through a deep healing and fundamental rewiring, then we can leave this ancient mind behind.

When evolutionary urges are frustrated and blocked, anger emerges as a buildup of energies, often fueled by unconscious fear and wounding. Anger is actually an attempt to mobilize energies for dealing with perceived obstacles, but is often wrongly projected outward from a mistaken perception that our anger is caused by conditions or people outside of us. A key part of anger, and its projection, is the belief that one is a victim.

Anger may compel you to react rather than act intelligently. When repressed, it is a burning irritation, a constant feeling of being eaten up inside. Under all anger is unresolved fear. Sometimes it is better to express the anger, not to throw it out onto someone else, but to express your experience, your feelings, and take full responsibility for your emotions and actions. Remember, if it is happening under your skin, it is yours!

If this impulse is closed down or rationalized, a fundamental expression on a primordial level is blocked that then results in resentment and further anger at the denial of one's own truth and unique freedom of expression. This can lead to deep complications along the pathway, and a twisting of oneself into many knots of belief, blindness, and fear.

Greed

The other aspect to the shadow side is greed. Greed is consumption, always wanting more of what we like. This is centered on the idea of lack, of using something to fill up the hole and the hunger we feel inside.

Greed is the ignorance about the nature of time, and its right use, which is to evolve and extend the good, the holy, and the beautiful. If we truly understand that we have many lives, not just this one life, then time is infinite.

Greed is the opposite of passion; greed is getting for the separate self, whereas passion is sharing your joy and zest for life with others in order to create more evolution and more passion. It is a giving and a catalyzing, not a taking and hoarding for oneself to fill up the lack we feel within ourselves.

Greed comes into manifestation in the action man or woman, thirsting for experience, craving for it, being attached to action and getting things done. Ultimately greed becomes greed for knowledge, for power, for spiritual tools, teachings, and the latest teacher or technique. Greed becomes the obstacle for the seeker on the seeker's path, as the seeking itself becomes counterproductive after a point on the path. Greed always wants more instead of being content with what you have, which if you really look, is everything.

Are you happy to be alive? What is blocking that?

What do you really love?

What consumes you, strengthens the soul, and gives you reason, meaning, and purpose to continue?

What fires your passion to its greatest extent?

What is stopping you from living this?

Greed comes to a halt when we realize the simplicity of life, and the true importance of relationship, of love, of family, of friends, and of nature. By attuning to the opposite of what man's greed is for, one finds the antidote for greed: contentment and the simplicity of life. Greed is resolved by residing in silence and in your true nature that is always present.

Greed never allows us to be empty, to simply be, to receive the greatest things, and to become truly filled.

Listen to the One, and greed dissolves. Greed serves its purpose up to this point, by pushing us to acquire more until we are satiated and have experienced what we need to experience on our life's path. When this is done, when we have finished our experience of acquiring, getting, using, then we are ready for something else. To relax, be in the present moment, don't know anything, give, and follow Holy Law.

When this happens, we let go and allow Holy Law to direct us, entering into the unknown, beyond what we can know, plan, direct, or account for, letting go into the free-flowing movements of creation that births all things, and which flow through us constantly.

The Anchor

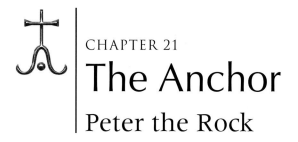

CHAPTER 21

The Anchor

Peter the Rock

I tell you that you are Peter, and on this rock I shall build my church, and the gates of Hades will not overpower it. I shall give you the keys of the sovereignty of heaven, and whatever you bind on earth will be bound in heaven, whatever you release on earth, will be released in heaven.

—Matthew 16:18

Yeshua made Peter the first pope of the Christ Lineage, the carrier of how the male aspect of the lineage was to continue in the world. He had specific Keys to spread Christ Consciousness into the awareness of the collective consciousness, and the power and authority in the world to do so.[1]

Peter holds the knowledge of the masculine side of the Christ Blueprint. In this strength, this reliability, this rock that is always immoveable, the pillar to always lean on and confide in, we can rest assured that all is well. This pillar anchors the acceptance of our fallible, human side. Yeshua knew this, and had faith in humanity, in the human side of people, in their innate goodness, despite their faults, to be caring, loving, and able to recognize love and act on it. He knew that this was what all humans want, above all else.

---

1. There are twelve people intimately associated with each Apostle and their quality in the world as part of that Apostle's soul group.

The rock upon which a Christ-oriented civilization is built is this simple heart that can recognize love, that does their best and lives a good life, who feels for, is kind to, and is there for others as a natural instinct, yet who struggles and has flaws. Peter represents the simple human side of us, the honorable masculine that is there for others no matter what, living in integrity, that would do anything for his loved ones, and is the pillar of strength that others can rely on and always come back to. Despite his flaws and naïveté, he was given Keys by Yeshua, who saw how love is understood most: through simple human values and the human touch.

Without these simple human values rooted in the earth, friendship, family values, and safety, the more transcendent or glamorous aspects of life can dissipate our vitality into a chaotic, ungrounded mess. Peter shows us that the human side is our greatest ally, and our greatest weakness. Yeshua shows that even the foolish and the cowardly can be friends with God, as well as the wise and holy. Indeed, it is the simple and foolish that will shame the wise and demonstrate to them the nature of love when the time comes.

If Peter can become the rock upon which Christ Consciousness is built, the simple soul doing what he can despite his flaws and weaknesses, then there is hope for us all. Yeshua felt that despite Peter's weaknesses, he could rely on him, as he saw this within him. How we manage to hold this space is through our innocence, our allowance of the unexpected, and our friendship with all of life. To be a friend with all life means we can talk to it, sing to it, communicate with it, and even argue with it. And life listens and responds.

Peter represents the aspiration to be more than what you are, and to be all that you can be. This is what makes us human, always open to growing, learning, and moving forward despite our mistakes and failings.

THE ANCHOR

Peter is the anchor of Christ: the servant, the action man spreading truth through any and all means. To anchor and ground something is to live and share it in all ways. To be grounded in Christ Consciousness takes all of qualities of the Christ Blueprint to be fluidly available at any time through action.

An anchor keeps objects in place, keeps things stable. It links heaven to earth through the human heart, securing and connecting one to the other. An anchor is the team member, Peter, responsible for the last leg in the race, taking the whole lineage to the finish line so it can land in the world and become grounded in all those thirsting for their freedom, their joy, their happiness.

To be grounded means we are engaged in relationship to all aspects of ourselves. Our passions, our visions, our soul get expressed, and we share this dynamically with the world rather than keep it to ourselves, or hold it just as a vision. Grounding means "doing" in the world. Grounding means we activate and create our Self-expression here and now, and share that with the collective consciousness. This could mean many things; we create a website, a book, or a new career, lifestyle, home environment, or relationship that complements our own evolutionary efforts so that we can manifest on earth in our full potential. Whatever it takes is what we have to do.

We all have Keys, like Peter, to ground Christ Consciousness. It is our responsibility now, not in some distant future, to enact this, to share it, and to grow it. For it is through our human vehicles, and our human inclinations, that we establish a Christed civilization on earth. It will not happen magically without our reaching out, without our extending out, in some way.

To be grounded is to move fluidly with all the forces of heaven and earth and not judge either one as more worthy than another. Meditating in bliss and paying the bills are both performed in a grounded perception of living the Divine. Having this as our ground, what we stand on, move in, and share leads to the uniting of heaven and earth. Being a friend to everyone, and sharing with them what they need to know in the way that they will understand, is grounded. Buying the groceries while sharing a moment of love with the grocer is grounded.

To be firm in knowledge, steady in mind, and clear in the memory of the truth is to be grounded in God. This firmness that is repeated through mind training and sealed into the memory through repetition and discipline allows the memory of the truth to resurface even in the times when we forget. This is a very masculine attribute. The mind is trained to remember and be reliable, something you can fall back on to assist you when you reach a situation where the mind is challenged.

HONOR

Peter embodies honor. Honor is best described by Yeshua as "the love that makes a man lay down his life for his friend." It is what King Arthur and the Round Table demonstrated: fighting for an ideal, for a cause, passionately, and without ceasing. This honor is a vital grounding aspect of love that never wavers, that never stops, that is felt deep in the noble heart. It is the quality that is known today as being "a man's man," full of integrity, masculine power, and strength.

The noble heart is a heart that always holds the highest potential, the grandest vision, and the deepest ideals as the truth. These deepest ideals are the foundation of an enlightened culture, built by men and women who may suffer scorn, failure, and ridicule, and be told to compromise by others, to fit into the world and its belief systems, but who never stray from what they know to be true.

This noble heart lives the truth that the world is one family. All peoples of the earth belong to each other, and *together* we share our triumphs and tragedies. You feel the others' suffering and tears and vow, deep in the heart, to do something in direct action about it, whatever it takes. Only by truly feeling this can effective and true action arise, by the heart being touched in alignment with the solar plexus deeply enough to act from this feeling directly.

Here, we move things forward, acting as a catalyst, putting love into action, working with others of like mind who share this feeling and vision and are ready to dynamically and wholeheartedly manifest this using their God-given gifts, resources, and talents to selflessly do so, despite the doubts and resistances of the world. This is compassion in direct, powerful action: love in dynamic and sometimes radical flow.

Peter is the honoring of the masculine side of ourselves. It listens to what the male side requires, and acts upon it. This masculine side is centered within Self, and needs nothing outside of itself to feel whole. This deep sense of centering, of immovability, of inner presence that is full and replete, gives to others as it needs nothing for itself. The rock arises when we are what we are without trying to be anything else. We stay with what we know to be true, and even if this is swayed, we learn and return to the essence of being a man: deep, centered, silent, organized, and everything else that means for us. We come to appreciate what we are more fully in this, and have this as a continuous thread in our life stream, a thread that becomes a constant source of Self.

The Sun

CHAPTER 22

The Sun
Lord Melchizedek

*Melchizedek is . . . without father, without mother, without descent,
having neither beginning of days, nor end of life, but made like
unto the Son of God.*

—Hebrews 7:3

One cannot understand Peter and why Yeshua placed so much trust in
him without understanding who Peter was guided by. Lord Melchizedek
is a guardian principle of the immortal Father, the Father of wisdom
and seeing. He first appears in modern history as the king-priest ruling
in Salem, today's Jerusalem. Melchizedek is the first model of Christ
Consciousness; his role is as a civilization builder, laying the foundations for Christ Consciousness as the "king of peace." He is the dynastic
head of a Godly civilization, and as such he was on earth long before
Yeshua, setting the foundations for the Egyptian and Atlantean mystery schools, and beyond that to the very creation of earth itself.

He has always held the foundation of Christ Consciousness, whose
aim it is to establish an enlightened civilization on earth. For Christ Consciousness is civilization-oriented, not just personal salvation–oriented;
it is for the benefit of all beings, for there can be no personal salvation
without collective salvation included within it as the true unfolding of
the One soul of love.

THE SUN

Or ain or
Or ain or
Or ain o

I am the sun. Gaze into me. Many millennia ago, I merged with what you call the sun, and through this portal I was able to tangibly connect my consciousness to many other stars, galaxies, and sentient planets in this universe and the next. In this process of merging with the sun, I anchored the solar power onto earth through human form.

To merge with the sun is to merge with the collective reflection of humanity, the collective transmission of humanity outward into the cosmos that is filtered through the sun, and which the sun reflects back to the earth, which then becomes purified through those beings whose role this is. One could call this process sacrifice, crucifixion, and resurrection.

Have the actions of Christ been done before on earth? Yes.

Will they be done again? Yes.

Are they happening right now? Yes.

There are many ways to purify the collective consciousness through your vehicle. Gaze into the sun every day. In this gazing, ask for its reflection, power, and light to be returned to you and purified through your vehicle, for the sun is the reflector and purifier of the feelings and thoughts of humanity, and a vehicle to bring the solar light down deep into your mind.

The One Sun, One Heart Practice

Create a triangle with both hands over your third eye.

Focus, and gaze just below the sun, allowing the light to penetrate into your third eye, for fifteen minutes at dawn or at twilight.

Breathe the energy down from this third eye–sun connection, down into the heart.

Open your shirt, and expose your chest to the sun. Hold the energy in your chest as you continue to breathe.

Feel the circuit between your third eye and heart. Allow the heat to expand.

Now visualize and create an infinity loop, a sideways figure eight, between your heart and the sun.

This loop is already there—you are just recognizing it, and further activating it.

Visualize the infinity loop as the same color as the sun, and send the loop out to the sun with each breath. The loop starts in the heart, with the sun as the opposite heart, another living being. It is like gazing upon the face of the Beloved, your soul mate.

Send the loop forth; it curls around the sun and comes back into your heart.

The two spheres connect through your breath.

After five minutes or more, turn this infinity loop down, with your breath, into the root, into your feet and the eighth chakra, down into earth, down into the spinning, hexagonal, crystal core of the earth. Send the loop down; it curls around the earth's core, rising up through the earth, and the feet, and comes back into your heart. The two loops connect through your breath.

So now you are breathing heart to heart with the core of the earth.

Focus on this breath; breathe into it. You are connecting the power of sun through your body to the earth's womb, living Gaia's core.

After a few minutes, relax and feel the difference in your body.

Thank the sun and the earth; touch the earth and relax.

Take up to thirty minutes every day to do this.

This is a remarkable and powerful practice, as you will discover. It makes you transparent to the energy of the sun, and ground's solar power into you, and the earth, as One. Do this practice first for seven days before the next practice.

A Practice for Christs

The next practice is to physically go to the most depressed, impoverished, crime ridden, sad area of the city or place where you live, on a sunny day. Go to this area in full faith; stand in this area and call forth through the practice, the power within your solar plexus, heart, and third-eye connection, and ask that you act as a magnet, a purifier through the sun, to whatever lies in this region of suffering, sickness, darkness, and death.

Do it only of you feel you can. It will give you a very good feeling-sense of what it is like to be Christ, not just in the idealized way that you may think Christ to be, but in the actual way that Christ and the twelve came here to do. It will give you an idea of what Christ did when he descended into hell with John the Baptist by his side, and the love that he shone forth.

Your Cornerstone

I am the sun. You are the sun. Using the sun's power, heat, light, and love through your whole vehicle renders you transparent, renders your vehicle fluid and open. If you do these practices well, it will almost feel like you have no body, for you are carving open a conduit for solar power to *be* who you are. These practices can lead to a full merging into the sun.

As Thomas says, "the cornerstone that the builders of this world throw away: that is what I will use to build my house." This is similar to you, your life. The cornerstone, the thing you are throwing away, overlooking, that you cast aside, is the very thing that will lead you to your salvation, the very thing that is the foundation of your soul life. Ask yourself: what are you overlooking? What do you have right now that you shove to one side or marginalize as less important, less worthy, less necessary than all the other things in your life right now? There is a huge Key in this for you. The very thing you make small is the foundation of your life in Christ Consciousness. Such as it is for you, so it is for humanity. The very thing humanity is overlooking *is* the foundation for a new society.

The first shall be last. And the last will be the first. This is why I am the completion of the path, and the guardian of the Christ Council. I was the first; now I come at the end times to complete the circle. I complete the path for all those who have dared to set foot on the path of awakening, and dissolving, into love.

Or ain amer or.

THE ORDER OF MELCHIZEDEK

Christ's priesthood is declared by God to be "after the Order of Melchizedek."[1] Paul justifies Yeshua's priesthood on the grounds that it is like that of Melchizedek.[2] The Order of Melchizedek priests came before Yeshua, which he was then given the Keys to in order to reestablish Christ Consciousness for this age on earth through any and all means appropriate.

When Christ took on human form, and experienced the trials of a man, he attained the status of high priest of the Order of Melchizedek. Melchizedek comes before Christ in the Messianic Lineage, and Yeshua had to suffer his trials before he was seen fit to enter into the priesthood of Melchizedek. "Although he was a Son, he learned obedience

---

1. Psalm 110; Hebrews 5–7.
2. Hebrews 5–7.

through what he suffered; and being made perfect he became the source of eternal salvation to all who obey him, being designated by God a high priest after the order of Melchizedek."

The Order of Melchizedek is one of the longest-running priesthoods on earth, stretching back to the first Christ-conscious civilizations on earth, and is composed of highly evolved beings who have dedicated themselves to the benefit of humanity wherever and whenever that is possible.

This priesthood is not conferred by any earthly authority but directly from the Holy Spirit and Melchizedek. Certain men and women have been called to this priesthood before the beginning of the world and are, by nature, true priests "according to the Order of Melchizedek." The feminine equivalent is the Order of Magdalene.

Like Melchizedek himself, the priests and priestesses of the order are intermediaries between Christ and humanity. The priest is a representative of the Christ, and his or her service is to act as servant and builder of a Christ-conscious civilization. They may not be known as priests or reverends, but their actions show they are here to help.

Yeshua gave Peter Keys to the kingdom, for Yeshua had been given them by Melchizedek before him, which he then renewed to bring fresh life to the Melchizedek priesthood. This is why Yeshua made Peter the rock of the church, because he was the link in the chain of the Melchizedek priesthood that was the foundation of Christ Consciousness on earth. It had been secured so that "Hades will not overpower it."

The Melchizedek Priesthood is eternal. Once a person has been ordained, their priesthood cannot be revoked but continues from incarnation to incarnation. The priest is a priest by virtue of what they are and what they have attained in this and past lifetimes. Any priest in the Order of Melchizedek feels humanity's suffering in their heart, and their fulfillment lies in the service and transformation of humanity as a whole. Being initiated into the various stages of the Order of Melchizedek gives a connection with the oldest solar initiate on earth, Melchizedek himself, and leads to more and more gifts being given through you to transform humanity.

Melchizedek gave Yeshua confirmation that the father on earth was now seeing and recognizing him as the Son of God. For Melchizedek is the name of the high priest of the Lineage of Christ, and Yeshua is this high priest. In essence, they are one and the same. And this is a potential that Peter held also.

Melchizedek's aim is to bring people together in Oneness as the foundation for an enlightened society. He fosters communication and encourages the sharing of our own unique talents to benefit the whole in a round table, where a circle is formed without feelings of superiority or inferiority. It is through this principle of an enlightened society that we recognize the common source of our own humanity, and can celebrate it with others in joy, enabling us as a collective to consciously link together in the eternal patterns of creation.

Bringing this principle into the physical, the principle of Oneness in many bodies communing together, is a gift of Melchizedek. As the new paradigm begins, Melchizedek reveals more and more in order to share the original Keys of love, and the technologies of light to humanity. He also shows that Yeshua was one of many Christ-conscious beings, and that we have the capacity to be like this also.

THE SHADOW SIDE

Peter exemplifies the inner battle that we all feel at different times in our lives—the inner fight between human and Divine. His human side, like all of us, could be confused, doubtful, and plain ignorant. Yet this is a parable to us all. Nobody is perfect, and we all have our foibles, our weaknesses. This is also what makes us human. Knowing yourself entails this as well.

The human side is what anchors Christ Consciousness. Acknowledging this allows us to join and work with others freely and as a family, not in isolation or aloofness masquerading as Oneness. When we all work together as One being in many bodies with the same purpose, we share and extend all that is good and beautiful.

The second aspect of the shadow side of Peter is reluctance to let go. The sense of duty that arrives through the father's principle is both noble and ignoble. Duty, service, and leadership become excuses for not including the feminine aspects of rest and receptivity. "He maketh me lie down in green pastures," as Psalm 23 says.

The Father

The father needs to recognize his role as supporter, as the rock, the pillar, the one you can rely on both internally and externally when the world comes crashing down. This also entails fluidity, gentleness, and humility. It is when a father's knowledge clamps down on his child, when a father tells a son or daughter what to do, instead of listening and responding to their needs, that control happens. To embody the father for a woman is to be both detached and caring. Instead of looking on the outside for the father, seeking approval or love, one looks inside to find one's own protector, comforter, caregiver, and power.

The reliable one who always gives unconditionally to you is within you, the one who is always looking out for your best interests is within you, the one who asks for nothing in providing you with everything is also within you, seeking to be called upon, used in action, and integrated.

A woman's lack of self-worth can also, in many instances, stem from this hole of a father figure. The father is God to his daughter; so if there is lack of care, recognition, attention, or love, the daughter feels she has not done something right, and tries to make up for it. She tries to make her father see her, approve of her, and love her. The daughter, or inner female, feels she has nothing of value, and feels unworthy. When she is not received, she starts to feel unworthy of even God's love, and starts to seek for this approval or recognition through a substitute father, authority, or guru figures in sexual relationships, and through exhibitionism of various kinds. This is a huge problem on this planet.

The solution is to look at what is filling up the hole for *you*. Look at your relationships with father figures, which we all have, but which you may have out of balance. Ask how they make you feel, what conflicts arise, what you need from them. When one starts to embody the father within, one becomes more spacious and witnessing of emotions, and is able to manifest more, able to land more on earth. One is no longer scared to be here, and one feels worthy and able to contribute fully.

Being Strong

Peter, like Thomas and Judas, stood more by himself, resolutely doing his duty and fulfilling his part of the Blueprint. This rock aspect shows the brave, invulnerable face that others can rely on and trust to be there, that is always immoveable. This responsibility to be strong for everyone can stop you from being open, vulnerable, and human. You can become frozen, no longer flowing with your feelings, becoming isolated, alone, and trapped in your role. Having to put on a certain face to keep things going can lead us into stagnation and lack of self-love.

Here, if we cry and express our weakness or vulnerability, we feel that others will feel scared, no longer having a rock to lean on, and we feel we have neglected our responsibility to others, to God, by dropping our facade of invulnerability. Here, we take responsibility for others also, denying them their lessons for growth and empowerment, rather than taking full responsibility for ourselves and our own feelings. We draw a subtle boundary line around ourselves, saying this is what I am, and this is what I am not—creating a separation. We cease to treat others equally as we feel we need to be an example for them, and we subtly place ourselves apart from others.

This creates a subtle separation, a subtle placing of yourself onto a pedestal, which then leads to resentment, as those placing you on a pedestal will try to knock you down eventually. This is because they are also separating from themselves in this action, and not fully venerating their own selves, projecting it outside, as often that is the easiest thing to do for many people, rather than to own it themselves.

Friendship with the human side means we share our good times and bad times with others. We open up and express our vulnerabilities, our loneliness, releasing our secret burdens of having to be there for others, without including all of our own selves. Humans bond through sharing the common thread of *all* that we experience, and we all come together in this sharing and empathy to form one common thread that cares for and loves each other.

When we cease to flow and embrace life, in order to be the pillar of strength that everyone and everything depends on, we lose a part of ourselves. Crying, being gentle with ourselves, and dropping deep into the vulnerable heart allows the rocklike confidence and attitude of "I don't need anyone, as I have it all" to become seen as "there is no one here for me, and I am alone."

To break this pattern is to commune, and be open to, all human beings. Yeshua himself did this, as he learned from everyone in the human experience. So go out now and share your time being present with another that you would not normally spend time with. This could be a beggar, a rampant materialist, someone you know you do not get on with, while at the same time being who you are, without having to teach or heal them. Enjoy, and have fun with it.

The Feminine

The leaving-out of the feminine side is the shadow of Peter. This feminine side provides us with great strength allied with sensitivity that is fluid and accepting of all. Peter asks us all to honor the masculine, to be the pillar of Self that needs nothing outside of itself. The male is Self-contained, needing no relationship in its essence, while the feminine is all about relationship and interconnection.

This polarity is reflected in the sparring between Peter and Magdalene two thousand years ago, and their mutual distrust of each other. Both have Keys to share, yet both never really understood each other. Both have to reconcile, trust, recognize, and honor the other for what they do, who they are, and what Yeshua left with each of them. Mary, an aspect of the feminine Christ, did not trust Peter, and held back, protecting her Keys from him. Peter did not understand her, and therefore refused to give her authority or power in the world. This game has continued for thousands of years in the collective consciousness, which is a symptom of why feminine teachings have been buried and have not been revealed to the general public.

Today, Peter is the midwife for Magdalene's birthing, whereas before Magdalene he was the midwife for Yeshua's birthing. The mirror has turned, and the Keys that Yeshua left them both can now be activated, as the male authority to activate things in public awareness can now be used to serve the feminine understanding of love and life.

In observing the strength of the feminine, of the flowing life force, men can evolve and deepen into their true nature. The masculine expression of love alone is not strong enough to withstand the pressures of the outside world; only the softer, yet stronger feminine love can do this.

Lack of empathy, softness, and kindness can make us close off into our shell of service, working hard in the masculine to make up for the relaxing into the feminine. Trusting the feminine instead of battling with it allows us to live a flowing lifestyle where the feminine qualities of feeling and sharing nonverbally and emotionally are equally balanced with the active doing qualities of the masculine.

These imbalances of yin and yang, of power and direction versus receptivity and rest, are the hallmark of modern culture. We are driven by a Peter culture, of yang, of achieving, of doing, of productivity, of "sharing the gospel," celebrating our busyness and how great and productive we are in our doing. We measure our sense of self-worth, or how little self-worth we have, through how busy we are and how much we can do. As a whole, inaction is seen as weak and ineffective in getting ahead with our lives.

This leads to self-destruction and depletion, for yang is limited. It needs constant replenishing by being harmonized with yin, which regenerates, restores, and fortifies it. Imbalance is destructive on a body-mind level as well as being destructive on a global level with the destruction of the environment, war, and conflict. Yin would never initiate a war or sustain one; only yang versus yang can create that, and yin would never deplete itself through outward action, as its innate nature is rest and receptivity.

It is yin that allows space and time in our schedules to be empty and spacious, not needing to fill in the gaps in our busy lives, because it is fulfilled within itself. Rest allows the right activity that will most benefit you and others to arise. Without this, we enter imbalance, where more and more stress related illnesses arise, as the body-mind is not built to remain in yang spaces for long periods of time. Thus we remain depleted and stressed. The rock then becomes stuck and inflexible, caught in its own thought structures and ways of being that do not allow itself to be challenged or rest in the feminine. The body-mind *is* built to remain in harmony between yin and yang for indefinite periods of time. We can do this by spending more time doing nothing, resting, and relaxing in a yin way.

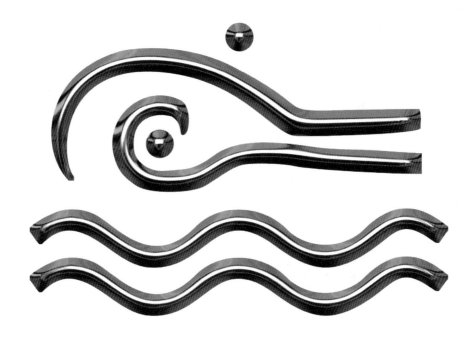

The Witness

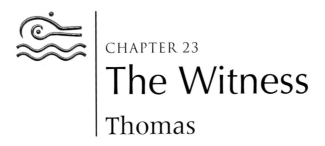

CHAPTER 23

The Witness

Thomas

Yeshua said, "Let thine eye be single and thy body full of light."

I am not the body
I am not the mind
I am not the emotions

There is but One Incarnation
There is but One being

What can I say of male or female,
This and that, right and wrong?

What can I say of relationship?
Mother father brother sister; all are not mine
Void and world are one

I have neither need nor lack of need
I have neither hope nor no hope
I have neither family nor friends
Yet all beings are my family and friends

There is neither a self nor is there not a self.
There is neither a you, me, a superior being, a teacher, or student.
I am the unchanging Self, the same in everyone.

One cannot even speak of something separate from the Self
How can there be two in the One?
One cannot speak of what does not exist
How then can I speak of similar, or dissimilar?

I have never been formless, or with form
I have never had a beginning or end

This is the peace that lies beyond understanding
The stillness where all understanding arises from
Here, everything is eternal
Everything is consciousness

Aham Purushottam ekam evam sarvam Om

Thomas was the Apostle for India, sent there by Yeshua as his natural character and disposition was most suited to the nondual teachings of Oneness. These teachings for him were centered on Purusha: limitless, universal essence, not subject to nature, nurture, relationship, and polarity—a totally detached witnessing of light and presence.

Purusha is seen in the Indian tradition that Yeshua was so much a part of as a cosmic man straddling and encompassing the entire cosmos: a Christ figure. When we forget this essence, when we identify with limits and with the body-mind, we suffer from grasping, fear, and attachment. We can lose ourselves, identifying with the appearance rather than the presence that underlies all appearance.

However, nature, the material world, the body-mind impulses, and the experiences it offers (known as the feminine Prakriti) provide Purusha with the enjoyment and delights of the world; Purusha enjoys the world through Prakriti. Prakriti is the temporal hologram presenting Purusha with experiences blissful and painful that are played over and over, lifetime to lifetime, until Purusha remembers the rules of the game (the Divine Play or Lila).

Purusha then realizes that, confused and deluded, he has mistakenly identified his consciousness with Prakriti's activity. He remembers and regains his true nature, which initiates a return to the first level of enlightenment.

This realization is the result of Purusha's power to separate the real from the unreal, and to stand alone, all-one. To do this, he withdraws from Prakriti, realizing he is pure and can never be affected by the swirling, ever-moving desires and raw material for experience that Prakriti is, by polarities such as good and bad, pleasure or pain, as he lies beyond the pairs of opposites in what is never created, never destroyed or affected.

When this happens, Prakriti becomes redundant, for her reason for existing has been to provide experiences for Purusha so that after enjoying the world he may, through discriminative knowledge, return to his original state. When Purusha recognizes Prakriti in this way, he loses interest in her, like a dancer who, having performed, leaves the stage. He enters the light of freedom, but not complete freedom.

WHAT IS THE WITNESS?

Thomas embodied Purusha through the Witness. Witness keeps one detached from the body-mind, and thereby allows the highest outcome and action without personal attachment or agenda to manifest. Thomas's position as Witness allowed him to calibrate the consciousness of the group mind of the twelve, just by the very fact of him bearing in mind certain questions in relationship to all he silently observed, allowed the navigation of the Christ Blueprint into manifestation.

Witnessing is detached awareness of the whole playing field of consciousness and all its movements. Your thoughts, feelings, words, and actions may be a part of the event, but it does not affect you. In this context, Thomas saw the underlying interplay of energies in the Christ Mind, and its energetic infrastructure or geometry. This then enabled him to synthesize these interconnections through complete detachment, while simultaneously seeing the inherent unity of each unique aspect of Christ Consciousness.

The Witness sees that who you think you are is nothing but a set of personalities, arising and disappearing so quickly that you cannot see it when under the influence of your thoughts and emotions. The Witness innately *knows* that it is not any of these continual processes. In this instance, the Witness that Thomas is "saw" the perfection of the Christ Blueprint, and this act of observation allowed it to manifest fully on earth.

The Witness prefers nothing. To prefer one thing over another, be it people, organizations, or countries, is to value life in subjective patterns that consist of the ego's need to belong, to feel special, to feel needed or validated, driving it to search constantly for love on the surface that offers a transient, illusory sense of intimacy, rather than the essence behind the surface.

Whether there are forms or no forms to cling to, essence remains the same.

The Witness does not emphasize one over another, comparing or contrasting. The Witness is all-inclusive, so aware of the unity that it does not prefer this or that; everything is equally acceptable. The Witness gives detached observation as the way out of the personal perspective, yet this can only become real in your experience if you no longer give credence, time, and energy to the personal perspective, needs, desires, and the idea of a separate, personal life. With the willingness to surrender, let go, and expose this perspective, the Witness becomes more obvious, gently pointing a way to the eternal.

Witnessing the choices, thoughts, and statements that you make in your daily life, and the subtle judgments that come with them, can be gently corrected through forgiveness. Forgiving creates the spaciousness for the One to reveal and manifest itself. You bless your creations, and set them free. By watching what you create, you also watch its potential dissolution. In watching both these movements, you enter eternity.

The body becomes something you no longer possess. The thoughts that you hold become meaningless, as you watch them drift by like clouds in the blue sky, without attaching any meaning, any value, any going toward the thought, or any pushing away of the thought. There is neither gain nor loss. This mind is a blank canvas, an empty page. Here you, as you thought yourself to be, have never truly existed.

Everything is a neutral event. What you observe around you is neutral, until you make a decision as to what it will mean for you. This decision allows you to stand back and see this mental process, of naming and defining what values and associations are true for you for that object or person. Witnessing this allows you to let go of what you think, allowing you to be present, rather than what you thought was present.

In Witness consciousness, one actually observes the movements, actions, thoughts, and feelings that the "I" has without involvement. It is pure detachment from any sense of self, dispassionately observing all that the body-mind thinks, does, or sees. The idea of "you" is removed from your ideas, attachments, and judgments about what reality is, which colors the surface of our perceptions.

The Gateway

The Witness is the gateway, the portal, to oneness. The Witness sees the big picture like an eagle, without judging, categorizing, labeling, separating, and placing people or events in boxes. The Witness leads into the underlying unity of all that is, and is in itself not separate from the dynamic ever-flowing ocean of movement that creation is, but is rather an integrated part of this flow, arising when necessary.

The Witness is clear perception without any personal distortion, leading to an all-inclusive seeing, a gateway to Christ Consciousness. As Yeshua said, "before you remove the speck out of your brother's eye, remove the log out of your own."

You can experience this. Try this practice with a friend whom you feel open with. Sit quietly, center yourself, and follow your breath. Open your eyes, the windows to the soul, and truly gaze at your friend, eye to eye: you will see, as you do every day, that they have a form, a body. Keep gazing, and you will see them blurring, becoming indistinct, a mass of colors, shapes, and gently vibrating patterns. As you keep gazing and concentrating, you will eventually come to see that he or she is a blank canvas, an empty space, not even "existing" as you would perceive "existing." They disappear completely into emptiness.

Witnessing this, what is already and always here, allows one the direct perception of reality behind the dream of form, of matter, of appearance. When one experiences this, and literally sees another person or object dissolve, how real can this body-mind, this reality, be?

The Dream

The Witness sees the dream. The dream of life is a group of images generated by perception, with a lot of emotional associations. Everything and everyone in your dream is an expression of the symbols and images your own nature is dreaming up: your own reflections. As soon as you identify with this dream figure, the body-mind, then it identifies with the images within the dream.[1]

The dream is the veil. And the key to the dream is not to judge the dream as good or bad; the key is to come to the observer, the dreamer, the witness state, and to see it as a dream.

The Witness is the Key to extract yourself from the dream of the

---

1. David Hoffmeister.

body, thoughts, and feelings being the only reality. It lifts you out of this suffering, of being identified with this perception, and allows you to realize you are not trapped in this dream.

The dream dissolves when one knows that they are dreaming. Think how happy, how free, how defenseless you could be if you were watching this dream, with monsters, or a whole army coming at you, and you are in the back, in the position of dreaming, so you know you are dreaming. And what does it mean to know you are dreaming? It is to know that what you are watching is not real.

And therefore the Witness knows that it cannot be harmed. No matter what the content of the dream is, the observer knows that it is not affected by it. You are the dreamer who is imagining everything, and everyone, in this dream. We appear to be many individuals in the dream, yet as separate individuals we are all expressions of one awareness that is dreaming itself to be everyone and everything.

In this understanding, there are no believers and nonbelievers, no enlightened ones or ignorant ones. In the Witness, everything and everyone is lit up, because everything is unified. The Witness sees the dream as designed to make you more conscious; the more you wake up, the more you become conscious that life is like a dream. Knowing this is the secret of enjoying the dream.

This leads to peace. Peace arises when we surrender unconditionally to the dream of the dreamer. Peace is the hallmark of the witness state, the gateway into genuine, permanent states of enlightenment. A quality of inner silence becomes permanent, present in the midst of all activity. There is no longer a dependency on external states, and no anguish at what comes and goes. There is no longer a sense of anxious striving, or need to get. Blame and praise are felt as equal and inconsequential, and the fear of death, of the body-mind perishing, dissolves. The body becomes an empty tool and vessel for the actions of your true Self to flow through.

The Regenerator

CHAPTER 24
The Regenerator
Babaji

Babaji is the guiding force behind Thomas. By witnessing your thought processes, you can lead yourself into love's dissolution, and regenerate yourself.

Babaji is an incarnation of Lord Shiva, the dancer and dissolver of illusion through love. His dance is the apocalypse of love, melting, burning, purifying, and separating gold from fool's gold, separating the glitter from substance, truth from illusion, soul awareness from ego. His dance is what transmutes poison into clarity, regenerating through the portal of death into the softness and power of loving awareness, found deep in the ocean of bliss.

In the Christ Blueprint, Lord Babaji holds the gateway into love's dissolution allowing regeneration to occur. This dissolution can be as easy or as hard as you wish to make it, depending on how much you are to willingly inquire into, swallow, and transmute the poison of your own discontent, of your own neurosis, of your own habits. How humble can you be to swallow and transmute your poisons?

There are many poisons in the body created over many lifetimes. These are very real biochemical substances that accumulate through suffering, fear, anger, and being a "victim" of life's experiences. There comes a time when we all have to experience these poisons and eject them from our systems. When this happens through Grace, through initiation, through spiritual fire, trial, test, and tribulation, this is the action of Shiva Babaji.

These poisons can manifest for clearing in many ways; through attacks of nausea and sickness, and also through traumatic experiences, accidents, or the abrupt wrenching of our physical-emotional-mental-spiritual bodies. As more light and love comes through, these bodies can be ripped apart to accelerate our openings.

This occurs through our willingness, our commitment and dedication to trample on our illusions. Once we have, then our task is to willingly transmute others' poisons and negativities through our clear and transparent vehicle. We become transmuters for others.

POWER OF REGENERATION

Babaji is the power of Shiva, the destroyer of ignorance and the regenerator of loving awareness. Babaji gathered into his physical form all the negativity and darkness of the karma, pain, sadness, and fear of all his students around him. He drew it from those who worshipped and loved him, and then transmuted it for them, handing them back the nectar and lightness of liberation. These were some of the most painful moments in the lives of his students, but some of the most rewarding also.

Yeshua was one of Babaji's students. Babaji initiated Yeshua to help him in his Divine mission, to do his task for the collective of humanity in the three days between the Crucifixion and the Resurrection. In these three days, Yeshua drew all the negative energy of the world into himself, both from the Crucifixion and his baptism by John the Baptist, which passed on the sins of the world to him, so that at the point of his death he could travel into the darkness of the hell realms, carrying with him the light of Christ.

Christ Consciousness entered, for the first time, the darkest part of creation, the lowest dimensional spaces of trapped matter identified with being only the body-mind. These spaces of guilt, of insidious darkness and shame are the lowest frequencies, the heaviest burden, the seemingly insurmountable barriers.

Yeshua's action showed those souls living in this deepest darkness that they could be forgiven, that the Divine did not judge, that they could be set free by having the vision that they created their experience of life through their own perceptions. It allowed them hope, it created a pathway born out of Divine power and love for them to find a way out of hell, reassuring us that the presence of love is in all places, at all times. In the darkest, deepest parts of humanity's self-created hell there is no point when we cannot be close to the presence of love. Love is in every program, in every part of consciousness. Even now, in Satan's eyes, Christ abides.

Many Masters since Christ have done this action, have descended into great ignorance, plunged into hell on humanity's behalf in order to pave a way for humanity's redemption. This is the essence of the Bodhisattva Vow, and its result: the birthing of the Golden Children and the establishment of the Christ Grids, which were reactivated by Yeshua's actions.

Lord Babaji has taken on many forms in many lifetimes. In Babaji's understanding, bliss and joy is the foundation of all experience. Love conceals this until you are ready to withstand the regenerative power of pure consciousness, until you are soft enough, open enough, and strong enough to be in this experience, which is the annulment of all experience.

We die; we resurrect. The only question you need to ask yourself is, how am I going to resurrect? Are you going to go through all the pain, all the suffering of dying, just to be reborn into the same patterns, attachments, and judgments of the limited ego? Or will you resurrect into the vastness of love? Are you going to allow the dance of love to occur? Are you willing to be trampled by the dance that love is?

Ask yourself how you are going to be born again, through which chakra and what action, right now. How are you going to manifest yourself?

LOVE AS REGENERATOR

Love allows continual creating to occur; it is constantly renewing itself, regenerating itself, perpetually creating new forms and new experiences, that on the surface appear different, but when one reaches their essence through the dance, are experienced as bliss. Love is the ultimate dissolver and regenerator. Power is used in service of love, but it is love that it leads to, for it is love that births power. One can do whatever they will if they allow this to be the ground of their life.

When we truly tap into this power, this link in the chain of flawless, Self-generating consciousness, all the other links become unified. Everything else is revealed, and it no longer conceals from us. We are given the power to create and sustain, with an invincible foundation that is governed under natural and universal law.

This link of dissolution stands in the middle of this chain of perpetual creation, of movement that leads into no movement. Here, love vibrates within the stillness, gently undulating, shimmering. When we still ourselves though love, we vibrate into the vibration of all that is. When we are vibrating in this silence that lies at the heart of all that is, we are able to contract and expand simultaneously. This paradox allows us to be inside, and outside at the same time. Which is what Yeshua meant when he proclaimed, "when you are neither inside nor outside, male or female, then you shall enter the Kingdom."

In this, we realize that we are the creative pulse of all life, the throb of life vibrating that guides us to be perpetually regenerated and whole within our own Self.

Babaji is a dissolver of what you have manifested through acts of ill will and ignorance of the nature of love. We do many things that we think or even feel are loving, are creative, are productive, are helpful, and serve others, and while these are all noble intentions, the road to hell is paved with such intentions.

Love sometimes need not act, and sometimes it does. Love dissolves as much as it creates. How easy it is for us to accept this dissolution; it allows us equally to regenerate into who we truly are.

DISSOLVING THROUGH LOVE

In this dance we come to see the true nature of ignorance, and the true play of creation. This is delight. In the suffering that is caused by the dissolution of the ego mind and the separation of the ego from the soul, in that moment, in that spark, in that opening, in that gap between veils, lies the power of the love that dissolves, the love that regenerates. In this moment, we become aware of love in action.

If you allow these moments to occur, then you can consciously recreate yourself in love's image. In these naked moments, one can choose to enter awareness, or one can choose the mirror that creates a vicious cycle. In these moments, in your relationships, in your meditations, in your interactions with the life force, one can enter and choose this unconditional love that serves to dissolve all that is not love.

We do this through conscious action. Choosing these moments spontaneously, one enters vast open arenas in which evolution is accelerated. It is like going from a small playground to an infinite playground.

Dissolving through love requires vulnerability, awareness, humility, and stillness. When all these qualities are present in a dynamic and spontaneous moment, then openings can occur consciously to regenerate our own Self in the image of God. This is vigilance, staying open to these moments, and acting, or not acting, in these moments, depending on what is necessary in the present.

Being aware that there is duality present in the moment can lead to a choice to dissolve that duality through a remembrance and expression of unity, be it in your own meditation, in relationship, or with a group of friends. You have the power in the moment to dissolve through love, regenerate yourself, and birth into infinite possibilities that which lies within the cracks, the gaps.

Duality in this sense is an artful reminder of how we can be more whole, more conscious, more able to use the dissolving aspect to regenerate ourselves. For love is always unfolding in every moment; we can choose to align with this perpetual unfolding, like a flower continually opening. The petals never stop opening, and in each opening lies another possibility of creating, and dissolving, through love.

When we are reminded of duality, we are reminded of our own innate nature of unity. Duality becomes our greatest ally, our greatest friend, in serving to show us the moments when we are not aligned to love, and then using the dissolving action of love to realign ourselves. Duality becomes the ultimate tool for remembering who we are, and serving others to become aware of their own spontaneous moments of love's opening.

All of this is always present, and it is through relationship and interaction that the possibilities for this transformation lie most readily apparent and easily accessible. Yeshua used this understanding extensively throughout his ministry. If we truly follow these openings, these dynamic moments, if we truly follow them to their full unfolding, then we too can embody Christ in any moment.

Om Babaji Om.

THE SHADOW SIDE

The shadow side of Thomas is detachment without true engagement, emotional coldness, staying stuck at a certain degree of enlightenment without fully including the feminine, losing oneself in an idea of oneness rather than engaging with life, and too much introspection.

Thomas never became particularly close to anybody in order to fulfill his mission of witnessing the Christ Blueprint, and serving to cocreate it through this observation as a form of participation. Thomas was very private, valuing his solitude, resenting intrusions into his world and his mission. Even if confronted, he remained quiet, appearing to agree while retaining his own viewpoint. He accommodated everyone, going along with what was suggested, while simultaneously doing whatever he felt to be true. He agreed to everything and did not outwardly disagree, as he did not want to create waves or stir trouble, as that would disrupt his inner world. When conflict arose around him he would avoid engagement, and sink deeper into his inner world.

Humanity

He left his human self out of the joy and juice of life. This eventually leads to a deep sense of disconnection and separation, which then manifests as a lack of vitality, dynamism, and joy. In staying stuck as the Witness rather than being fluid, we witness everything, including our own life. This leads to holding back from holy desire, expressing it fleetingly, rather than moving with it. The positive aspect of this is that Thomas then directed this energy into his work of fulfilling his roles as the Witness and as scribe, leading to his partial Self-realization.

When one's whole life is dedicated to observing a cosmic drama being played out on a stage right in front of you as part of your soul purpose, there is going to be a sacrifice on the human side: not actively participating in living life to its fullness of expression and feeling. Thomas's fear of engaging and involving himself too much with the play, detaching himself from the direct experience, also isolated parts of him from himself, as well as from others.

This isolation of different parts of himself resulted in him living a lot in the mind, out of touch with others, yet also in touch with Holy Spirit in this, as it is the Holy Spirit that was guiding his actions as a mystic, lived experience. This prevented him from becoming too intellectual, dry, and cut off from Divine experience. However, this is not the case for many attempting to live in the Witness experience today.

Knowledge to Thomas was vital as the Key to fulfill himself and his mission, as seen in his Gospel. In his work, analyzing, observing, and synthesizing all that was presented to him was the Key to unlock the deeper faculties of intuition, insight, and understanding. Yet the aloofness that can arise from this is also tinged with arrogance and disdain for others, who know not what you know. His knowledge and detachment was a source of safety for him.

Relationship and the Feminine

The fear of being engaged in relationship, and his quality of nonattachment, also meant that Thomas never got seriously involved with a woman, as the energy and engagement required of intimacy meant that he would have had to surrender his Witness world. Relationship would have meant Thomas would have had to go beyond the first degree of enlightenment into seeing God in all life.

His sense of losing independence, being swallowed or engulfed by the fires of intimate relationship, and thus losing part of himself in this dynamic, is one of the key holes of Thomas, and one to be aware of on the spiritual path. The opposite side of this is going headlong into relating without this awareness, and losing oneself totally in it: the shadow side of trying to engage in sacred relationship.

Immersing in the Witness can lead to a separation from empathic, feeling qualities as one gets immersed in one aspect of Christ Mind rather than the wholeness. In this we can also leave out an aspect of our humanity, and become stuck in detached observation and a certain state of peace than can become an impediment to further evolution.

Thomas left out the feminine, the life force, and relating on the human plane. The Witness discerns through the use of the mind, and leaves out emotion. There is no male and female in the Witness, and no polarity. While this is true, on a relational plane these energies are the juices of life and creative energy itself, of love that connects us as humans, that the feminine plays with in order to create experience and matter itself.

Meditation and certain aspects of mind training can be used as a strategy to hide. Going up and out from the body, reassuring ourselves that we are spirit, that we are light, that this world, this relationship, does not matter, that we are beyond, is our electrical nature. This split of the magnetic, personal, relating feminine from the detached masculine creates a deep sense of separation, the greatest form of harm.

Meditation is essential ... *but* when it is used as a means of hiding, and closing off from relating, it will always lead to more heartache, and more heart closure. Meditation is not about running away, or disappearing into emptiness in order to avoid intimacy, to avoid relating to life. It is about embracing and including *all* aspects honestly and vulnerably, with spaciousness and detachment, that leads to full healing and communion.

Vulnerability is the lesson for the witness to learn: being vulnerable, and learning from the dream, as well as seeing it as the illusion that it is. One can become attached even to seeing life as a dream! Seeing everything as a symbol, including woman, negates what woman is. And this stops one from embodying love.

Matter is not an illusion; it is an appearance that we can become attached to. When we are not attached to it, when we are fluid in the Witness, we can truly enjoy matter for the purpose that God created it for: for delight. The Witness sees this without getting entangled in the mind yet still vibrating with the life force, the pulse of the feminine, engaging with life in passion, detachment, and sacredness.

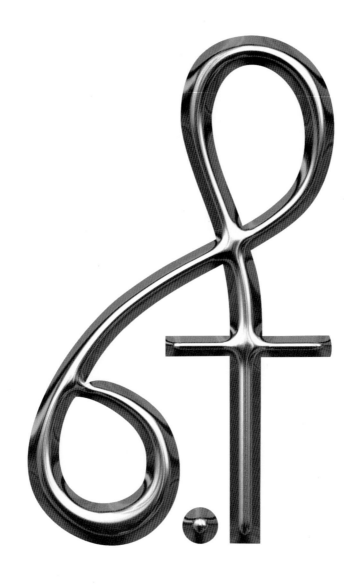

Original Human Being

CHAPTER 25

Original Human Being

Christ Yeshua

My Friends,

Much has been said about me, talked about me, and written about me, much of it exaggerated, much of it others' perceptions about what I was experiencing or sharing. One thing is for sure: everyone relates to Christ from their own knowing of who they are, and how much they love. And this, my friends, is the crux of the matter.

For you are creating, moment by moment, all that you experience. You are totally responsible for everything that is happening in your life right now. You have created these experiences and events in order to learn how to use the mind, and how to become Christ, for all events are neutral. They only acquire value by the value you give to them.

Place your value and loyalty in love, that which lies at the center of your heart, the stillness within. Let this guide you, and let this be the value you place in your relationships. You can choose, at any moment, to withdraw the value you have placed on conflict, being right, dominating and judging others, and forgive yourself for doing so.

There is nothing to get from others or the world; no one can fulfill you. Only love is the cause of your fulfillment, your peace, and your healing. Claim and know your power to awaken now. This arises through your connection to your Creator.

Remember that God has created you, and that no matter how great the light that flows through you, it is God's, not yours. Rest in this humility for a moment. It is from this space that you can truly know, listen to, and act on your heart's desires.

Observe your previous choices, and choose again. Be clear in your intentions. Allow and embrace all things that come to you. Loosen your grip, and allow life to flow. Surrender to the will of life, the movements of the life flow. Stand up, show up, and be counted.

There is only love or fear. Choose only love, in every moment, for only love heals. Love alone is real. Embrace your shadow in love and honesty, for love alone trusts, allows, and embraces all things.

In this, the world and the dream no longer have any power over you. The world is innocent and harmless—it is what you make it. Rest in this innocence; play with it, delight in it and what it reveals in each moment.

Use time wisely to grow, to expand, and to share love.

Choose at every step to live as love.

Bring your attention back to this when in conflict, or when choosing suffering.

Ask, "How do I extend love in this situation?"

Be what you are created to be, for you are born to create. You are here to be a Master, to be Christ in your own unique way, to extend your love into creation.

This is the greatest joy, as you are extending your uniqueness to others, and flowing with the movement of Life itself.

Choose and decree that only God exists. And God is but love, an open invitation to rest in the deepest peace. Ask for more and more of God to come to you every day, and remember in asking, you can *always* receive.

THE TWENTY-FIRST CENTURY

As the hub of the Christ Council I say this to you: the risks that you take, the edges you go to, the daring you have to go beyond the known, will mark you out as another Christ in a long lineage of eternal Christs.

The opportunity is now; seize it. Those who do will receive help that they could never have imagined, a vast quickening more than they ever thought possible. Up to this point I have taught and shared what was necessary for the time. Now there is nothing more to hold back. There is no more teaching, save the living of it. The Golden Age is the return of this innate state, the Original Religion, without doctrine. When you are ready, write your own books, realize your own teachings, and become them all. Write yourself into your own expression of God.

Be yourself; this is God's desire for you, to be yourself, to be your own unique expression of the one fire, of the one Living Light, of the one holy breath. I have traced out the path for you; when this path becomes traceless, then I will be you, and you will be I. Contemplate what this means for you.

As the hub of the Council of Christ, I, and the entire council, are now ready to be called upon, to pave the way into those areas that you do not wish to go into, that you do not wish to see, the areas where you are presently content and secure. Be sure and definite in what you command to come into being. Become the Master breathing Holy Spirit, walking side by side with the student of your soul, for this is living the teachings.

All things come to a point. If you are ready to bring your doubt, your lack of self worth, your false pride, and your belief that I am greater than you to this point, and into release as power to move into your uniqueness, then you will realize we have always been right here with you. This can be done in one moment of daring, for the basic truth is this: everything is open. Allow yourself to be friends with this openness.

THE COUNCIL OF CHRIST

The Council of Christ is an infinite hologram. I sit in the center. There is an infinite number of Christs stretching above me, below me, and beyond me. I am within all of them, and they are within me. We are jewels within the same eye, shining our light to each other, reflecting it back off our own Self and into the other that is also our own Self, and so on . . . into infinity.

The Council of Christ holds the space for Christ to anchor in, and through, all thirteen aspects. The Apostles ground the limitless Christ by holding their positions within this mandala. As I looked at myself each and every day in these twelve faces while I was embodied, it allowed me to breathe more freely, and to remember that even though I am One, it is relationship that makes this so.

The deepest reminder of this came through my own relating with Mary Magdalene, my Beloved. She reminded me through her silence, through her holding, through her slightest glance, that we are One, and that holy relationship is the Key to this reflection that All is me, and I am this, now.

A true, deep, intimate sacred relating is the way to anchor all parts of yourself onto the earth. This is what I came to establish with my family, with the Apostles, with Mary Magdalene, and with this planet. All was done through sacred relationship; I did nothing myself. And yes, it was my role to stand alone, to be crucified alone, and even then I was in relationship.

The individual becomes the expression of universal love. If you truly rise in love with another, you can taste the universal love. Just as you commit to God, so commit to your Beloved. Then you will realize the fullness of what I am sharing, for this is what I did with my Beloved, and my Beloved with me.

Sacred relationship, then, Beloveds, is the Key of the Christ Blueprint. Within yourself, within your family, within your community, and with your chosen Beloved, the art of sacred relationship allows you to surrender to the desire to merge, and to merge with the intent to realize yourself as Christ.

This is the path, and it is possible for each and every one of you to do this. And then you can create your own path, and then this path will dissolve into the pathless path, the path that leaves no trace. We wait for you to stand up, and go beyond what you have been taught.

Christ manifests through action. In the doing lies the prayer, and you then create your own living prayer. This prayer is music to our ears, a music that never ceases, for it is the living breath of all masters.

Beloveds, you are not here to create any more teachings. You are here to live them, to breathe them, in your thoughts, words, and deeds. This is my message to you for this Christ Blueprint, brothers and sisters of the heart.

Peace be with you.

CHAPTER 26
The Antichrist

The Antichrist is a key part of Christ Consciousness. It was anchored two thousand years ago as part of the Christ Blueprint. It consists of the twelve shadow sides of the body of Christ, all embodied into one living thought-form. It is the polar opposite of the Christ, here to provide the tension, the friction, the push and pull of duality, to propel us into unity consciousness. The Antichrist is an energy field that surrounds the whole earth, and it is controlled by various beings mentioned in the Gnostic Gospels by Yeshua, called Archons and Aeons. These are the rulers of the collective consciousness of humanity, the manipulators behind the scenes of our unconscious, that which we cannot see or do not wish to see.

Until we are resonating at love and joy, we are still feeding these rulers, and have a negligible effect on the collective consciousness. As soon as we rebirth and step into joy, we can change the collective, balancing thousands of people by our mere presence alone.

From an evolutionary perspective, the Antichrist has to fully embody on earth before Christ Consciousness can fully reappear. The darkness is necessary in order for the light to appear. Circumstances have to get so critical as to reach a climax point in order for a more enlightened civilization to sprout phoenixlike from the ashes of the old. Therefore the Antichrist has a definite purpose: to serve as a catalyst, a point of tension. In any state of heightened tension or friction (at a certain wave band of consciousness) there is far more possibility of transformation, as well as a new creation, as you are accessing deep emotions and energy in this stretching. We have to stretch and challenge ourselves in order to really grow, to reach our full potential.

The ways that this stretching, or additional tension, are occurring has become obvious on a planetary scale: ecological crisis, wars, terrorism, mass extinction of species, loss of nature, pollution, mass media controls over public thought and opinion, and personal upheavals and transformations, all designed to wake us up to what is happening, and do something about it in our own way.

The matrix created by the Antichrist is a chrysalis constructed by our own thoughts, fears, desires, and subconscious, in order to prepare us for our next phase of evolution: the next wave. Its dissolution can only happen once we have learned and mastered the lessons from it, which is when it will have served its purpose. This is when humanity, as a collective, issues the cry that "enough is enough."

This matrix is the training ground that Yeshua himself exhorted us to "not get lost in, for it is only a way station, the in-between stage to heaven and the higher worlds." In essence, we are now rapidly externalizing and manifesting the collective thoughts and subconscious of humanity over thousands of years in order to experience something new, something that we can claim, either arrogantly or with soul purpose, is ours.

THE PORTAL TO CHRIST

In order to fully embody Christ, one has to meet and embrace the Antichrist, and know it in its fullness. Yeshua did this in the forty days in the desert. We will all have to do it in our own way at some point in the unfolding of our soul. This can take many forms, but rest assured it will be both a personal and a universal unfolding, felt on all levels of your soul. In our own unfolding, just before we embody Christ, we have to embrace the darkness of creation, the anti-life force that is also Christ.

It is all God. In this, we embrace, and surrender to the All, extending love to those who are extending the cry for help and healing.

The creation that is the Antichrist is humanity's. God is love, and is the expression of this, and we, as a species, have created the Antichrist, that which is anti-life, anti-love, and anti-flow, the rigidity of matter without the conscious awareness of light, the opposite to being in the present, organic, ever-unfolding moment. It is the deepest darkness that Christ Yeshua descended into after the Crucifixion for three days, bringing the spark of Christ, Divine love, into the places of despair, guilt, shame, and body-mind identification, of identification with matter alone, that had never felt love before.

It is that which we have created over millennia that has said no to love, no to life, no to embrace, and no to surrender, the fear that was birthed from the first thought and feeling of separation. It is the ancient mind of man built on fear. It is the forgetting of the truth of who we are, the demon that Shiva dances on, the demon of ignorance and forgetfulness. This demon is seen as epileptic, spastic, and prone to fits of rage and anger, very similar to how Hitler behaved.

WHAT IS THE ANTICHRIST?

The Antichrist is the incarnation of temptation, luring you away from truth and promising you everything that the world has to offer. The Antichrist manifests when we look away from God and turn all our attention to ourselves, putting ourselves first and foremost, so that we are independent from God and others in the web of life in all we do.

Here you feel you have a separate will to the One, and want to occupy for yourself what is yours. You feel you are a separate doer from God, independent in identity and authority, and above God. You feel that your unfolding is separate from everyone else's, and that love is about being more focused on one person alone.

You feel you are unlovable and are wrong, leading to you feeling ashamed, guilty, unworthy, humiliated, helpless, and in despair. Feelings and thoughts of abandonment and rejection from God may haunt you, as you feel lost, doubtful, insecure, and isolated from everyone and everything else.

You try to manipulate others to make you feel better, acting and seeking to enhance your sense of self through deeds, interactions, and relationships with others. You try to make your ego self look bigger, feel better in your interactions with others, as that is where your self-worth arises from. You insistently defend your points of view, reacting to any perceived attack on your sense of self. You plan your life in detail, and blame others when things go wrong. You are suspicious and wary of all, and try to get the best for yourself at the expense of others. You create alone, and in isolation from others. In this you refuse reality, the reality of the soul, the interconnection or Oneness of all life, and the Creator of all.

The Antichrist can take many forms, yet is unique to the individual. It has no basic trust in life, in others, or in being held, supported, and loved, even from the stages of early childhood and the womb. It is against love but really wants love, which is why it is the beast that puts down love. The Antichrist needs love, when we are ready to do so. The Antichrist personifies hatred and cruelty, and is hard and rigid in body and mind, although adept at hiding it under a veneer of social respectability.

If we were to imagine the Antichrist as a single embodied being, he would be living in fear. Lust and greed would be his dominant instinctual drives: acquiring, consuming, and getting for himself. He is a voracious sexual predator, always skipping from woman to woman, although secretly, so he does not ruin his reputation.

He is in a position of great worldly power, as he perpetuates the lie that the world promises *you* fulfillment in time, and that you will get all you want in the future. It promises you that the world can fulfill you, so keep seeking, but do not find. This promise, of needing the future to make the present viable, always leads us to try to get somewhere, apart from here, now.

His goal is separation created from his pride that he can take God's place and create what he feels is right. He is inherently jealous of God for having created what he cannot, but that which he wishes to be ruler of, and is jealous of others' successes and virtues, which he also wants and wishes to acquire.

This brings him into a sense of isolation, of aloneness, of being cut off from everyone else as he feels he is so much greater than everyone else. This paradoxically brings him into a codependent relationship, as he does not want to feel alone. He wishes to control all aspects of his life, and those around him, creating it as he sees fit, made in his own image. His guilt at all that he does devours him regularly, where he is racked with remorse for doing what he knows is not true . . . but he cannot help it. It is his job. This stagnancy leads to ever-deeper states of despair, fragmenting his mind, which becomes even more unstable. He becomes deeply polarized.

He is full of noise and bluster, living in the pollution of the city and the hustle and bustle of people running around to be everywhere apart from the here and now. He is lost in the world and in the sense that he has to do something all the time to stay away from the deafening roar of the silence, and peace, that underlies his restlessness and ideas of the future, based on the wounds of the past.

He is cynical, closed to new possibilities and ways of doing, very much part of the "old guard," which fondly remembers the good old days of slavery, apartheid, discrimination, and inequality. All the women around him are subservient, and he indulges in sadomasochistic sexual practices. He revels in disempowering others, and is standoffish in his emotions.

The Antichrist is incarnated in many forms on earth. He comes directly to those who have the wisdom, power, light, and love to make a difference to the mass consciousness on this planet. Two notable examples are Yeshua in his forty days of temptation, where he deliberately wanted to meet and get to know the Antichrist so he could find out more about himself and the true nature of reality and the holy trinity of wisdom, power, and love; and the Buddha's encounter with Mara just before his enlightenment.

The more love that arises on earth, the more the Antichrist is provoked as a form of hatred that has originated from the loss of this love. It is the force of resistance and opposition to love that wishes to annihilate and stop love flowering at all costs. It is death that constantly wants to keep you small, in fear, and denying reality. This beast can be felt as an ominous eye, a huge demon that is a cruel, cold, calculating force of destructive hatred and great pride.

Love heals all. Power is an essential aspect of love, and this power is distorted by the Antichrist force. This is why we have to claim our power from the darkness by traveling deep into it, learning the lessons from it, and reclaiming our sovereign power.

In one sense the Antichrist is a guardian of our greatest power, and if we can feel this power and hatred without resistance, then we can reclaim this power. In this process we can see some of the deepest levels of why our soul originally disconnected from love. Love illuminates these parts of self, relaxing and opening these aspects of our psyche and soul to receive and embrace all parts of ourselves. When we understand the Antichrist, we can then access the loving nature of reality through embracing being as it is.

The Antichrist is a part of God, created as part of the Divine Plan. In order to reach Christ Consciousness, one must, like our illustrious predecessors, get to know him fully and become friends with him, showing loving wisdom and our own sovereign power with him so that he too can see we are all one.

Everything is God. In every program of consciousness, in every being, lies the spark of God. Realizing this experientially when encountering the varied aspects of the Antichrist is to step more into your Godhood.

Golden Child

CHAPTER 27

Golden Child

Yeshua said, "Become again as a child to enter the Kingdom of Heaven."

Play with me
Learn with me in laughter

Sit with me in silence
Gaze upon your own innocence
Rest in your own delight

This is you
And I am what you are
Reminding you of your own child
Nestled in the folds of the heart we share
In this moment

Sit and abide where there are no boundaries

Our eyes touch across a crowded room,
Melting the distance of the heart
Allow yourself to care for me
As I care for you

Allow me to caress you
And open the cracks in your heart a little wider
So we can play together
Free, and easeful

I am Grace
The flow of ease
The heightened sensing
Of what is possible now

No more striving
No more working
The process is almost done
So we can all join without preference
In the One

We come to share through being
What you have never dared
The easiest flow
Radical in approach
Simple in design

As the veils of illusion begin to dissolve in the eyes of humanity, and enough minds become unplugged from the ancient collective mind-set of fear, the way is clear for the birthing of a new paradigm. It is through this new paradigm that the Golden Children make visible Living Light on earth.

These new children started to incarnate in 2007. They arise as conscious representatives and manifestations of the Black Light, and their expressions of this are as golden or diamond minds. They incarnate the Original Human Being, activating all those that come into contact with them and within the areas they live in. They act as conduits for transformation, serving to dissipate negativity wherever they venture, literally creating quantum zones where anything becomes possible, where anything can be manifested, wherever they are.

They resonate with the underlying fabric of creation, serving to wipe away the distortions that are out of alignment with the Source of Creation, that are out of alignment with male-female union, that are out of alignment with the Original Human Blueprint. They create *only* according to this. They bring forth the unseen into the seen. Wherever they go they are the Great Mystery Incarnate. The great mystery of these Golden Children is that they see the world with such different eyes, even to those of the Indigo Children.

THEIR ACTIONS

It will be hard at first to even comprehend what these children are. To some, these children will seem serious and withdrawn; to others they will seem magical, delightfully refined, and exquisite. When you are faced with the Source of Creation in a human child, one can become polarized, according to your own beliefs, projections, and cynicism. For those who are wise among you, you can actually harness this energy like a cosmic battery, using it to fuel your own evolution in many ways: as many ways as you can think of, such is possible.

It is through their actions, not through their words, that they transform; it is mainly through their presence and telepathic abilities that they change people and environments. It is from their sheer presence and power of being that people will learn the greatest lessons. They act as magnets for silence, for they embody silence. People will be drawn to go into deep silence around them, and thereby come into communion with Self. One potential is that these children can simply sit, and groups of people can gather around them, going into deep silence.

Another potential is that these children can literally transmit their silence to geographical locations and areas, neutralizing polarized areas into their original wholeness. They can be part of workshops or teachings holding the space of the Black Light, for others processes and transformations to be accelerated and made whole. They come to give the world what it needs, which is a return to the Source of Creation, the remembering of the silence from where all things arise, and all dissolves back into.

They are the creators of a new wave of technology that will harness the sources of creation, from space travel to free energy and the elimination of pollution. They create environments and atmospheres in tune with the original creation, creating viable infrastructures in alignment with this original creation, allowing humans on this planet to be governed by these laws again in a practical way.

They are the leaders, teachers, and Masters, and the Indigo Children are their support.

All of their creations are based on simple laws and simple ways of seeing things that will appear obvious to them, and miraculous to most people. The ease and grace of their beings, and expressions, will allow rest for humanity, allowing the struggling, seeking, and striving to cease.

These children are only birthed and nurtured in a womb that has been opened, purified, and prepared. They will not incarnate without knowing they are welcomed, safe, and fully received by conscious parents, with the womb ready to hold, support, and nurture them in their purity and Divine essence.

It is through these children that the collective consciousness will awaken, and the world as we know it will disappear. It is through the fruits of these children that humanity will awaken and rejoice together in unity, peace, and harmony.

The Golden Children are the fruit of Grace, the product of the Christ Blueprint. All the work that Yeshua, Mary Magdalene, and the Apostles did was to help pave the way for these children to arrive on earth, to weave their magic of innocence, joy, and cocreating the Divine Plan in this age. They are delight and play embodied, emanating pure joy, seeing in innocence. They may be perceived as "special," but they simply reflect our natural God-given essence and Divine birthright.

AVATARS

"Often He did not appear to his disciples as Himself, but was found among them as a child."[1]

The Golden Child births in us through the opening of the Womb of the World, or the revelation and application of the feminine mysteries through the integration of male and female. In this sacred marriage the third is born: the Golden Child, both within the bridal chamber of our own hearts, and in the physical flesh and blood Golden Child.

The Golden Child is the Golden Ball energy. This Golden Ball was created via the collected energy of many enlightened masters of all times who have walked on earth. These masters have given freely of their awakening to the collective consciousness of all humanity through the energetic vehicle of what is known as the Bodhisattva Vow. This promise and vow is to help and serve all others to reach their awakening. This selflessness, literally having no self or having One Self, is the strand that unites all spiritual traditions, as all traditions speak of service as the way to realize God. This sincere desire, passion, way of life, and deep knowing is that we are born on earth out of compassion to realize God, and then to help others do the same, as once we are awake there is nothing else left to do.

The Bodhisattva Vow was created in order for humanity to realize its own freedom and the laws of the universe, as the limitlessness of the aspiration to help limitless realms of sentient beings is the limitlessness of all those beings themselves. Thus as we awaken, all those we love awaken in their own way, as no awakening is just personal—it affects all worlds, in all times. The spark of one awakened being is rejoiced in all universes, as the light generated by this is seen all over the universe.

The Golden Children are the results of this consciousness. Their lineage has been on earth in previous golden ages, where they were known

---

1. Gospel of Judas.

as the Four Kumaras, the Four Golden Children who are the ancestors of the Christ Lineage. The Kumaras are shaktyavesha avatars, or incarnations invested with the transcendental power and law-making abilities of God, charged with bringing new energies and principles into manifestation for earth and humanity. They are the firstborn sons of the Creator God, Brahma, and are described in Vedic literature as "shining as brilliantly as the sun, appearing like fire blazing on an altar." They are always seen as eternally youthful, joyful, and innocent, no more than five years of age, naked, and eternally absorbed in meditation. In the *Bhagavad Gita* they are "glowing effulgence, the masters of all mystic power . . . the only friends for persons who are blazing in the fire of material existence."[2]

As such they have been known throughout history as the eternal, changeless youths, princes, and saviors. Yeshua was the last of this lineage to be incarnated on earth as the way-shower for the rest of the Golden Children coming now, children born to create a new world.

---

2. *Bhagavad Gita* 4.22.15, 4.22.2.

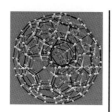

CHAPTER 28

Christ Grids

The Christ Blueprint is anchored by the Christ Consciousness Grids. These Christ Grids are anchored across and in the earth in thirteen primary sacred sites and ten secondary sacred sites. This grid was reactivated and set up by each one of the Apostles two thousand years ago upon guidance and initiation from the Divine Mother. The Apostles were guided to different parts of the world to anchor their quality of consciousness, their strand of the Christ Blueprint, into the earth itself, activating these sites as receiving and transmitting stations for the energies of the Christ Blueprint.

The Christ Consciousness Grids are part of the template and support for our merging into Christ Consciousness, for they hold the imprint and memory of Christ itself. They were reactivated through Yeshua's choice to descend into the deepest darkness, the deepest hells, in the three days between Crucifixion and Resurrection, and bring love to where love had never been, thereby including all aspects of creation in Christ.

His mission brought light and hope to the deepest darkness, reassuring all those souls who were lost in the body, lost in the mind, lost in guilt, shame, and

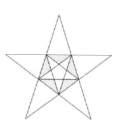

the torture of their own self-created hells, that God is indeed every-where, even if we cannot see it. This had never been done in our pres-ent thirteen-thousand-year cycle of time until two thousand years ago. Therefore the Christ Grids exclude nobody from them, as they are designed to stimulate us to move into Oneness, acting as a reminder of our true nature, where all are included. We all evolve together.

The Christ Grids hold the remembrance of group unity, for the Christ Grid is a unified collective consciousness. When humanity is in unity, then God reveals itself. This is the Key to the Christ Grids, and how we can access them.

THE THIRTEEN SITES

The thirteen primary sites of the Christ Grids are connected to the thir-teen planets of this solar system, and each of these sacred sites anchors into the crystalline core of the earth. The Christ Grids are part of the Key to awakening Christ Consciousness in this age, receiving and trans-mitting Christ frequencies to their local areas, to the planet, and to this solar system.

Each Apostle was given specific instructions on how to descend the Christ Light into the earth using their own vehicle as a vessel for the Holy Spirit to descend. This descent anchored their strand of the Christ Blueprint into the core of the earth, while Holy Spirit anchored it through the Apostles' crowns into their respective planets. In other words, their higher selves were physically connected through their light bodies to the resonant fields of these places.

All these sacred sites are places where it is easiest to plug into the Christ Grids. The Masters of the Christ Council are overlighting these places so that many more can directly access the Christ Light. Activa-tions in these sites, which have been happening for some time now, accelerate the frequency held within the crystalline core of the earth.

ACCELERATION

This does not mean that they increase the frequency of the collective consciousness of earth in the beginning, for the Christ Grid is beyond the collective consciousness frequency. These grids actually increase the friction between the earth and the collective. As the frequency of the Christ Grid increases, as the frequency of the crystal core increases, increasing tension and pressure is placed on the collective thought mind-set and grid frequencies.

In this increasing dissonance, the living intelligence of the earth rises up to cleanse and purify itself, so it may come into harmony with that which it really desires to come into alignment with: the Christ Grid, the higher frequency. In reaching for this higher frequency, all that stands in its way must necessarily dissolve, and be released. In this case, what is to be dissolved is the mind-set of the collective consciousness.

This mind-set of the ancient mind is what keeps humanity in fear. As this fearful mind-set is placed under even more pressure, even more desperate measures will be taken by those who wish to maintain this mind-set. These desperate measures will then be counterbalanced by the forces of the earth itself, which will strive to push and purify itself through the form of natural disaster, as well as through increased warnings through many kinds which are being initiated *now*.

The Christ Grid was fully active by February 2008. This was about the time that the full descent of the Antichrist happened. This created enormous stress and pressure on the collective consciousness, and the crutches that were holding this together. These crutches are like threads holding a blanket together—if one thread goes, the whole blanket can start to unravel.

This tension, pressure, and friction creates the push for evolution on the three-dimensional level. This push and pull tears apart what was held previously to be true, and allows a new reality to emerge. This tension will be released through volcanoes, earthquakes, and tsunamis. As we move further into the Christ Grids, our DNA also changes, allowing us to tune into more frequency bands of consciousness, raising our awareness.

The Christ Grid is unlike any other grid of consciousness. It has been established by the Council of Christ with both Yeshua and Magdalene as the key players in establishing these sites. This is why they traveled so much, not only to learn and be initiated, but also to establish the Blueprint into that which would not dissolve—the matter of the earth itself.

Both Yeshua and Mary were assisted by the devas of the earth to establish this Blueprint, and it is they who also guard it. This Blueprint has been kept concealed for two thousand years, and is now being revealed, for it is now active, and nothing can disturb or touch it once it is active.

Now that the Christ Grid is active, Christed Servers can visit these sites and amplify their energy. By giving, here you do indeed receive. To truly give to these sites and the Christ Grid requires three Keys: the application of light, the integration of the shadow within you through awareness, and the application of the Thirteen Keys of Christ Consciousness.

One does not enter Christ Consciousness without first going through the hell realms. It is the same with light: one does not reach Christ by just striving for heavenly light; one has to have gone down into the darkness in order to learn compassion through experience, in order to rise phoenixlike up to that which is even beyond the heavenly light.

Similarly, if one enters a Oneness state of consciousness, one cannot transform certain aspects of the subconscious while in this state. If you utilize all three Keys, then one has a full spectrum. The Christ Grid was laid in order to provide a mass transformation for earth at this time.

The dark night of the collective soul of humanity is a necessity. It is only through the creation of tension, and the releasing of this tension, that transformation can occur. This is nature's law. In order for a new creation to arise, the old must dissolve. This is what Yeshua and Mary saw, and were told two thousand years ago, and it is what they seeded in order for it to bloom *now.*

THE FALSE MATRIX GRIDS

To connect fully to the Christ Grids requires that you unplug from the collective consciousness grids of fear, the ancient mind of humanity or false matrix, as anchored by the thought-forms of the seven rulers, the Aeons, and the Archons. These energies keep us feeling separate, alone, hurt, scared, ashamed, unworthy, or incapable.

THE SEVEN RULERS

For thousands of years the human consciousness has had seven main supports for its ego structure, which over time have become living, breathing thought-forms, or sentient beings. These have become planetary-level entities that create, manipulate, and feed on these archetypal collective ego forms within the human matrix. These seven living beings of lust, fear, greed, envy, sloth, ignorance, and pride feed on your life force to keep these thought-forms alive, and to keep you imprisoned within the planetary light body, incapable of expanding outward.

For millions of years humanity has lived with these seven primal supports of the ego mind, and year by year these seven grow in size and power as more and more people feed, and are fed by, these living thought-forms in a vicious cycle of parasitic, interdependent relationship. For example, after 9/11 the rise in fear expanded the Ruler of Fear tremendously, resulting now in the mass consciousness of the United States residing at the frequency of fear. All seven rulers are based on false body-mind identification, which, if not rooted out from the depths of the psyche and ego, results in us being unconsciously controlled and manipulated by forces buried deep within the human mind-set.

Archons, or Ancient Earth Rulers

Archons are demonic rulers, and are mentioned extensively in the Gnostic Gospels as one of the prime reasons for suffering on earth. They have been behind the scenes for millions of years, manipulating and orchestrating the movements, fears, and emotions of the collective consciousness in order to feed themselves, and keep separation in place.

Archons are ancient, powerful demons that live at a high frequency of power between the seventh and ninth dimensions, inaccessible to most people who are not fully conscious of the Galactic Body of Light. Several Gnostic Gospels, and much of John the Baptist's and Christ's work, focused on dissolving many of these demons' holds on the earth and its people. However, many are still left.

Archons are attached to almost every human's body of light, preventing the crown channel from being fully open. They form a thick, black, oily blanket 1,300 to 23,000 feet above your physical body in your light body, preventing light, love, and full empowerment from reaching your body-mind consciousness. When an Archon is removed, major changes can happen in many areas of your life, particularly the loss of fear.

Archons are also attached to the twelve planetary fields, several star constellations, to the earth's fields, and to many individual countries. They can be several miles across in size, and are drawn to zones of terror or war to feed on the energy flows there. Some of the biggest Archon numbers on earth are at Auschwitz, Iraq, Sudan, and Israel. Conversely they are also drawn to areas that hold great light, to create chaos there.

Aeons

Aeons are mentioned in the Gnostic Gospels as the rulers of earth. Their lieutenants are the Archons. Aeons are huge demons that hook directly into the central nervous system and spine of most humans, feeding directly on your life force. One can only be disconnected from them when you are ready to be unplugged from their matrix; they cannot be destroyed except directly through a fully Christed being, as they are enormously powerful, and a deeply ingrained aspect of the collective consciousness of humanity.

They are sustained by your very life force, until you are ready to be exorcised from their grip, and become "unplugged" from the collective consciousness grids. When you leave the collective consciousness, you leave the ancient mind of fear that has governed humanity since the last golden age.

This ancient egoic mind has always been the same, always craving to change, always angry, fearful, judgmental, competing, and comparing. The nature of the mind has never changed—this is what makes it the mind. There is no point in wanting to change this structure of the mind. You cannot get rid of this mind; you can only be free of it by realizing that it is not yours. Then you will stop trying to change it.

This ancient mind is what has characterized humanity since the time of the Neanderthals, for this ancient single mind is based on fear. This fear, supported and nourished by the Aeons and Archons, is at the core of the human mind. Earlier it could have been the fear of a tiger or lion; today it is fear of relating, fear of opening the heart, fear of being vulnerable, fear of losing your job. Fundamentally, man has not changed; only the objects of craving, desire, fear, and anxiety have. But fundamentally, it is the same old mind, living continuously in fear.

When we are unplugged from the collective consciousness, through a fundamental change in the brain itself, then we can leave this ancient mind behind. This does not focus so much on a transformation within the mind, such as what psychologists and philosophers do; this is becoming free of the ancient mind itself.

CONNECTING TO THE CHRIST GRIDS

Once we are unplugged from these fields, which can take lifetimes, then we can become fully plugged into the Christ Consciousness Grids through the removal of the Aeon, the reconnecting of the alta major chakra to the grids surrounding the earth's energy fields, and the reconnecting of the foot chakras to the feminine web of life, the living soil and intelligence of the earth.

Everyone is connected to the Christ Grids, and can access them at any time. However, without being unplugged from the false matrix grids, one does not fully access the totality of the Christ Consciousness Grids. To do this means one is clear and resonating at the frequencies of love, joy, and selfless service as a way of life, not as an ideal or concept.

The alta major chakra is the feminine entrance to the third eye. It is a part of the Shakti Circuit, which I extensively discuss, along with its relationship to the womb and heart, in *The Shakti Circuit*.

THE EIGHTH CHAKRA

The eighth chakra is our connection to the earth's grids and the feminine energy of the web of life. It is located just below our feet in the earth itself. It resonates with the living intelligence and movements of Gaia, as well as the ley line patterns of earth. The eighth chakra also connects us to our roots and origins. It helps us access deeply buried and karmic patterns, as well as the genetic blueprint that we receive from our parents and ancestors. The eighth chakra creates a balance with the crown chakra and the Christ Grids around the earth, linking heaven to earth through our root chakra and our bodies, and powerfully grounding high vibrations through the web of life. The web of life and light, held within the earth's womb, the trees, nature, and the moon, is also reflected in the ley lines that connect and crisscross the planet.

Working with the web of light allows one to be completely present with the energies of the earth, and in doing so one accesses many other dimensions beyond just this earth.

The web of life connects all dimensions, and is anchored on earth in the Womb of the World. This connection is feminine, and it is from this web and womb that the leaps in spiritual evolution throughout history have occurred. Webs are nonhierarchical and nonpatriarchal; they are cooperative in nature, and connect us to earth and beyond.

In the past it was through the use of perpetual choirs, choirs that sounded earth's tones and chants all day and all night through voice and natural instruments, that we connected to this web of light and vibration, harmonizing our own rhythms, souls, and sexuality to Gaia's womb and callings.

It is through this connection that we become aware of, and respect, our environment. It speaks to us, and we speak to it, as one. The web of light is oneness. By connecting to it we heal and align ourselves to the natural rhythms and motions of life, clearing anything out that stands in the way of this. We connect to the web of life by offering and giving ourselves to it. Gratitude is the attitude of the web of life. Within the web, everything can be seen as a glowing silver-white web, threading, weaving, and sustaining harmony in all things. Your body, your flesh, your nerves, your cells, your very being is permeated by this web, the same light that is giving birth to every plant, every tree, and every star that is spread throughout the cosmos.

Breathing down through the soles of your feet while standing or sitting barefoot on the earth is a simple, effective way to access the eighth chakra. Just below the feet is your connection, a star-shaped geometry. As you are breathing down, focus on this star, and then visualize the web of energy that extends out and down into the earth. See it. Now ask, and pray to Mother Gaia, in your own words, from your own heart, to feel and extend your connection to her. Offer her yourself, offer her your service, and thank her for being your foundation, your anchor, your home. Initially, the best way to do this is while visiting a sacred site you feel attuned to, where you feel at home. After receiving this connection, one can access it anywhere, anytime.

CHAPTER 29
The Second Coming

Christ Yeshua, the last so far in a long line of Christ-conscious beings throughout history, is one who proclaimed that many will come after him, and they will do greater things than he. This is the new wave of consciousness sweeping our planet even as you read this. Christ Consciousness is about building a Christ-oriented civilization for all humans, not just for our own liberation. This is the next big evolutionary step for humanity; it is for all of us to create a unified movement based on action, communication, and communion, rather than just words and ideas.

This is the Second Coming of Christ. This Second Coming happens when you follow your deepest heart's desire, and act on it spontaneously and immediately. The Second Coming happens when we are no longer just students, but step into our mastery. The master is equally a student in this context. This is when we realize that we are here to do greater things than Yeshua himself, and are open and willing to embrace this possibility.

The Second Coming is the return of our naturally blissful, creative, and miraculous selves, where miracles happen every day and are the norm. It is the actual fulfillment of our wildest dreams that if we act on *now,* will manifest. The Second Coming occurs when we reunite with our soul families and with our true partners, our deepest kindred spirits from which effortless creation flows, the creation that manifests more love, beauty, and God.

The Second Coming happens when we move purposefully in action, uniting with others who passionately feel the same desire. The Second Coming occurs when we leave behind the old world, the old relationships of the collective consciousness; when we sort out the wheat from the chaff, and get radical in our ways of creating and expressing more transformation, more love, more beauty.

It is time to feel and know that only the best for God will do; do not think in limited or small ways. Do not restrict the possibilities that can happen. It is from all these ways of being that we cocreate ourselves, and a new human civilization can be birthed. God wants us to be totally who we are in our own unique way, not what someone else is or was.

Now is the time to accept that only the best for God will do. Over too many years you have been accepting the scraps, the bits and pieces off the spiritual and fiscal table, compromising on the place to give God in the world. This is the time when we only do the best for God; nothing else will suffice any more, nothing else will lead us forward, nothing else will satisfy our souls.

Holding this space and intent means it actually manifests, as you are ready to step up for Self and put Self in its rightful place within the chaos and delusion of the modern-day world. If you do not compromise, and go for it, then Christ will come to you, stirred by your passion and commitment for excellence.

In saying "only the best for God will do for me," we invite Christ into our lives fully, as Christ Consciousness means no compromise. Keep with this truth, hold this intent, and you will be amazed at what happens in your life! Experiment, take a risk, learn what you have always wanted to but never dared to, follow the whispers of your soul that pop up now and again but which you dismiss because you are too busy... leave what no longer serves your highest potential, and *trust* that you will be looked after.

The Second Coming is the revelation that we are Christ, and we are here to be all that we have been created to be. The collective consciousness of humanity in unity is God itself.

When we unite, we reveal God in action. This Second Coming is the next step in the Divine Plan for evolution on earth, and is the Blueprint seeded within our very souls.

The Second Coming occurs when we integrate all aspects of Christ Consciousness within ourselves, and in action with others. This then forms the foundation for a Christ-centered civilization on earth, a culture and society that is based on love, equality, wisdom, and awareness. A Christed civilization is based on group consciousness. It starts with groups coming together freely to pool their collective talents to create something far more than its parts. This uniting creates the highest potential, revealing unimagined transformations and illuminations for everyone, no matter which spiral of evolution they are residing at. This union of working together will surpass anything earth has ever seen before.

The Second Coming is awakening from the collective dream into our highest potential. The Second Coming is the birthing of the Golden Children on earth within us, and in the new children that are coming here, now.

CONCLUSION

The Christ Blueprint is about embracing being both human and Divine, feeling your humanity, exploring it, and diving deep into it without shame or regret. To balance both your mortal human heart and your immortal consciousness, to feel both without negating either, is to embody and enjoy Christ Consciousness. This is the greatest balancing act: to know when to be mortal and when to be immortal, which is what each Apostle and Master represent.

It is not about embodying one, two, three, or even four of these qualities, those which are your strong points, the aspects you already know and love about yourself, the aspects you feel most comfortable with, the ones you already have. You will feel more affinity with certain qualities than others, but your joyful task is to integrate all of them so you can fluidly move from one to the other. Only this can truly fulfill you, and this is an open invitation for you to live in every day. You will eventually be able to shape-shift into any quality according to what is appropriate for the highest potential to manifest in that moment. You become fluid.

The Christ Blueprint is about embodiment: being in and with your body, and igniting the soul presence within your very cells. It is not just about the heart or mind or consciousness; it includes all parts of you, reweaving many forgotten and isolated fragments of yourself back together into remembrance and connection, using your body as the barometer for this.

This is a book of relationship, with perhaps the most important relationship of all your lifetimes being paramount: the relationship with your true Self. In this light, Christ becomes a living force of loving wisdom and power within you that then gets shared and expressed into the world in giving: the passion of love, which moves, inspires, and transforms.

One can either live to give or live to get. In loving oneself, one loves Self as reflected in others. Many things that block this can be found in this book once you apply it with investigation, dedication, and discipline, which then can flower into the primordial trinity of love, wisdom, and power from this solid foundation that needs to be sustained and is ever-ongoing. The more one evolves, the more one is aware of, and the more discerning one has to be, as all the notes on the scale of creation become available to you. You can then play any note without judgment. So which notes do you choose to play?

The Christ Blueprint allows you to actively identify which aspects of Christ Consciousness you need to integrate, and then work with the light and shadow of that aspect. This then becomes the foundation for you to explore the remaining qualities that you have not yet integrated, and the shadows that you are still living with. This is a continuing journey, a journey you have been on for many lifetimes, and with this unfolding much can come to you, some of it wanted and some of it unwanted, but all of it absolutely needed.

The Christ Blueprint is not about becoming like Yeshua or even like Christ was. Evolution itself is changing in these accelerated times, and much of what was applicable two thousand years ago has been surpassed, and much of it is still timeless. To bring the timeless into the present in a way that is understandable and relevant is what thirteen noble beings strove to do two thousand years ago, and now that effort is bearing its fruit in you.

There was only one Yeshua; but there will be many Christs. As Christ said, "There are many who will come after me who will do greater things than I." This could be you, and in fact is your birthright, and what the

Christ Blueprint is all about. In this age the true empowerment of humanity beyond any guru, any authority is coming to pass, so in this spirit we share this with you:

Many are called, but few choose themselves.

APPENDIX

The Practice

The Christ Blueprint is put into practical application through retreats and healings given by the Christ Council. They are offering help, support, guidance, and practical transformation on an unprecedented scale right now to you. To gain access to direct teaching, one must be available by clearing away all obstacles along the rainbow bridge or antakarana, which connects your crown chakra to Source. These clearings open up the way for the descent of the bodies of light into the physical body, allowing for direct guidance into the different qualities of Christ Consciousness.

Thousands of people have already received these healings, and their lives have shifted as a result. All these distance healings are available on the website www.christblueprint.com. We would love to hear from you.

The practical application of the Christ Blueprint is achieved through the Shakti Circuit retreats. These retreats are powerful direct experiences, openings, and healings from the Three Marys and the Feminine Christ. The feminine is now holding the Christ teachings, and provides the platform for experiences of Christ Consciousness to be integrated and anchored deeply and permanently into the body-mind through timeless and enlightening practices from the Egyptian, Aramaic, Hebrew, and Tantric traditions of the East. All these practices and healings have been done by the Three Marys, who hold the resonance and space for them, and guide individuals throughout the retreats as an active presence.

Once you experience this experientially, you will understand in your very cells what the Christ Blueprint is about. The resonance and loving power of these retreats quickly open you to your essence and connection to the galactic center, the womb and heart of this galaxy. They are not intellectual teachings, as the core reason for the Christ Blueprint is to bring people into the direct knowing and experience of Christ Consciousness.

The Shakti Circuit details more of what occurs in these retreats, which contain the direct experience of the loving power and wisdom of the Christ Council in action. They are deeply transformative, and if you are committed, miracles can happen in these retreats. In addition, *The Nine Eyes of Light: Ascension Keys from Egypt* shares many of the teachings of wisdom and practices that Yeshua, Magdalene, Joseph, and John also undertook, culminating in the Isis Pyramid initiations.

All these retreats are established to train and initiate women and men into becoming leaders and teachers in their own right, We welcome and honor you, and look forward to spending more time with you.

—*Namastute.*

ACKNOWLEDGMENTS

Thank you to Laura Araya Re for her support and scientific calibration of the text: for holding the space, for recording all the sessions with the Christ Council, and transcribing them. Without her, this book would not have happened, and without her, valuable human lessons would not have been learned by me through her reflection. I would also like to thank Gene Thompson for his generous support and open heart toward the Christ Blueprint.

Thank you to my agent Ja-lene Clark for her enthusiasm and angelic ministrations in making sure this book got published; thank you to Michael Hawkins at Findhorn for his loving editing and embodying of service. Thank you to David Hoffmeister for his transmission of Thomas, and to Jayem for his transmission of John Zebedee; and thank you to the people of Saintes-Maries-de-la-Mer for living in such a marvelous place and being so kind to two strangers.

Thank you to Anne and the team at NAB for their splendid work in making this book look beautiful and justify its content. Thank you to David Andor for his artwork and his endless patience with my requests at all times of day and night under impossible circumstances! He has been with me since the beginning of this ride as Web master, graphic designer, e-book designer, illustrator, advisor, and more . . . always looking out for me. Thank you, my friend, I could not have done any of this without you . . . you are a diamond.

Finally, I would love to thank my dearest soul brother Yeshua, always loving and present for when asked and allowed to Be, and his Beloved

Magdalene and the Feminine Christ Masters, who inspired, ignited, and opened the Way for this Book to be written. I am eternally grateful for them, to them, and for what they are now bringing back again to this world.

—Ameyn, Amen, Amun.

ABOUT THE AUTHOR

PADMA AON PRAKASHA is a passionate, powerful, and enlightening presence creating transformation wherever he goes. A twenty-first century evolutionary guide and author, he offers potent and experiential transmissions from the world's sacred traditions that catalyze an alchemical experience of the divine within. He teaches worldwide and has led initiatory pilgrimages to sacred sites in fifteen countries over the last ten years.

Prakasha started early on his path. After being initiated into the Brahmin lineage at age two, he read the Bhagavad Gita at age four, followed by the Koran and the Bible by age seven. When he was twenty-one he had an experience of God Consciousness that changed his life forever. Shortly after this, he was initiated into Saivite Tantra through the Head Priests of Kedarnath and Pashupatinath in India, and into the Sama Veda through the Arunachala sampradaya. Other initiations came through Sri Om, a Tibetan Buddhist teacher in the Lineage of Tsongkhapa and Maitreya in London, after which Prakasha sat in the highest form of meditation, samadhi, for two months continuously. He is also a Priest in the Order of Melchizedek and closely aligned to the ancient Egyptian lineages.

Prakasha combines all his lineage teachings and skills into being a catalyst for rapid growth. His unique, experiential blend of Christ Consciousness teachings, multiple forms of Tantra Yoga, pure energy, and light transmissions, and sacred sound in Sanskrit, Tibetan, and Aramaic form an alchemical experience of the divine within.

As a globally distributed music performer, Prakasha has produced two world music albums for the label Sub Rosa/BMG: *Rhythmic Intelligence* and *Song of Light*, as well as his forthcoming album, *Life Cycles*, based on the teachings of a new book in development, *Wisdom of the Womb*. He has appeared on BBC TV, Dutch TV, and Radio One, and in *XLR8R*, *Straight no chaser*, and *Variety* magazines, to name a few. He currently lives in the Greek Islands with his beloved wife, Anaiya. He is the author of *The Power of Shakti* and *The Nine Eyes of Light*.

Discover more about the Christ Blueprint at www.christblueprint.com.

FINDHORN PRESS

Life changing books

Consult our catalogue online
(with secure order facility):
www.findhornpress.com

For information about the Findhorn Foundation:
www.findhorn.org